Excursions with Kierkegaard

Excursions with Kierkegaard

Others, Goods, Death, and Final Faith

Edward F. Mooney

B L O O M S B U R Y

NEW YORK • LONDON • NEW DELHI • SYDNEY

Bloomsbury Academic

An imprint of Bloomsbury Publishing Plc

175 Fifth Avenue   50 Bedford Square
New York   London
NY 10010   WC1B 3DP
USA   UK

www.bloomsbury.com

First published 2013

Library of Congress Cataloging-in-Publication Data
Mooney, Edward F., 1941-
Excursions with Kierkegaard : others, goods, death, and final faith / Edward F. Mooney.
p. cm.
Includes bibliographical references and index.
ISBN 978-1-4411-9034-5 (pbk. : alk. paper) -- ISBN 978-1-4411-4632-8 (hardcover : alk. paper) 1. Kierkegaard, Søren, 1813-1855. I. Title.
B4377.M655 2012
198'.9--dc23
2012022572

ISBN: HB: 978-1-4411-4632-8
PB: 978-1-4411-9034-5

Typeset by Fakenham Prepress Solutions, Fakenham, Norfolk NR21 8NN
Printed and bound in the United States of America

CONTENTS

I saw the world as the unimaginably layered thing it is, full of strange likenesses, but also impenetrable, available to comprehension in the merest flashes, if at all.

SVEN BIRKERTS

ACKNOWLEDGMENTS

No book is a solo. It's a pleasure here to name colleagues and friends who have helped these excursions along paths from passing thoughts to passages on the way to chapters – chapters then stopped, somewhat arbitrarily, I confess, midway in the arcs of their potential, their aspiration. Kierkegaard sets us on paths of unending thinking stopped only by the need to move on. One might, of course, have said more. And what one writes in excursions with him lives on after the walk is done and the pen, set aside.

Alastair Hannay, George Pattison, and Patrick Stokes gave unstinting attention, critical and encouraging, to these chapters separately and to the flow from one to the next. Some of their remarks immediately altered a step in a particular exposition or prompted a revised sequencing. Others were harder to assimilate into the body of the texts, and live on in footnote reminders of work to be faced later. I thank them for sympathetic insight into what I was doing, and for their helping hands. For encouragements and assistance great and small, I also thank, in particular, Tony Aumann, Dana Barnea, Jack Caputo, John Davenport, John Lippett, Gordon Marino, Rick Furtak, Haaris Naqvi, Tyler Roberts, Marcia Robinson, Anna Strelis, Joe Westfall, and Clark West. Of course, there are unnamed others to thank, as well. Their cumulative and singular support has memorably cheered the labor of this writing.

**

The chapters that follow have evolved in bulk or in part from the following sources: I am happy to acknowledge their role in the genesis of this book.

"Kierkegaard on Self, Others, Goods, Final Faith", *The Graduate Faculty Journal of Philosophy*, Fall 2011.

"Kierkegaard's Mirrors: Interest, Self, and Moral Vision", *Kierkegaard Newsletter*, 56, Nov. 2010

"Style and Pseudonymity in Kierkegaard", *Oxford Handbook to Kierkegaard*, ed John Lippitt and George Pattison, Oxford, 2012.

"Transfigurations: The Mysterious Agency of Death," *Kierkegaard and Death*, ed. Patrick Stokes and Adam Buben, Indiana, 2011

"Hidden Inwardness as Interpersonal," *Why Kierkegaard Matters*, ed. Mark A. Jolley, Mercer University Press, 2010

"From the Garden of the Dead: Climacus on interpersonal inwardness", *Concluding Unscientific Postscript: A Critical Guide*, Rick Anthony Furtak (ed.), Cambridge University Press, 2010.

"What is a Kierkegaardian Author?", *Philosophy and Social Criticism*, 35, no 7, 2009

"Julia Kristeva: Tales of Horror and Love," *Kierkegaard and the Social Sciences*, ed. Jon Stewart, Ashgate, 2010

AN INVITATION

Final goods, embraced for their goodness alone, not for what they otherwise achieve or buy, easily pass by unnoticed. One final good is the wonder of communicative mutuality, where shared words seem part of a couple's dance flowing flawlessly in ways that would seem, were we to notice, infinitely apt and pleasing. When this happens with colleagues or friends, with children or lovers, it marks an instant of faith not just as promise (we *do* strive to connect) but as harvest. It's not the shared achievement of a negotiated settlement or new piece of observational knowledge or interesting philosophical result, important as these may be, but rather a wedding of persons, words, and worlds, grounded experientially, radiating the sense that we belong to each other and belong to the world.[1]

Whether or not we find such mutuality in philosophy, we are happy to find it *somewhere* – perhaps in music, sport, companionship, love, or frolicking with pets. When he plays with his cat, Montaigne famously wonders whether his cat isn't just as much playing with *him*.[2] Of course, it is – in a wonderful rapport! Communicative rapport with my cat, when it happens, just *is* my cat's communicative rapport with me – a dance of hand and paw declaring indubitable reciprocal understanding. Yet Montaigne shares his thoughts in an age tilted toward skepticism and worry over connection. For an instant he plays with the voice of disconnection or difference (between human and other animals) and of doubt (about communicative connection). Yet in the long run, I'm sure, he lets himself marvel. He knows his cat plays with him, and reclines in that finality – we need nothing deeper.

It is subjectivities, face to face, hand to hand, voice to voice, eye to eye, that undergo and constitute moments of communicative mutuality. Kierkegaard defends subjectivity as a first-personal stance from which we meet others and the world and even ourselves – insofar as we are issues, or marvels, to ourselves. To endorse the truth of subjectivity is to endorse the truth – the conviction – that to live is to assume such a first-personal stance. This is not the adolescent mantra that if I believe something then it's true, and that the opinions of others are superfluous. "Truth is subjectivity" claims a stance we assume as we meet the demands of the day, as we weigh in, now and again, on whatever we say, do, or feel. To be subjectively alert is to refuse being always on automatic pilot, to refuse conceding all authority for the way things go to the stream of social reality. Subjectivity needs continual affirmation for we habitually flee its fragile alertness to self in its openness to itself and to otherness.

Kierkegaard invites us to acclaim subjectivity-as-stance, and live out that stance in our own particular ways. Imagine the opposite. As Kierkegaard deploys the subjective/objective idiom, to live under the truth of objectivity would be to bury any personal urgency in the question how I should live or where it is, at the moment, I stand. It would be to attend dispassionately, mechanically, to the way anyone else in my position would live – and leave it at that. Objectively, professors live thus and so; therefore I fall into living thus and so. From another angle, to live under the lights of objectivity could mean to pursue only objective truths. Kierkegaard ridiculed these substitutes for living and knowing. We need something more intimate and heartfelt than just "doing what is (objectively) done," "doing what, in this milieu, one does," acting always "*comme il faut*," as one "must." We are certainly more than clerks collecting and sorting objective knowledge into academic or bureaucratic bins, awaiting distribution and consumption by anonymous others, or aligning facts with the latest theory, or just distributing theory itself.

We must take time – subjective time – to decide, one by one, minute by minute, how we will shape or receive or reject a life, in its many phases, down to its tiny temporal moments. "How should I live?" and "Am I what I seem to be?" are as inescapable as "What should I – or in fact do I – feel, right now?" For Kierkegaard as for Socrates, these are subjective questions, with answers that, so far as we form them, are also subjective. That doesn't mean they are mere fluff or opinion. On the contrary, they are the truths of our living and dying, moment-to-moment, decade-to-decade. They possess us as the convictions, the struts and beams, of a terribly vulnerable life that would be more so without them.

Our "essential truths," the distillate of our wrestles with claims on our heartfelt embrace, appear in our living them out. They answer to the insistent plea that we take our subjectivity as non-trivial, as truth, as truly valuable. My "essential truths" might be on the order of "Care for your family" or "I am, after all, a teacher!" – or "Care for the poor" or "I know, after all, I'm in love." These are truths to be endlessly explored and revised in the living of them, for although I may have deep convictions, I may still ask, who are my poor, how much care is enough to count as care, by what marks do I know I'm in love, am I sure I'm a teacher? These truths are demands that endlessly explore and challenge us, each "solitary individual," as Kierkegaard would say, one by one. They are truths of subjectivity.

*

Kierkegaard deploys various genres, some of which he invents, as frames to bring out truths that might properly matter for us. He varies the mood and tenor of his writing in the conviction that thinking close to experience, from the variety of angles that different genres of experience afford, will give us fresh looks. Sometimes he writes in the manner of a poet, at others, in the manner of a philosopher or religious thinker – often in a parody or burlesque of a pastor or professor or man-about-town. Varied styles carry varied pedagogical powers. Yet why do we need the fruits of his pedagogy? Why do we need his instruction?

Our deepest need, he holds, is for a personal sense in one's life of what matters (and what doesn't) – a sense we can believe in, stand by, pledge as our own. His different genres apply pressure towards recognition of the personal dimensions of experience and sense, and against cultural forces that subvert these dimensions: the imperium of science and technology, of instrumental thinking and careerist strategies, of consumerist hunger, celebrity gossip, entertainment distraction, and a politics of rancor and despair. These familiar forces promising connection with goods in fact disengage us from meaningful life. They fail to answer our need, Kierkegaard holds, and only *increase* the urgency for subjective attention to richer and deeper goods.

Writers in the tradition of what Stanley Bates calls "great moral philosophy" (Schopenhauer, Carlyle, or Nietzsche – not to mention Plato and Kierkegaard) deserve the widest possible hearing.[3] Kierkegaard wrote before philosophy became an academic specialization with endlessly proliferating sub-fields. Whatever ethics, metaphysics, epistemology, social philosophy or political philosophy mean today, before specialization set in a century and a half ago, their meanings were skewed differently. The outcome is that Kierkegaard (and others) disappear from view for lack of a "place" in the current warren of sub-disciplinary philosophical apartments; and his fate is no better in the warrens of religious studies or of languages and literatures.

It is a telling curiosity that one of the best Kierkegaard commentators in the last decade writes from a department of sociology. Another fine commentator relies on his experience as a practicing psychotherapist (as well as a philosopher).[4] In an earlier decade, this would not have been a "curiosity." In the United States in the 1960s, one could read Rollo May, Eric Erikson, Carl Rogers, Martin Buber, or Eric Fromm without being a specialist in psychology or philosophy or literary studies. Each of these writers relies heavily on an understanding of Kierkegaard, and each is unabashed in venturing forward with him without concern for establishing credit as a full-time Kierkegaard scholar. I would praise them as non-specialists (though thank God for specialists, too).

In the chapters that follow I crisscross through landscapes that are at once literary, psychological, religious, and philosophical, each site of interest developed to call out for first-person response. Each prospect calls on readers to join, not through the compulsion of reason, but through the allure of invitation and promise. Like the poetry of Rilke or the prose of Melville, the essays of Montaigne, or travels of Thoreau, this writing becomes irresistible.

Kierkegaard has an uncanny ability to call his reader into question. This locates his impact in the peculiarities of my position and stance. If his aim is to agitate, then his aim is not primarily to argue for an abstract principle or a particular way of faith, but to make his reader disquiet regarding her own principles or faiths. We might say tentatively that he works from a position that is Christian and Socratic, Romantic and Ironic. He can be Poet or Philosopher, Preacher or Pundit, at a moment's notice, or all rolled into one. We should not anticipate his thought to be a well-organized system. It is thought on the move, changing, to be savored and wrestled with, each reader monitoring her or his individual response, gaining something new or forgotten – then sharing it, perhaps, with others.

*

The excursions I include in these pages open on prospects that hang together as aspects of a continuous and varied landscape – not, say, as views of different cities in different parts of the world. What matters most is the almost visceral feel of the view, and the way it confirms or inspires us as viewers. We are walking with a sharp and often silent guide, not for insights that are poststructuralist or existentialist, continental or analytical or phenomenological, but for shared moments that have the power to startle or unsettle. Sometimes moments are strung into tableau or scenes. Aspects are evoked – they ring true – that's it! – at least for the moment. Then for longer stretches, we settle in to absorb. Thoreau or Montaigne write this way, Rousseau does in *Reveries*, and a stricken Gillian Rose does in *Love's Work*.[5]

We should not discount insight lodged in what Kelly Jolley calls "the considered experience of its author" (rather than exclusively in meticulous reasoning or argument). A writer gives out a prospect we're invited to share, all the while knowing that it is, in due time, "open to analysis and to disagreement."[6] Therein we encounter "experience as something to which we can be loyal, something to which we can rally, something that can obligate us, something that can be educated, … [experience] as accumulating, as having weight."[7] If the upcoming excursions lead us to memorable prospects caught in an ephemeral glance, this is as it should be, for starters. Kierkegaard's is not school philosophy, but it is none-the-less philosophy, artful and alluring.

The essays ahead feature particular themes: subjectivity, the maternal, faith as assurance, irony and self-deception, pseudonyms and the elusiveness of selfhood, genres from burlesque to analytical, the enigmas of authorship, how to think about death (… just as a start).

We move with the modulated stance of any "I" – open to any "you" or "it" – open to any "we" or "they," even to any other "me." The immeasurable importance of this subjective stance has been lost in the wake of ever-colonizing cognitive styles that groom the sciences and their allied technologies, styles that further bureaucratic-administrative idioms that dismiss both commonplace sentiment and deep passion (something murky and dangerous) – that refuse instruction from the personal idiom that is a power of literature, philosophy, and the arts. Artistic, literary, or philosophical production and reception are relegated to the provinces of entertainment or pastimes. After all, there is no yardstick to measure the social or career benefits of loving Shakespeare or Wallace Stevens or wondering at the genius of Ella Fitzgerald, Basho, or Kierkegaard.[8] But why should there be?

These are final goods.

Notes

1 See Cavell's words which mine echo here, Chapter 2, p. 28.

2 See Michel de Montaigne, *Apology for Raymond Sebond*, trans. M. A. Sreech (Penguin: 1988), p. 17.

3 See Stanley Bates, "Stanley Cavell and Ethics", *Stanley Cavell*, (ed.) Richard Eldridge (Cambridge: 2003), p. 39.

4 See Harvie Ferguson's *Melancholy and the Critique of Modernity: Søren Kierkegaard's Religious Psychology* (Routledge: 1994), and *Modernity and Subjectivity: Body, Soul, Spirit* (Virginia: 2000), and Jonathan Lear's *Happiness, Death and the Remainder of Life*, (Harvard: 2002), *Therapeutic Action*: *An Ernest Plea for Irony* (Other Press: 2003), and *A Case for Irony* (Harvard: 2011).

5 See Gillian Rose, *Love's Work, a Reckoning with Life* (New York Review Classics: 2011) and Rousseau's *Reveries of a Solitary Walker*, trans. Peter France (Penguin: 1979).

6 See "A Philosophy of Considered Experience?" Quantum Est In Rebus Inane, January 12 kellydeanjolley; http://kellydeanjolley. com/2012/01/12/a-philosophy-of-considered-experience/

7 Ibid.

8 Stanley Fish has recently argued that the only justification for teaching literature, philosophy, and the arts is that professors find them pleasing. The argument is simple and cynical. Since there is no utilitarian justification (better jobs, better citizens), then the only alternative is imagine them as pursued only for private and sophisticated pleasure – as if, after we subtract utility, pleasure is the only remaining good: " ... the humanities 'don't do anything,' if by

'do' is meant bring about effects in the world. And if they don't bring about effects in the world they cannot be justified except in relation to the pleasure they give to those who enjoy them. To the question 'of what use are the humanities?', the only honest answer is none whatsoever." "Will the Humanities Save Us?," *New York Times*, January 6, 2008.

1

Subjectivity: Exposure, Care, and Response

For many, "Kierkegaard" is synonymous with a pair of catch phrases – words we think we understand but don't. There is the notorious "truth is subjectivity" and then the oft-cited reference to a "passionate leap of faith." Setting aside the popular confusions around "leaps of faith," what is Kierkegaard promoting under the heading of subjectivity? My aim here is to bring alive its proper grip and bite against the pressure of counterfeits, and to fill in some of the cultural contexts that have made subjectivity of any sort suspect. I try a retrieval of Kierkegaard's worthy notion, a sort of subjectivity to welcome in from the cold.

Kierkegaard's subjectivity is a variant of an ordinary subjectivity that may go unnamed but should be familiar in the back and forth exchanges between subjects, between persons, that ravels out the weave the everyday world. It does not exclude objectivity but enables it. It is because we expose ourselves to ongoing passionate exchange with others in a mutuality of subjectivity that we come to embrace objective truths and realities. As subjectivities in pursuit of what's real, we become initiated one by one into the protocols of objective reporting, of objective lab testing or measurement, and so on. It is only certain sorts of objectivity that Kierkegaard shuns, and only certain sorts of subjectivity that he pleads with us to embrace.[1]

For Kierkegaard subjectivity is prominent in faith or in ethical judgment but it is fully evident in less contested domains as well. It is present in ordinary life as an everyday background, silently entangled in a person's sense of agency and passivity in a nexus of relations to herself, others, and an environing world. It is caught up in the daily stream of walking and hearing, cooking and dressing, paying bills and running for the bus. It is opening ourselves, exposing ourselves, to the endless realities, aspirations, and dreams of the everyday.

This sense of subjectivity should be distinguished from the idea of a judgment that is "merely subjective" – one that is defective. In this narrow use, "subjectivity" attaches to instances of error, miscue, and mere fantasy. It then marks a person's unfortunate distance from the real. But everyday subjectivity has a different and wider reach. It affords fortunate and flowing contact with the real.

An overview

Contact and immersion

Let's set textbook definitions and discussions aside and start afresh with an evocation of my immersions in life. Say I read a passage from Heidegger (a philosopher, as we know, who is harsh with specifically Cartesian subjectivity). After a difficult stint with *Being and Time*, I'll want to know where to shelve Heidegger's tome, whether to loan it, whether its call to resoluteness means staying in or out of politics – and of what stripe. Answering the phone, I won't mimic the text to chirp "Dasein here!" I'll think of myself as someone in this town, at this address, happy or unhappy within this family and this job, disgusted or delighted by this evening's news. There's nothing tendentious in my thinking of myself *as* a self, a "me," a subjectivity of some sort.

Perhaps at other moments I'll succumb to reverie. I'll picture myself walking with Dante, a soul mid-way in the journey of my life, lost in a dark wood. Or in less reverie, I'd think of myself as subject to the allure of philosophy and French cuisine and the crushing glory of Leontyne Price. Or perhaps I'd think of myself hard at work to become a successful writer. Long after the collapse of atomistic Cartesian subjectivity – an influential configuration to which I'll return – I'll think that Heidegger addresses me as a subjectivity in his writing, even as he avoids any picture of subjectivity as isolated, atomic consciousness – isolated from others, isolated from the world. I might find that he calls me (as a subject, from his subjectivity) to monitor technological imperialism. If I return the favor, addressing him as a receptive subjectivity, I might tag him for avoiding his implication in political realities between the wars. Yet I'd also think of him as deeply, "subjectively" concerned with the roots of Greek culture and with Hölderlin's poems.

Subjectivity is an animated field already inhabited precisely by we who are openness to that field. Yet this reciprocal openness-to-otherness – an inestimably worthy subjectivity – gets occluded by cultural regimes that slide into taking the objective deliverances of science as all that's needed for the world (and ourselves) to be intelligible. Or such subjectivity is occluded by administrative, bureaucratic regimes that reduce selves or souls to numbers or exchangeable parts in economies of production or consumption. Or such openness gets blocked and denied by self-refuting "theory" – in disquisitions on the death of the author, of the human, of ethics, of philosophy, not to mention the long-heralded yet still lingering death of God.[2] Kierkegaard sets to revive lost subjectivity, and so sets out to mark limits to science and scholarship as sole paths to intelligibility of things human and personal, and to mark the error of living one's life swallowed by the human *en masse*, or by mindlessly consuming fashion, gossip, or shallow opinion. I'll bracket popular academic pronouncements of multiple deaths from the 1980s and beyond, pronouncements that have shifted recently to advocate anti-humanism.[3] Whatever the virtues of these fashionable academic trends, their object should be exposing bad theories of human existence, not a frontal attack on explorations of authorship, say, or of a self's agency or passivity at an experiential level. Why reduce persons, viable meanings and successful communications, to ghostly after-images that intellectual sophisticates urge us to set aside? As I see it, these suspicions of fraud at the root of subjectivity, whatever their kernel of insight, quickly approach over-kill. They become hyperbolic and theatrical, hiding essentials from view. Living uncritically with fashionable critique is, one needn't point out, uncritical.

Of course, there are real-enough fissures and enigmas at the edge of self- understanding, and of shared meanings and communications. In the pages that follow I return time and again, in a Kierkegaardian vein, to these enigmas and fissures. But the bare fact of anomalies in our understandings of authorship, writing, or death is no reason to jettison these realities, or to censor our talk of them: quite the contrary. The surfacing of anomalies ought in many cases to trigger the question, how can we fruitfully live with such fracture or discordance? This is something quite other than discarding or scorning it.

There's no way (and no need) to banish pedestrian subjectivity – the idea that we are individuals who are responsive to each other, that we are subject to each other's help and hindrance, responsive to aesthetic, political, ethical, and personal invitations and demands. The challenge is to welcome ordinary subjectivity and to disable a specific Cartesian picture of knowledge and consciousness that distorts it. I take Kierkegaard's role to be a fierce critique of trends converging on the weakening or elimination of pedestrian subjectivity. To have a grip on Kierkegaard's sort of subjectivity is to acknowledge selves as caring, responsive participants in a field of reciprocal psychic and social exchange – all sorts of misfires included; it is to enter a vibrant space of conversions, of delight in marriages, of enjoyment in morning tea (sunlight streaming over the desk).

Truth and subjectivity

Kierkegaard's improvisations on "subjectivity" will reappear from several angles in chapters ahead, but let me prepare the ground with these introductory strokes. To say that truth is subjectivity is to emphasize the worth and inescapability of personal immersion in life. The dictum is less an epistemological insight than a practical appeal, a plea that I turn away from those public distractions that take me to a no man's land of impersonal non-existence – a place of barely conscious despair. It is a plea to return to myself, to others, and to a world, a return that with luck will expose what matters to me – as I expose myself to *it*.

There is a mistaken view that subjectivity, passion, concern, and immersion will always mark misalignment and distortion in our effort to attain an accurate sense of what comes to pass. This denigration of passionate immersion or subjectivity is only reinforced by the imperatives of an administrative culture that closes down the intimate and personal. Front and center are institutional imperatives: career advancement, bureaucratic progress reports, preparation of tax returns, endless "objective," quantitative performance evaluations. Anything we'd call personal, intimate, or subjective gets buried under protocols of administration. What matters is not the pleasure I take in my kids but whether they qualify for scholarships, not devotion to classical music but whether better "time management" will save the day. Intimate, subjective space then shrinks in importance. For Kierkegaard this loss is disastrous.

The region of non-institutionalized "privacy" diminishes as it comes under attack by the public and political. All that we hesitate to own as intimate or personal gets ceded to an institutionalized "public" space and style of critique and comprehension. My subjective "feel" for my world and convictions, and my attempts to communicate my intimate immersions, insofar as they lack admission to respected modes of public articulation, lie fallow or die. They resist the coin of the academic realm. The journalism of "true confessions" and intimate scandal, replace nuanced accounts of our complex embeddedness in an intimate social world. Rather than embrace our subjectivity in resistance, we collaborate in its silencing. Rather than trace out the lineaments of ordinary subjectivity and affect, or following Kierkegaard's ventures in this regard, we fall back on the safer ground of the "objective." The "objectivity" that Kierkegaard finds so ridiculous and dangerous is not the world of objective news or research. It is in part what he calls "the public," a transpersonal force that feeds on and reproduces for mass consumption reams of impersonal gossip and chatter, reminders of "what one must do" in one's objective roles, or under administrative edicts. To absorb without reserve the objectivities of disciplinary and professional pursuits buries our more personal, private selves – our spans of pedestrian subjectivity.[4]

Closer to home, a fragmented university, especially in its pre-professional programs, serves as an impersonal training school for assimilation into wider political and economic structures. Even in graduate programs in the humanities, the professoriate is self-replicating, producing new scholars to replace departing ones. The university takes pride in the production and distribution of objective knowledge of utility to outside institutions, or as often, of utility to other academic institutions. Professors write for other professors and deans in efforts to validate each other's merit for corporate advancement. All this has its legitimate purpose, but a cost is exacted if the intimate or personal is utterly suppressed. Excluded are central virtues of the humanities: cultivation of sensibilities, engagement in self-reflection and Socratic exploration, and husbanding poetic expression. Practices of producing and consuming data, method, and theory leave out evocations of simple things of great depth or radiance we might otherwise encounter experientially, to our betterment: quietly bringing the intricacies of my specific immersions in life to bear on my reading and viewing and teaching, letting that reading, viewing, and teaching realign my desires (and aversions) and inviting students to feel how that realignment works. Under the restrictive prompts of a preemptive and all-consuming objectivity, my writing can't reveal what it's like to let a poem or a philosophical meditation look into my soul, and make it come alive, or blush in shame. Yet I know that a paragraph from Emily Dickinson or Kierkegaard takes my subjectivity in earnest: I can be swept away, and called up short.

Kierkegaard refused to embark on a university career in part because he wanted knowledge that would let him come alive, that would quicken his sense of the inescapably human, and of intimate self-recognition. He wanted knowledge that would key him to dimensions in his complicated, singular existence that *he* should attend to (alone, and with books). A tepid interest in tracing the objective footprints of world-historical figures – their texts, and the trails of their promoters and detractors, was not enough, and existentially, irrelevant. With regard to his readers – in particular, let's say, his regard for my reading – Kierkegaard prods me to set aside the objective world-historical and impersonal and take up with *my* subjectivity, even as I do this in tandem with a mentor: say, Socrates, Cervantes, Gillian Rose – or that marvelous writer, the immortal Johannes de silentio, who pens *Fear and Trembling*.

Wounds of subjectivity

We can illuminate subjectivity by tracing its roots to Plato's account of Socrates, and pause with a new conception of Socratic irony. Kierkegaard loved Socrates, and averred, late in life, that his thinking was always as much Socratic as Christian.[5] He learns from Socrates how to keep subjectivity alive, and what is at stake in doing so. It will repay us to see Socrates as someone who values subjectivity, and carries the banner of living ironically. We can clarify Kierkegaard's praise of Socratic ironic living by drawing distinctions.

Verbal wit, ironic capability, and living ironically

A prominent philosopher and practicing psychotherapist, Jonathan Lear has written extensively on Kierkegaard's practice and theory of irony, not to mention Kierkegaardian "subjectivity."[6] He takes irony to be *the* fundamental structure of evaluative consciousness for modern subjects. He uses Kierkegaard's account to illuminate Socratic irony, which in turn gives us the structure of Kierkegaardian subjectivity. Briefly, there are three levels of sophistication in the play of irony. First, and least important philosophically, there is the ironic quip, or wise-crack. At the verbal level, this can be a moment where stable evaluations are rocked for an instant, as a speaker takes a jaded or tender unexpected angle on things we value or disvalue. Its jolt for an instant can destabilize our routine uptakes on gender, say, or age, ethnicity, size – on family, eating, kissing, politicians, and so forth). It can teach but it mainly entertains.

Irony can be more substantial, however. Here, in its second manifestation, it is the capacity, exercised seldom or often, to take a wry backward step that fosters critique of one or more of the parade of evaluations that weave the fabric of my life, and life in general. Ironic remarks or perceptions, arising from a step-back position, put conventional evaluations under scrutiny, and can put them at risk. A capacity for irony is a capacity to wield its deflationary powers. As a feature of moral reflection and agency it deflates routine judgments and slows down overweening assurance by creating gaps between practice and aspiration. Putting ourselves under ironic scrutiny, or letting others put us there, we squirm in recognition of a gap between how we typically perceive ourselves and others, and how, in contrast, in late hours, for instance, we can take ourselves (and others). Perhaps we aspire to an excellence in writing; others take us to be successful, but without being neurotic or pathologically perfectionist, in the dim hours we can wring our hands in dismay at the gap between what we desire and the little we seem to achieve. We exercise our capacity to see our work under the aspect of deflationary ironic detachment.

Lear is innovative. He notes irony's step backward (to assume a potentially corrosive or negative stance). He then adds a forward step of wholehearted immersion that leaves deflation aside, and readies the self for action. He attributes the delineation of this capacity for a step forward into life to Kierkegaard. Kierkegaard wants to have irony be a way of life, a Socratic way of life, where critical evaluation is always latent but does not interfere with living forward. There is little time for ironic evaluation as Socrates strides through a battlefield, or sends the women packing before beginning his death-watch meditations. To inhabit a stance that holds commonplace evaluations under a critical lamp requires a moment of distance and suspension of routine action, yet life requires more than stalling in irony. If Lear is correct, ironic living includes powerful exercise of one's capacity for irony, and also a powerful capacity to keep that exercise in reserve, at the ready, but not dominant. A master of living ironically does not let that capacity bring life to a halt. She can leave the sting of deflationary exercises, the stall of scrutiny, well off the map. Without controlled irony, its detachment becomes iterative: irony breeds irony on irony, critique breeds critique and critique of critique; living grinds to a halt, despair or cynicism sinks in, sloth or worse obtrudes.

To live ironically is to live forward effectively, affirmatively. One is fully aware that one can take up irony as a mode of critique, timed to circumstance. Irony can have its day in court, but it does not hold court interminably. It is a phase – only a phase – of life. What one takes to be central to one's life – one's key evaluations – can be viewed sideways, from a skeptical angle. One might recall moments of holding one's dearest commitments under irony's withering light. Yet living ironically cannot mean continuously stalling life in exercise of a vigilant distance from immediate engagement. A distanced view is necessarily suspended (not abolished or repressed). Ironic capability remains a capability, even as one enters the fray, steps into life, wholeheartedly. A professional and nearly flawless young skater knows she may very well miss her upcoming leap, but she shelves this critical distance on her performance as she glides out on the ice.

In Lear's account, Socrates and Kierkegaard go beyond ironic word play and beyond the ironic distance ingredient in sharp critique. Socrates models wholehearted ironic existence.

Kierkegaard is the first to see this, and in fact adopts it as a necessary feature of Christian existence. As I see it now, the capacity of subjectivity to split from itself in deflationary evaluation is the capacity of subjectivity to wound. To bring life under withering judgment is the wound of Christian existence. It endures, welcomes, painful inner tensions that Kierkegaard identifies with living ironically. One overcomes the fright of ongoing reevaluation and transformation, of dying and reviving each day, wherein what otherwise are the wounds of subjectivity can appear as fleetingly beautiful fault-lines.

Trauma in Athens

Lear sees irony played out in the drama of Socrates' life; his confrontations with the city call its convictions in question. His critique wounds the city, and Athens retaliates. Lear's earlier *Happiness, Death, and the Remainder of Life* spells out this trauma.[7] Of course Socrates in Athens is Kierkegaard in Copenhagen. Both are interrogators who interrupt normal life, whose stings cause cultural trauma, with its associated anxiety and disquiet.

The baleful impact of Socrates on Athens is like the wound to my self-understanding that arrives with an awareness of my death. Schopenhauer and Freud, not to mention Plato and Kierkegaard, are acutely aware of the destabilizing effect of exposure to the inevitability of my death. Freud speaks as if death is an instinct bent on raising uncanny havoc on my evaluative center of gravity, on my conception of life.[8] Death shatters my ordinary subjectivity the way Socrates shatters Athenian subjectivity.

Death snatches life, and is traumatic also because it defies simple comprehension. In considering my own death, it can't be just another event that I watch transpire. But if not, how *do* I think of my own death? It's not exactly unthinkable, but it's surely uncanny. I'm here, and then I'm not, not even as an onlooker: I disappear totally, without a trace. But if I try to think of my death, I have to picture myself both dead and undead – I must be undead to do the picturing of my death. This enigma is uncanny because we half-see, half don't see, what's going on. We wrestle with death the way we wrestle with great sea storms or whirlwinds. One of Kierkegaard's scenes of wrestling with death is set at a graveside, where a child and grandfather mourn.[9] A hidden onlooker is suddenly, uncannily, caught up with his own death. To consider my death, Kierkegaard seems to say, is to undergo a kind of uncanny trauma that brings my entire life to the fore.

If I can undergo trauma, so can a culture. Lear argues that Socrates gives Athens a foretaste of her own demise. He numbs subjectivities. Citizens just don't understand the Socratic irruption in their midst. For self-protection, they trump up charges against him to restore their balance. Just as I would banish death, if I could, so Athens would banish Socrates. It does. And yet in a deeper sense, Athens fails. Thanks to the charm of Plato's words, the city launches Socrates into a spectacular, ever-expanding post-mortem career.

The unsettling idea that puts Socrates to death, and that survives his death, is the disquieting insistence, echoed by Kierkegaard, that I have a life-as-a-whole, I am responsible for it, and it needs scrutiny. The charge is that Athenians fail to acknowledge this. Each citizen has a life-as-a-whole to put under radical questioning and to doggedly own up to. Truth is subjectivity – that is, alert responsibility for who I am. But Athenians were accustomed to being tried only for ignoble *deeds*, not for the span of their lives. Furthermore, trials were to be conducted through oratory, exhortation, and emotional manipulation, not through the trickery of logical examination.

Socrates needs to be silenced because he has exposed a raw, uncanny thing (life-as-a-whole) in a raw, uncanny way (cross-examination). Kierkegaard likewise is pilloried. His charge against Copenhagen is raw, uncanny. They call themselves Christians – in fact, they are not; they picture themselves individuals – but they aren't. Interrogation, mimicry, dialectic, and humor are his stings. In turn, Kierkegaard is Socratic, boisterous, polemical, literary, and lyrical.[10]

Athens, like Copenhagen, is frightened and humiliated. Socrates asks for definitions of piety or friendship, of moderation or justice, drawing his interlocutors into doubt and confusion. The sting is to leave those accusations hanging, to leave his interlocutors stumbling publicly, in shameful disarray. Socrates breaches their threshold for tolerable moral anxiety. Perhaps he could barely know himself what sort of answers he was groping for – always opening issues he couldn't close, starting fights he left unfinished – leaving Athenians to finish things off.

Copenhagen didn't finish Kierkegaard off, but they found him a bewildering irritant. Just as death (as Jonathan Lear has it) is an uncanny disruptor that we just can't come to terms with, so philosophy and philosophers can be uncanny disruptors we just can't handle. If as readers of Plato or Kierkegaard we attend to this arena of subjectivity and its disruption, we may likewise be dispirited and disrupted. But perhaps such confusion is a prelude to resolution, to new immersion in life. If so, transformation will be a response to trauma, a recasting of subjectivity itself.

Descartes

Loss of sociality and cares

A sensibility that is antithetical both to Socrates and to Kierkegaard, a modern sensibility, emerges with Descartes. The advent of Descartes' revolution inaugurates a new face of subjectivity, one that strips the subject bare, and in its own way is as traumatic to European culture as Socrates was to Athens. The Cartesian revolution, in concert with new technologies, effects what Max Weber identifies as the "disenchantment" of the world. Let me give a rough outline – a cartoon – of the Cartesian subjectivity that Kierkegaard (and others) will inherit and resist.

Descartes enthrones subjectivity first as a center of skepticism. What can I trust? Yet in the same breath he exhibits an exorbitant self-confidence, a kind of tacit declaration of the power of his independent isolated mind to deliver from its own pockets two things: the proof of its own existence (the *cogito)* and then the existence of God. Shouldn't we sense chutzpah? Descartes sets aside schooling, history, and language, disregards the necessary role of others in one's thinking (and in one's existence), and pays no heed to the matrix of material sustenance and civil security so necessary to learning and thought.

The self established solo by Descartes is disembodied, asocial and conceived as an autonomous site of individual consciousness and mental performance. This is not a Socratic subjectivity, embedded in public dialogue with differing figures, focused on comportment (the place of love, justice, or friendship, for instance). Descartes has solitude, but none of Rousseau's or Thoreau's deep immersion in a rich natural world – a Creation that encourages or consoles as one walks in meditation.

To be sure, Descartes' accomplishment is astounding, both world-shattering and world-making, and elicits astounding rejoinders and rejections in Marx, Kierkegaard, Nietzsche, Heidegger and Parisian poststructuralists. Hobbes and Spinoza are anti-Cartesian, and German Idealism and Romanticism are too. For Marx, consciousness is neither individual nor autonomous but molded by social and economic forces. Nietzsche, Weber, Durkheim, and Freud take further turns in dismantling an individualistic, asocial, consciousness. On a related front, psychology discovers science-based ways to study persons that seem to bypass consciousness. Philosophy has its own recurrent fixations on a world of pure matter, where both God and subjectivity leave the stage.

By dint of an unfortunate simplification, a passion for the scientific study of things human and otherwise comes to mean breaking free from all religious and even moral conceptions of the psyche, self, or soul. A secular chauvinism posits only one world, and lets the natural sciences tell us what it is.[11] Subjectivity comes to mean the failure to meet the objective standards of scientific inquiry. In a similar vein, we say of a journalist or judge who becomes "subjective" that she has succumbed to cognitive or moral vice. Cartesian tenets also become tethered to acquisitive individualism, where rational self-assertion mixes with egoism oblivious to dependencies on community, class, gender, or education. The inescapable field of a rich subjectivity, of humane exposure and responsiveness, is forgotten as its counterfeits take center stage.

Any number of twentieth century critiques (Heidegger, Wittgenstein, and Freud, for a quick sample) target Cartesian subjectivity, but as I see it, they don't target and they don't deflate the everyday subjectivity we all affirm. This everyday weave is the place of reading and responding, of being me and not you, of speaking at conferences, or disputing my hotel bill.[12] Even as Cartesian varieties die out, there is plenty of garden space left for healthy alternatives, not least, for a Kierkegaardian subjectivity.

Demise of care

Subjectivity and what matters

Kierkegaardian subjectivity is tied to my sense that I care for
things that matter. I am summoned and struck by things that make
demands on my responsiveness. To be subject is to be summoned,
struck, and responsive. Subjectivity is not an epistemological
concept focused on how I know this or that, nor does it name
a kind of propositional truth. It is a broadly moral, existential,
and experiential concept. One has more or less subjectivity as one
takes more or less responsibility for one's life, or is more or less
affectively and morally responsive to others and one's ideals, or is
more or less subject to passions, benevolent or malevolent. It is an
openness to be affected by (subject to, and responsive to), interven-
tions and pleas, calls and demands, whether moral, religious or
aesthetic.

Kierkegaard undoes a raw Cartesian isolationism by evoking a
porous interiority. In facing a simple request, another's words enter
my socially tuned consciousness – I am not alone. Kierkegaard has
angst, care, and mood circuit into the world and return back to the
self. In a long passage from *The Concluding Unscientific Postscript*,
Johannes Climacus, overhears a man at a grave-site grieving a
son.[13] Mood travels from the stranger "over there" to enter and
upset Climacus, who rediscovers it permeating the heavens and
whispering trees. Mood is both outside and inside in seamless
animations. When Heidegger places us primordially always already
"in the world," he is taking a page from Kierkegaard.[14] Emerson
will say a person "*is* place."[15] Person and place are mutually articulate.[16] In class I am, in a sense, my classroom.

Of course, Kierkegaard and his pseudonymn Johannes Climacus
speak approvingly of "inwardness," which sounds alarmingly
Cartesian. But "inwardness" is an *outward flowing* wholeheartedness or cordiality.[17] It is not a Cartesian screen of consciousness
on which disembodied images float, images that are only conjec-
turally connected to an outer world. We're implicated in a world
that already implicates us. A loving parent faces a loved child;
a desperate soul faces desperate straits. Furthermore, when
Kierkegaard talks of "inwardness" the point is less *about* something
(a metaphysical region) than it is an earnest plea – that I *enact* the

truth of wholehearted (inner) responsiveness. I am asked, as it were, to bring wholeheartedness into the world. Under the auspices of inwardness there is no move toward self-enclosure or ascetic withdrawal.

Losing contact

Kierkegaard laments a loss of subjectivity. He sees that one can lose care for self and others, lose care for one's God, one's neighbor, and one's world, lose a sense that one's time and place matter, and that one matters to oneself. Cartesian subjectivity is tied to the epistemological certainty that I think. Kierkegaardian subjectivity is tied to broadly moral-religious convictions I can muster – or not – in the face of objective uncertainty. It is tied to whatever cares summon me or make demands of me or call me to become who I am. It's a sense that can wax and wane, a passion that will run full tilt or die a trickling death.

A suffering child pleads for my response, calls on my responsiveness, my subjectivity, asks for help or compassion. To record this dispassionately, to "make a mental note" – "a child's voice was heard asking" – and feel or do nothing in response, would be to stand in good stead as an objective observer. Writing down my observation, the result could be passable as "true to the facts" – though it would still be, I suspect, true to only a stripped down and cruel, even alien view of "the facts." To be only an objective observer in this circumstance, however, would be to stand utterly false to what I could and should be, false to my recognition that I hear a call to respond from my heart. It simply follows, then, that if the highest value anyone can aspire to is being morally, religiously, humanely responsive, then truth (our highest value) is subjectivity.

To lose subjectivity is to lose the sense that things matter or summon the heart. Short of nihilism, numbness or indifference, one might feel an intimate pain of absence, like the pain of unrequited love. To restore lost subjectivity is to restore, if not an unqualified "Yes!" to life, then at least the hope that a heart wounded is not dead. One might hope that love can be requited, that despite desolation a Whirlwind's voice can return a world (as in the Book of Job). One might find that dialogue, even as it addresses lost love, or the bleaker prospect of nihilism, can bespeak a fragile intimacy alive in that address itself.[18]

Subjectivity as interpersonal

Let me add – again, in broad strokes – another dimension of Kierkegaardian subjectivity. His manner of writing works to bring subjectivities alive. I approach this more fully in Chapter 3, but here let me sketch words in flight and at rest.

Living words and voice

A passage born in writing is reciprocally born in being read or heard – born in the moment it breaks a deadening drone to jolt and ignite a soul. Each launch invites interpretations along contrasting registers of hearing. Each intimates an unfinished world as an adumbration (or refiguring) of my world, and intimates an unfinished source as an adumbration (or refiguring) of my source. Words get intercepted as I read or listen. They fall under my purview, yet are not hedged thereby from becoming any others' words just as well. My gain in self through words is no one's loss. In the best of circumstances, we rise together. Speaking of the poet Wallace Stevens, Simon Critchley avers, "Words of the world are the life of the world, and poetry is the highest use of those words."[19]

As traveling arcs of subjectivity, words can shape an intimate communion that forms part of a communication – that then radiates outward and aspires to realize universal community. If they ring true, the conditions of the soul that a Kierkegaard and Plato bare for us in the charm of their writing begins to resemble a general condition. I gain access to a soul that is not mine, that begins to become mine, that can belong as much to others as to Kierkegaard, as much to the present age as to another, as much to me as to him or to my neighbor. It's as if spirit lies in common trust, even as I avail myself of it as the particular and irreplaceable individual that I am. Of course, community and communion can fail in the familiar ways.

Complacency, selfishness, power, desire for fame or riches, dull imagination, lack of contact with the better world of words – each or all can deny me salutary transformations. The bulk of words that cross our paths hardly carry transformative powers, and the transformations offered can be illusory or violently destructive. We know, too, that words are not the only force in town. There's brute power, blindness, and famine to contend with.

Living voice and words work seas of subjectivity. Launched by a friend or a Socrates, words take on power from deep cultural roots. It's as if they flow with an indigenous strength from an opaque, even mythic or archetypal timeless past. If my friend admonishes "To thine own self be true," its force is powered in part from Shakespeare, and in part from even deeper roots, for Shakespeare borrows "true self" from cultural strata earlier than his own.

Such words seem to carry transforming power on their own, as if my friend, or Shakespeare, were exploiting a collective source quite apart from a particular awareness of a deep provenance. Though we may stumble at giving an account, that such words can have immense effect is hardly in doubt. If someone says on a dark street, in effect, "Your money or your life!" the impact is as certain as a physical blow. When my friend says, "To thine own self …," words likewise carry power, yet without a physical threat. We can acknowledge that words realign selves – and manage with humbling ignorance when it comes time to say *how* that is done.

My friend's words are not his alone, but "the words of others" through which he calls on me. This confirms our lives as cultural creatures, at the disposal of language. We avail ourselves of words other to ourselves in becoming selves. Heidegger's *Dasein* gets translated recently, *"the-openness-we-are."*[20] Among other things, we are openness to time. We are the very undergoing of this passage from a present, soon to be former self, and a self that speaks now to us as other, as future, stranger, or neighbor – in words that are other, first and last.

Kierkegaard puts all this aphoristically: "the 'I' is oneself and one's neighbor at once."[21] His words arrive through evocative depictions, first as neighboring us, then as words and worlds to make our own, then abandoned to others who may or may not await them (or return them). They impinge from an unknown past as old as Faust or Socrates or Abraham, and arc toward a passing present contact with us – from which they may (or may not) find new lease on life to form a future now unknown.

These are inter-animating moments in fields of widening (and contracting) subjectivity. We should find them in our classrooms, those minor animated worlds. But is living voice, a transfiguring moment, a transporting word or melody, at all welcome in a modern secular university? Far from starting a digression, this question asks us what role Kierkegaardian subjectivity might play – or not – in a locality most of us know too well.

Teaching humanities

The domain of the performing and expressive arts is one academic site for exploring feeling, action, gesture and perception, where ordinary subjectivity might be a focus of attention. We wonder objectively, but also intimately, how to perform Hamlet or read aloud a single line, how to hear Beethoven, how to see Chagall. We acknowledge the need to get ourselves subjectively into their lives or worlds or creations, and wonder how to come alive within the varied domains of popular culture. Literature is another place we encounter modulations of ordinary subjectivity. We wonder at the acuity of Toni Morrison or Jane Austen in depicting the inescapably human in its great and compelling variety.[22]

We might think that matters of personal aspiration, passion, or meaning – matters of subjectivity – don't belong in the academy. They get nurture elsewhere in sports and entertainment, in the melee of public politics or the pieties of religion. Immersion in things that give importance to life (a big part of what I mean by ordinary subjectivity) can take place outside the academy, and certainly does. But why take from psychology, philosophy, literature or the arts their capacity to join happily in joint ventures of understanding, celebrating, and mourning the human?

Intimate classroom exchange

Kierkegaard found the barren intellectuality of his university comical and distressing. Professors might take a detached, impersonal approach to the matters they teach, especially in the natural sciences or technical disciplines – say academic medicine or engineering – where a cool impersonality can be an apt and prominent ideal. Yet even here we'd want teachers to model passion, a love of truth, love of discovery, or a love of the many small details of the discipline itself.

Mathematics can be a calling that animates a life, not just a machine-like mastery of specialized techniques. But in the humanities and in those sectors of psychology, religious studies, or philosophy that belong there, we engage in more than the transmission of hard fact, elegant theory, and necessary technique. We engage and are engaged by subjectivities, and our own subjectivity is altered in the process. In our texts we encounter grief or anger or halting tenderness, and in successful teaching, such grief or sweetness will come alive, echo in the room. To win this success in teaching requires intimate touch with a mood or passion, and depends on modeling that intimacy in diction, pace of speech, apt analogy. And it requires recognizing its transference to a student. It means monitoring the receptivity of a class to what's at stake. All this is not just cool objectivity. It's warm engagement.

To evoke possibilities and hopes for renewal and repair, and to evoke, with some regret, the multiplicities that conspire to shut down hopes or possibilities, requires intimacy with the terrain of affect and aspiration – not to mention the capacity to convey it. Part of understanding in the humanities is laying out facts and context, and putting methods of analysis to work. Yet understanding here is also to enter repositories of yearning and desire, of imagination, aspiration and tact, of tainted love and rash conceit. To understand, we enter a treasury of cultural resources, and listen from a place of immersion and exposure. Psychology and history, poetry and philosophy, art, dance, and music ask us to imagine very particular instances of requited and unrequited love, betrayal and steadfast courage, fluid grace and tempestuous disorder, arrogance and single-minded vengeance, innocent delight and deep despair.

Intimacy is the opposite of abstraction and *also* the opposite of fact or method. It opens to realms of understanding, appreciation, and worth. It's imagining the feel of possibilities, regions one's soul might inhabit, that one's friend or enemy might live in and from – say, envy, tenderness, or brashness. In its own way, the university would be for Kierkegaard, and should be for us, Plato's city of words – a place where imaginative conversational exchange both critiques the present and gives allure to the future.[23] We might even believe, against the evidence of money and guns, that "words of the world are the life of the world."[24] Unhappily, classrooms can become just another site where intimacy and soul have fled. The Socratic and Kierkegaardian aim is nudging persons, one by one, toward their better selves, toward inhabitation of unforeseen realms of openness and response.

Not long ago, an Amish schoolhouse was invaded mid-day, the children terrorized and several shot by a local deliveryman. The next day, the grandfather of one of the girls killed said, within his inconsolable grief, "We must not think evil of this man." I passed on these words to my class, letting them sink in, and quietly alluded to the Christian injunction to love one's enemies. I moved on. But from the hush I could tell something essential had been communicated.

Institutions tend to sideline sites of intimate or passional encounter, contact with Hamlet's doubts, Mozart's grace, or the terror of unnecessary death. A figure of ridicule in Kierkegaard's *Postscript* is the teacher utterly blind to a pedagogical aspiration: the desire to let affect or insight, eloquence or affliction, come alive and vibrant in a class. The credentialed Adjunct unknowingly damps down all soul as he distributes trivia tests on Plato.[25] Knowledge that bears on "care for the self" would resemble what Clifford Geertz calls local knowledge, aspiring to a fine-grained sense of things as they lie ready for one's responsible attention. We might call this "tactile" or "visceral" wisdom, the sort of acquired and practiced intimate knowledge a rock climber has of a granite wall, or the unexpected fleshly knowledge Jacob has in wrestling his angel, or the knowledge Thoreau has of his Concord paths and ponds. It might be the intimate pain and joy resonant with the life one knows only in giving birth.

Kierkegaard, like Plato in the *Symposium*, thought that any knowledge worth its salt comes from love and gives birth – to new thoughts, new ways of response, new configurations of soul. This sensuous knowing shows one's attunements and convictions, one's world and others, as one is exposed to them. It's an undergoing linked to a quick readiness for the next step or grip or moment in one's impending future. It resists propositional formulation (hence Socratic ignorance is its ally). Yet it can give bracing or terrifying intimacy of the sort one has in confidently knowing one's way about, knowing how to go on – or in fearfully or joyfully knowing what one undergoes, as one meets a mettling challenge or a moment of renewal.

Passion for truths and texts

Here's a startling announcement that sounds a death-knell for subjectivity – for humanistic ideals of refining moral, aesthetic, or literary passions, of refining imaginative inflections or perceptions. Here is the credo of a contemporary university. Just listen: "The University of Malta is geared towards the infrastructural and industrial needs of the country so as to provide expertise in crucial fields."[26]

With a brush of the hand, we abandon the humanities leaving them unfunded and forgotten; we drop imaginative variation or the inflection of lyrical perception, and abandon sites for curates of past lives and souls, welcomed from this culture and the next, brought from the dead into presence. We shut down fleeting dialogue with this companion figure, with this striking line, this image, this chord sequence. Nor does this credo honor sites for futures flowing in as dark or lifting winds apt for souls taking their next tremulous step into an unknown where questions are so much more than answers and even silence has its place. No space is saved to lift and fall with this Van Gogh crow, with this line from Rilke, with this Socratic exchange, Emersonian invocation, or Hepburn moment – no space for this gasp of King Lear's incomprehension. There is no hearing Kierkegaard's plea for knowledge that will "come alive in me."[27]

Cultivating intimacy or affection in the humanities is cultivating subjectivity as openness to texts, suffering exposure to them, as they display the arts of conversation and praise, of attentiveness, gratitude, and compassion; the arts of grieving and outrage; the arts of seeing and coping with affliction, injustice, and estrangement. Subjectivity means allowing oneself responsiveness to demands that appeal to us as initiates of poetry, wonder, grief, and love. Contacts here become pedagogical moments, dance movements, steps initiates can learn from (though this learning is never simply imitation). The good or radiant, the beautiful, serene, or frankly sublime would beckon not just on the scale of a city, of a hero, or of a sonnet of great power, nor just on the scale of a violent storm or vast thunder soundscape. The scale could be far smaller, a glimpse of easy wonder, grief, or love, or of an early lily, the smile of a child. It could be the dazzling feel of granite at one's fingertips, the air above, below.

Truths thus imparted or evoked (This is beauty! This is tenderness!) are not propositions to test at arm's length – or to pocket greedily as a creed. They're an intimate touch that's quite compatible with a Socratic "propositional ignorance." They're truths resonant in athletic or musical wisdom, in love, or in hearing just *this* line of Dickinson. Such intimate, passing contact is called "truth" because it has inestimable value and fitness for and to life – as when we speak of a true love or true path, or of a dedication that's true, or of truly living. Or as we speak of Hamlet enacting and suffering truths of the most capacious consciousness (or subjectivity) we've had the fortune to know (and not to know).

In being at home at sea, in being true to our intimate knowledge of death and of giving (and undergoing) birth (to ourselves and others), in being exposed to and grasped by lives and their truths – in such cases truths appear as apt attunements to varied worlds. And they appear as beckoning possibilities that in our brief time afloat we marvel to uncover or meet in moments of illumination.

Self-knowledge, subjective care, pledge

Postmodernism is born in suspicion of grand narratives, and in challenges to overweening confidence in epistemological and metaphysical pursuits. It too often culminates, I'm afraid, in suspicion of the very possibility of self-knowledge, authenticity, or wisdom. Self-knowledge can't be a matter of holding oneself as an object at arm's length and then observing. That would leave in darkness the self doing the holding and observing. Nevertheless, more than a grain of truth remains in the Socratic maxims, "know thyself" and "the unexamined life is not worth living." Socratic self-knowledge, and the variant Kierkegaard would hold, has to be a matter of sensing which experiences claim one, getting confident in one's intimacy with those claims, pledging them as one's own, and having one's actions be faithful to that pledge.

Self-knowledge is not propositional. It doesn't rest on knowing *"these truths to be self-evident"* (or otherwise justified). Self-knowledge seems more like a species of contact, tactile, or visceral knowledge, knowing our way with our experience, and then having trust in it, standing by it, having it morph into a pledge or promise. Socrates claims ignorance of everything but love. Perhaps he's intimating that he's in visceral touch with a love of friends, of his city, and of wisdom – even if he could only stammer in ignorance if asked to give grounds for his loves. To know his love is to be close enough to it, and responsive enough to it, to pledge fidelity to it (to stand by a love of inquiry and ideals, of justice and the good, and of friends and city) despite lacking even the semblance of an "enlightenment-approved" proof or justification of those ideals that one's action and one's life might embody – the elusive objects of one's trust and pledge.

We know that Socrates knows himself because he's loyal to Athens, pledges his loyalty, and is at ease in steadfastly living out that pledge. He's in intimate contact and at one with himself, oblivious to any temptation not to honor that pledge. His self is that pledge. He neither pines for anything, nor agonizes over options he might have followed out. He wins strength from saying, pledging, "Here I stand and can do no other" – without a trace of false bravado. The "necessities" his pledge entails are so much a part of who he is that they don't strike him as restrictive – any more than the biological necessities that breathing entails strike one as restrictive – they can be pure delight. Socrates shows only poise, composure, self-possession, and freedom. He lives out the truth of (his moral-religious) subjectivity. That's as good as it gets, and is good enough for assurance that he knows himself.

Notes

1 I develop a taxonomy of sorts of objectivity and subjectivity from a different angle in *Selves in Discord and Resolve*, (Routledge: 1996) pp. 86–7).

2 Foucault is often associated only with the idea that subjectivity and the subject disappear once we grasp the role of powers and institutions in their formation. For an argument that disassociates him from any proclamation of "the death of the subject," see Amy Allen, "The Anti-Subjective Hypothesis," *The Philosophical Forum*, XXXI, 2 (2000); for an argument that disassociates Nietzsche from the demise of subjectivity, and defends a picture of multiple subjectivities (or masks) as capturing Nietzsche's standpoint, see Robert Guay, "The 'I's Have it: Nietzsche on Subjectivity," *Inquiry*, 49, 3, (2006), 218–41.

3 In *An Atheism that is Not Humanist in French Thought* (Stanford: 2011), Stefanos Geroulanos gives an eye-opening account of 'anti-humanism' in France – a perspective that was dead set against "liberal" views that put individual consciousness (or subjectivity) center-stage. This move against Socrates, Descartes, and even a Kierkegaardian subjectivity started in the 1930s and resurfaced after

World War II, especially in Heidegger's "Letter on Humanism" and Derrida's privileging of *texts* over contexts, persons, or authors.

4 In a strange misplacement of focus, and as if to satisfy a craving for our *own* fugitive subjectivity, we gorge on the details of someone else's all-too-glib subjectivity – guests of Oprah or Dr. Phil who so often vent predictable feelings, or celebrities disheveled in scandal magazines at supermarket checkout aisles. Distracted from, and fearful of, our own intimate life, we lose ourselves in the shallow revelations of figures that remain anonymous to us even as they seem vulnerable and accessible.

5 I discuss Kierkegaard's collaborative Socratic-Christian identity in the first four chapters of *On Søren Kierkegaard*.

6 See Jonathan Lear, *A Case for Irony* (Tanner Lectures on Human Values) (Harvard 2011), and *Therapeutic Action: An Earnest Plea for Irony* (The Other Press, 2003).

7 Lear, Jonathan, *Happiness, Death, and the Remainder of Life* (Cambridge, MA: Harvard University Press, 2002), pp. 101–5.

8 Our understanding of Freud's "death instinct" should be modified in light of the Socratic experiment in Athens. As Lear sees it, the death instinct is not an *instinct* at all. Freud falls victim here to the widespread assumption that all forces in a life or a culture must have a purpose or manifest a drive or instinct. Lear's counter is that death (for instance) can disrupt massively. It can be a major force in shaping individual life and culture. Yet it is not a drive or instinct: it is "without purpose," *without teleology*, "just a fact." Death's "irruption" is linked both to the execution of Socrates and to the trauma Socratic questioning brings to the city. (This "irruption" then bears comparison to a momentous Heideggerian "event" or "happening" (*Ereignis*) – a Kierkegaardian *Augenblick*.)

9 See Chapter 9.

10 Socrates' protestations of ignorance – his claim that he's not really teaching anything, that he's not a teacher, that he knows only that he knows nothing – take on new meaning here. Given the inherited conceptual landscape, Socrates' questions don't make sense to his audience, so he defuses the barbs by protesting that he knows nothing. How can it be a crime to *know nothing*? That makes him seem innocent.

11 To better approach the ideal of the natural sciences, psychology becomes grounded in physiology, biology, and the observation of behavior. Philosophy approaches the mind through the lens of behaviorism, pragmatism, naturalism, or more recently, cognitive

science. Only quite recently has consciousness and a loose
phenomenology returned as exciting fields of study among academic
philosophers and psychologists. Stokes speaks of a "resurgence of
interest in consciousness and subjectivity in philosophy of mind
in the last twenty years or so" and points to Chalmers writing
on 'the hard problem' of consciousness (Private correspondence.)
And there has been "a return to religion" among a number of
continental post-structuralist thinkers. On the other hand, these
movements toward a "rehabilitation" of consciousness or subjectivity
is countered, from another cultural corner, by a suspicion of
"humanism," where that term is a stand-in for the sort of subjectivity
and life of the spirit of such concern to Kierkegaard, Buber, and
so many others thinkers continuing a tradition of philosophical
anthropology or the first-person standpoint so crucial to existentialist
thinking

12 Patrick Stokes gives us this caution: "Obviously Heidegger and his
descendants reject Cartesianism but it's not clear to me that they
thereby give up on subjectivity *per se*" (Private correspondence).
Generalization has its risks.

13 See Chapter 9.

14 Here I borrow from *On Søren Kierkegaard: Dialogue, Polemics,
Lost Intimacy, and Time* (Aldershot, Hants: Ashgate, 2007),
especially pp. 62–5. In a story that remains to be fully told,
Kierkegaard provides Heidegger's Ur-text for *Being and Time*.
Angst, *Augenblick*, care, openness to otherness, repetition, silence,
fallenness, appropriation, decisiveness, attunement, leveling,
chatter, temporality – all these (and others) are lifted directly from
Kierkegaardian texts. The argument that *Being and Time* is a version
of Kierkegaard's *Unscientific Postscript's* "religiousness A" (pagan
religiousness) is defended in Hubert L. Dreyfus and Jane Rubin,
"You can't get something for nothing: Kierkegaard and Heidegger on
how not to overcome Nihilism," *Inquiry* (30) 1987. Kierkegaard's
A Literary Review (London: Penguin, 2001), formerly translated
The Present Age, is the place to find "leveling," "the crowd," and
"chatter." In a personal note, John D. Caputo writes, "Augenblick's
importance is found in Heidegger's GA 29/30, pp. 224–5 (translated
under the title *Fundamental Concepts of Metaphysics* (Indiana
University Press), pp. 149–50). Heidegger interprets "the moment"
("the glance" "Augenblick") as the moment in which Dasein is
disclosed to itself in the *Blick der Entschlossenheit*. Rather like
the moment of truth." I thank Professor Caputo for this reference.
I discuss Kierkegaard's version of "Augenblick," *Øieblikket*, or

"the glance" in *On Søren Kierkegaard*, Chapter 6. This cluster of concepts or themes becomes central to the development of continental philosophy from Heidegger through Tillich, Buber, Sartre and on to Derrida and after. It also becomes central to psychology through Jaspers, Binswanger, and Carl Rogers, among others.

15 See Robert H. Richardson, Jr., *Emerson, The Mind on Fire* (Berkeley: University of California: 1995), p. 312.

16 In this vein, Henry Bugbee will say that our best thinking comes as a "meditation of the place." Henry Bugbee, *The Inward Morning, A Philosophical Exploration in Journal Form* (Athens, GA: University of Georgia, 1999), p. 139.

17 In Chapter 9, I argue that "inwardness" (better, "wholeheartedness") is interpersonal – not a private Cartesian box wired up to God or Truth. To lose subjectivity is to fall into public "chatter" or run with "the crowd".

18 For the role of intimate conversation in the constitution of a moral self, see my *Lost Intimacy in American Thought: Recovering Personal Philosophy from Thoreau to Cavell*, Continuum Books, 2009, Chapter 9.

19 Critchley, Simon, *Things Merely Are* (London: Routledge, 2005), p. 10.

20 "Dasein" is rendered "the-openness-we-are" by Thomas Sheehan, "Reading Heidegger's 'What is Metaphysics?'," *The New Yearbook for Phenomenology and Phenomenological Philosophy*, I (2001), p. 196

21 *Kierkegaard's Papers and Journals, A Selection*, ed. and trans. Alastair Hannay (New York: Penguin, 1996), p. 92, (7 October 37, II A 131).

22 Not so long ago, philosophy and psychology would be part of a joint venture in contemplating and studying ordinary subjectivity. In the nineteenth century, Nietzsche identified himself as a classical philologist *and* as a psychologist. Kierkegaard has mentored psychologists and psychoanalysts from Rollo May and Carl Rogers to Erik Erikson and Jonathan Lear. A radical divorce of psychology from philosophy and an abandonment of subjectivity would be unthinkable to William James, not to mention Plato, Kierkegaard, Nietzsche, or Socrates. More recently, both Pierre Hadot and Michel Foucault take philosophy in the old Socratic fashion as care for the soul – a practice at once psychological, religious, and philosophical. See essays on Rollo May, Carl Rogers, Eric Fromm, Erik Erikson and Julia Kristeva, *Kierkegaard and the Social Sciences*, Jon Stewart, (ed.) (Ashgate, 2010). I entered graduate school in philosophy

to follow the author of *The Self in Transformation: Philosophy, Psychoanalysis, and the Life of the Spirit*. Later, Herbert Fingarette authored *Self-Deception,* a minor classic in which Kierkegaard, Freud, and Sartre play trans-disciplinary parts untangling the riddle of a self against itself, of a split-subjectivity. As an undergraduate, I studied in a seminar room whose door bore the copperplate, "Philosophy and Psychology." The bookshelves held a mixed collection of nineteenth and early twentieth century volumes from what have now become distinct disciplines.

23 In the *Republic,* Socrates promises to his friends "to build a city of words," a city in speech or dialogue. For Socrates as simultaneously religious and philosophical, see Chapters 1 through 4 of my *On Søren Kierkegaard.* Parts of the second half of this essay are adapted from Chapter 4.

24 Critchley, Simon, *Things Merely Are* (London: Routledge, 2005), p. 10.

25 Climacus ridicules the "privat-docent" – not exactly an Adjunct, but an instructor who is paid by attendance.

26 This is the opening sentence from the mission statement, found at the website home page for The University of Malta, Fall 2006.

27 *Kierkegaard's Papers and Journals*, 33, (Gilleleje, 1 August 35). On the connections between "knowledge that comes alive" and avowals (or pledges) related to authentic identity and self-knowledge, see Charles Larmore, *Practices of the Self* (University of Chicago Press, 2010).

2

On Self, Others, Goods, and Final Faith

In philosophy as in other intellectual and artistic endeavors, we stay alive by relating to the living and also to the dead, bringing them alive for us. In different times and places, Søren Kierkegaard travels under different cloaks, serving different ends and warming readers' aspirations in ways that are typically understood only retrospectively. We can be grasped by Kierkegaard's words long before we understand what has grasped us, or why. His impressive longevity through various resuscitations rests partly on the power of his texts, available first in Danish only, and now translated into every major language. It rests also on ready ears and eyes, distant in time and space from Copenhagen, on those who find a living core in him, even as he brings their eyes and ears alive.

This mutual fit of writer's and reader's needs is testament to a kind of pervasive and primal communicative mutuality. Miguel de Unamuno discovers Scandanavian writers who can speak to him: first Henrik Ibsen and then Kierkegaard. He learns Danish to better hear and respond. He knows in his bones that Kierkegaard's knight of faith is none other than the heroic (and anti-heroic) Quixote.[1] Ludwig Wittgenstein finds a writer who touches his troubled soul, and seeks out a translator's help in Minnesota for getting closer to Kierkegaard's *Works of Love*.[2] His notes on Kierkegaard in *Culture and Value* bring Kierkegaard alive in new ways.[3] Kitaro Nishida happens on words of Kierkegaard; he enters a communicative exchange that brings him alive in unexpected ways, this time in Kyoto, Japan.[4] It is as if we are suited to live in such communicative mutuality.

Here is an instance of what I am calling "communicative mutuality" taken from a classroom experience passed on by Stanley Cavell:

> Here was serious mirth in progress, and what I read as perfection was the projection of my utter faith, then and now, that the mirth was impersonal, that here a class had witnessed not the private defeat of an individual's experience but the public victory of sweet and shared words – mirth over the happy fact that the world is working out and that we are made for it.[5]

The world works out as we come alive in a "we" of dialogical and hermeneutical community that stretches back to the dead, even as the dead stretch forward to us. In it we entrust our restless questions and desire to live.

**   **   **

In the compass of a short essay, these spidery channels of mutual revival can't be traced in detail. Nevertheless, I want to trace Kierkegaard's relevance to philosophy over the last hundred years or so before turning to his overt and tacit presence today. I give a brief satellite view of the terrains he has inhabited since his biological demise, focusing on his philosophical afterlife (though he has been endlessly relevant to literature, theology, psychology, and social-political critique, as well). His reach has been global, embracing North and South America, Spain, and Japan; England, Scotland, Ireland and France; not to mention Australia, Israel, Russia, Poland, and Iran.[6]

Inevitably, we discover the terrain marked "the analytic-continental divide." I am interested in how that chasm emerged, and how Kierkegaard is a figure bridging it, for Kierkegaard's writing on the self (not to mention Wittgenstein's engagement with him), makes the old maps obsolete. Thus Kierkegaard wears two hats in my narrative, first as a major figure in the genealogy of continental philosophy, and also, a major figure in smoothing over that divide. After some quick historical sketches I consider Kierkegaard's picture of the self as a constellation of unfolding expressive relations to itself, to others, and to constitutive goods, including one he designates an "establishing power."

I conclude with a reading of "establishing power" in terms of what I call final faith – a mood or way of being that can be rendered theologically (God is the establishing power). But perhaps unexpectedly it can also be rendered non-theologically – otherwise than as a gesture toward Christian divinity. Absorbing some powerful words from Stanley Cavell, we can read a relationship to an "establishing power" as our need to acknowledge, to faithfully concede, our multifold roots in ways of life construed in an anthropological register.

Glancing back

Kierkegaard revived

Kierkegaard was interred in Copenhagen 1855, but he lived on as a writer in Europe, including Denmark, as well as in North America, and Japan during the first half of the 20th century. In the United States, one thinks of the influence of W.H. Auden, Reinhold Niebuhr and H. Richard Niebuhr, and the émigré Paul Tillich, who were all serious readers of Kierkegaard. He also lived among readers of Rilke, Ibsen, and Unamuno; he lived under their skin.[7]

In the 1950s and 1960s it was as "the father of existentialism" that English-speaking intellectuals would know Kierkegaard. Existentialism was global.[8] In its heyday it thrived in Paris, London, New York, and San Francisco, as well as in Berlin and Kyoto. By the 1980s, postmodernism and deconstruction kept Kierkegaard alive. The attractions were his social critiques, his de-centering and complicating of "the self," and his indirect communication, a device prompted by his sharp awareness of the inadequacies of solely representational discourse. Through all this, a suspicion lingered that a dangerous Christianity lay underneath his otherwise brilliant expositions. He was cited only sparingly in an increasingly secular high-cultural world.

In the 1920s in Spain, Unamuno and José Ortega y Gasset were devoted readers. In Germany, Heidegger took up with Kierkegaard, who provided him with diction for Being and Time. He picks up Kierkegaard's "leveling," "repetition," "prattle," "angst," "being toward death," "temporality," "augenblick" (or "moment"), and much more.[9] Heidegger's later discourses on poetic thinking owe something to Kierkegaard's theme of poetic living. To the extent that Heidegger is an inescapable figure for twentieth century philosophy, Kierkegaard becomes inescapable, too.

Less well known is his presence in Japan. In the 1920s and 1930s, a number of Western-looking Japanese philosophers discovered in Kierkegaard a champion of "the single individual."[10] They found in the Dane an intense religious pathos well out of reach of stifling religious institutions. Here was a way to escape the dogma that personal, "existential" identity is just a negligible ripple – if even that – beneath identities cast in terms of social powers and roles. Personal existence, they surmised, needn't be imprisoned in tradition and ritual – even as traditional forms retained beauty and inspiration. Quite incredibly, by 1930 there were more Japanese translations of Kierkegaard than there were English ones. Overall, in the 1930s his presence in Japan, France, Germany, and Spain was far greater than it was in the Anglophone world, where philosophy was bent on logic and linguistic analysis rather than on anything as vague as a restless human spirit.

The seedbed of "continental philosophy"

In Paris, between the wars, Kierkegaard figured in debates on the fate of Europe after the disasters of 1914–18.[11] At issue were the prospects, if any, of democracy and socialism in postwar Europe, and more generally. Perhaps these options were dead. If so, the issue was whether cultural and personal life could survive nihilism, despair, and ennui. Was this the decline of the West? Kierkegaard, Hegel, Marx, Husserl, Buber, and the rising luminary, Martin Heidegger, figured in these debates. In this intellectual ferment, a number of now-famous writers were cutting their teeth – among them, Emmanuel Levinas, Jean-Paul Sartre, Merleau-Ponty, Jean Wahl, and Gabriel Marcel.[12] In Germany, The Institute for Social Research morphed into the Frankfurt School, that blended philosophy and social science in a progressive agenda. The Institute was reborn in Manhattan as the New School.

Acute awareness of the perils of human existence stoked the flames of what came to be called "continental philosophy." Interpretations of Hegel, Marx, and Kierkegaard were at the center. Kierkegaard appealed to those who sensed a crisis of spirit, not least in religion, yet doubted that faith could be summarily dismissed. His psycho-social analyses of "the crowd," of dread, love and hope, of self-deception and anxiety, gave his readers a diagnosis of the times. His subtle mix of skepticism and hope was endlessly alluring.[13] Certainly the genius of his writing – its cutting irony, psychological acuity, and astounding intelligence – could not be missed.

In Britain, "continental concerns" were under-played or absent in academic philosophy. Between the wars, a physics-inspired logical positivism thrived alongside emerging "analytical" and "ordinary language" styles of philosophy. Here, the names of Russell, Moore, Ryle, A. J. Ayer, Wittgenstein, and John Austin loom large. The epistemological structures of physics, logic, and language were at issue. The drama of human existence was left to literature. Nothing of interest was revealed by anxiety or despair; these "mere emotions" were unhappy signs of pathology. Philosophy's high aspiration to become scientific cast aesthetics, ethics, and political philosophy to the bin of only third rate importance. Philosophy as a way of life was unintelligible, a glaring and inept *non sequitur*. If the gap between non-continental and continental philosophy grew wider in the period before World War II, it became impassable and poisonous after the War. Its festering reality is still evident today in academic job markets – though signs indicate lessening hostilities.[14]

** **

The story of mutual incomprehension between British-analytical and German-French-continental philosophy makes for an intriguing, if somewhat embarrasing, saga. It has recently been expertly told in great detail by a number of philosophically sophisticated historians.[15] For our purposes, however, the presupposition of an inevitably impassable rift is a poor basis for evaluating or framing a Kierkegaard who can speak in the present. Whatever he can mean to us today is not abetted by placing him against a divide that no longer divides – or no longer needs to divide.

Kierkegaard's contemporary relevance has to be established in new terms. Apart from the interest of cultural historians, to whom should he matter today? I bank on his pertinence to all who set the analytical-continental divide aside as they explore the contours of self and community as they historically unfold, linked by ties of sensibility and affect as much as by reasoning and dispassionate knowing.

"Analytic" explorations

Do all philosophers fit neatly on one side or the other of the continental-analytic rift? Wittgenstein is usually taken to nail down the "analytic" end of things – yet Kierkegaard profoundly influenced him. Perhaps their affiliation casts some doubt on the adequacy of the "two camps" picture across the board. Perhaps they belong to neither camp, or to both simultaneously. This is worth exploring.

Wittgenstein on ethics and religion

That Wittgenstein shaped Anglophone philosophy from the 1930s on, peaking in the 1970s but continuing into the present, is a relatively familiar story. What is less familiar is a notable revival of interest in the ethical and religious bent of his thought, found, for example, in his notebook comments on Kierkegaard, Schopenhauer, Spencer, and Tolstoy. From recent scholarship, we can compose a pessimistic, "existential" figure – a Wittgenstein caught up in spiritual struggles that are part and parcel of finding one's way in philosophy and in one's life.[16] Glimpses of Wittgenstein's disquietude, as well as of Kierkegaard's importance to him, leap to the fore in the collection of notes titled Culture and Value.[17] Kierkegaard is also a presence in Wittgenstein's early "Lecture on Ethics,"[18] and is a player in the works of Stanley Cavell, Steven Mulhall, Hilary Putnam, and George Pattison, all of whom write well beyond the analytic-continental rift.

These philosophers are deeply sympathetic to both Kierkegaard and Wittgenstein. Cavell, Mulhall, and Pattison have written on Heidegger, as well.[19] Yet none would be called a continental philosopher. From an immersion or training in Wittgenstein, they find Kierkegaard a great philosopher, more or less a contemporary, "one of us."[20] They would understand (though they might respectfully contest) Wittgenstein's view that Kierkegaard was the greatest philosopher of the nineteenth century.

A turn to the self

If the Wittgenstein-Kierkegaard connection circumvents the analytic-continental divide, contemporary Anglophone discussions of "the self" repeat the lesson. Charles Taylor's influential "Responsibility for Self" appeared in 1976, just a few years after Harry Frankfurt's "Freedom of the Will and the Concept of a Person" (1971).[21] These essays begin an groundswell of interest in personhood, love, care, and a self that reflects on itself, its ideals, and its responsibility toward others – and acts in light of these. This brings Kierkegaard on stage at the center of Anglophone philosophy. Taylor's compendious *Sources of the Self* (1992) and *The Ethics of Authenticity* (1991), paired with Frankfurt's *The Importance of What We Care About* (1988), *Necessity, Volition, and Love* (1999), and his instant classic, *On Bullshit* (2005), point toward a constellation of excursions that might as well be called "existential." They pair handsomely with Kierkegaard's portraits of the self.[22]

While the literature related to the "Frankfurt-Taylor" unraveling of "selfhood" is now enormous, Kierkegaard citations are relatively sparse. Nevertheless, Kierkegaard can be found, or at least plausibly imagined, as a shifting presence in these contemporary discussions. Wherever the focus is the self's expressive capacities and identities, Kierkegaard is close by. What emerges is a relational view of self unfolding narratively. Most of these Anglophone explorations are only among academics, though Taylor's reach has been enviably wide, and Frankfurt's *On Bullshit* sent him well beyond the walls of the academy. I return to its connection to authenticity in a later chapter. A bestseller, it reads, in the present context, like a companion to Kierkegaard's critique in *Two Ages: A Literary Review*. Therein one finds his scathing attack on chatter ("B.S.") – in media and social-political-cultural affairs, the ugly swamp of fraudulent, "inauthentic" prattle.[23]

Constellations, ensembles, rivers

There is a rich constellation of Kierkegaardian themes that weave in and out of the Frankfurt-Taylor trajectory. This constellation includes taking "the self" as an inner and outer interweaving of multiple self-factors or threads. There is a continuous embodied outflow of expressive threads that flex backward, drawing on those self-fibers, and forward, into the world of expressive others. This inflow-outflow brings the fibers of the self into embodied contour in the world, into a social interplay with others, and into receptivity toward what Taylor calls higher goods and Frankfurt calls "necessary ideals."[24]

If the self is a pattern of interweaving relationships, it is not a Cartesian mental substance, or a substance of any sort, mental or corporeal or spiritual. Nor is it a core around which elements in a constellation swing. It is not a Zen-like nothingness, nor a Nietzschean useful fiction, nor a dubious cultural construction in dire need of deconstruction.

This schema of "the self" as a constellation of relationships is elaborated by Anti-Climacus in *The Sickness Unto Death*. To prepare the stage, let me consider three images that interpret this constellation. It can be seen as a fabric, a musical ensemble, and a watershed. Interweaving self-fibers can twist into threads that weave into a fabric. A number of self-strands with beginnings and ends weave in and out of a shirt or scarf made of nothing but other strands – there is no underlying core or substance.[25] This image allows us to picture revision, conversion, or transformation of self as the extraction of a thread, or a number of them, or the addition of new ones, sometimes altering the fabric as a whole: the unraveled shirt knits up anew as a shawl.

We can also envisage the constellation of self-factors as a performing musical ensemble, playing without a designated director. This figuration lets embodied auditory motion upstage what might otherwise be taken as a static constellation of only "inner" elements. Of course, these figurations are not competing. A musical ensemble can weave strands of melody and supporting harmonic or dissonant lines into the fabric of an unfolding piece. And the unfolding can be pictured as an unfolding constellation of temporally extended auditory elements (and the spaces between).

A third figuration that can clarify the relational self comes from Climacus's remark that passion is a river, constantly in flow, whose beginnings and ends remain in dark obscurity.[26] We visualize a self, then, as a system of streams, or rivers of passion – or, from some height – as a flowing watershed.[27] "Self" is not an anchoring rock but a fluid tangle where streams and brooks become larger rivers, where movement slows in ponds, swamps, and lakes, and self springs from the earth, empties into oceans unknown, and reflects skyward through mists and atmospheres toward heavens.

We don't need to ask, in the old Cartesian way, whether self and passion are body or soul, corporeal or psychic. That's like asking whether waterfalls are liquid – or rock-face, whether ponds are water – or geological kettles. To ask whether a passion for music is an emotion or a cognitive attachment is like asking whether, hearing Bach, our hearts are stirred – or our minds are impressed by infinite harmonic improvisations. We needn't ask whether a Kierkegaardian self looks inward – or outward. His vaunted "inwardness" is a heartfelt way of relating to others and the world.[28]

For Taylor and Frankfurt, the self is necessarily related to defining goods. One's identity is tied to goods that call on our receptivity to what can present itself as initially "outside" us. To an autonomy-fixated culture, this attentive receptivity to ideals can look like a swooning abandonment of self to external ethical-religious demands, a moment of child-like dependence. Bold self-assertion and choice seem absent. We are skittish about yielding to ideals. Yet in ordinary life we yield to sleep, pleasure, or reading without a dangerous abandonment of action or autonomy. The expressive flow of an assertive self is typically punctuated by spans of quiet and withdrawal.[29]

Narratives

What we are may turn out to be less a central core of decision and assertion than an ongoing unfolding, marked by intermittent unraveling. We render affinities or clashing disharmonies among self-strands in the many stories we tell (or don't tell, or are incapable of telling) about ourselves – our actions, tastes, passions, reflections, friends, maladies, deep sorrows. These multiple stories are modulated by what others might tell of us.

What I called communicative mutuality is an ongoing negotiation among ways we find ourselves, and ways others find us, between our sense of what we have written, and another's sense of it, between my sense of my bravery or love, and another's. "A self" is still like an ensemble, fabric, or watershed, but now we may superimpose on these images a narrative flow of telling and retelling. We are story-telling, conversational creatures. Tracing the self is tracing interweaving strands of telling and retelling, partial stories and their revisions in the light of what we, and others, make of them over time, while longer and shorter strands are added, removed, or knitted anew.[30]

In the past 20 years and more, there has been a move to set aside the ancient quarrel between philosophy and literature, begun dramatically with Plato's banishment of the poets.[31] In the tradition of Shelley's "A Defence of Poetry," Shakespeare can now be read philosophically, and Plato, as a dramatist. There are affinities between writing out a life autobiographically, and writing philosophy responsive to texts and one's deepest intuitions of their carriage and content. Literary, autobiographical, and philosophical interests need not be at odds: each may run stronger in acknowledgment of insights, and practices and tropes of the others.

Cavell, for example, speaking for himself, proposes that autobiography and philosophy need to be "told in terms of each other."[32] This renews the Kierkegaardian demand that philosophical reflection stem from the heart of the writer, and that the writer be ready to undergo transfiguration in its light. Reading a philosopher can change me unexpectedly.

Writing philosophy can change me too – mark conversions, great or small. Words and gestures open into narratives arcing inward to texture the self's lights and darks, and arcing outward toward another's subjectivity, there to be acknowledged or refused. A child, neighbor, friend, lover, or oneself (under scrutiny) might be so addressed. Kierkegaardian literature, philosophy, and autobiography contour a self nuanced to being one among others in a context where readers and writers, listeners and speakers seamlessly switch roles, all open to transformation in the process.

A relational self is a skein of interests, passions, and affinities that unfold bodily and among others: an embodied relationality. My singular shames or joys unfold from these blushing or radiant cheeks. A relational self is socially embedded. We need others as we emerge from infancy, and as we launch into adulthood, and as we enter the fullness of age to help negotiate who we are, who we have been, who we will be – others who are new raveling and unraveling strands of relationality. The relationality that we are aligns itself responsively to constitutive goods: I am my love of Bach and of grandchildren.[33] Finally, an unfolding relational self is best rendered in narrative episodes carrying spans of a life.

Modes of relation

Kierkegaard sketches a relational subjectivity. His plea that "truth is subjectivity" suggests that for humans the deepest call is to be responsive to oneself and others – to be responsible.[34] It is a plea to own or internalize moral-religious demands as they appear, to act on them, make them part of one's moral-religious life. To act "in the truth," as Climacus demands, is to act in light of the truths (or goods) that claim us. If "truth is subjectivity," we acknowledge (or dismiss) goods or demands as they appear. This highlights limitations in an exclusively executive self.

Executive self and receptive soul

When I acknowledge goods, my gesture is less an instance of autonomous will or decisive action than the exercise of a receptive, attentive, dependent soul. As early as *Either/Or* II, Kierkegaard has Judge Wilhelm contrast activity with receptivity in self-formation.[35] In one idiom, the self must "choose itself," affirm its history, take responsibility for what it will be. In a contrasting idiom, the self "receives itself" as a gift. In his short book *Repetition*, a pathos-ridden young man awaits the gift of self, even as Job, in his patience, is an unsuspecting recipient of new worlds.[36]

In acknowledging the warmth of a child's smile or the majesty of a descent of geese, or the radiance of simple justice, I find myself glad for their gifts, dependent on realities I cannot command to appear. If compassion becomes a good in my life, I find myself less an executive making compassion happen, than receptive, ready to answer its call. Shelving the executive self resembles shelving self-assertion in yielding to the voice of another. For the moment, I just listen. Or it resembles a movement from willfulness to willingness or will-lessness, when awe, surprise, or indignation supervene. I'm thrown out of activity, as it were – into stillness or quietude, or in the case of indignation, the shock of anger. To fall asleep I must relinquish the executive self, let myself fall – as in letting myself fall in love, or succumb to simple goodness or beauty. For something to be good in the eyes of subject, if that subject is more than an impassive observer, it must have allure, a magnetic force. Then to see the good is to give in to its allure – not to endlessly second guess it.

Typically, yielding will be a momentary phase that's followed by action. After a startle of indignation, one may utter a curse (or not); after love strikes, one may break into a run or a smile (or not). Some lives seem to follow a path where receptivity, attention, contemplation, and listening provide the tenor of becoming; others may follow a path where decisive action, deeds, self-assertion, and public achievement mark the tenor. Yet a life tempered toward action cannot altogether lack moments of listening receptivity;

nor can a life tempered toward acknowledgment or contemplation altogether lack moments of standing decisiveness and action.

Relations to goods, self as ensemble

There are any number of goods I might acknowledge, listen for, or attend to in a life: justice or creativity, athletic prowess or camaraderie, bravery or honor, service, family, or contemplation. These possibilities are offered in the course of communications with others and traditions, possibilities, to be sure, that I can come to own and affirm. They are not self-made but offered as inheritance, as strands in an identity not yet my own, woven through lives I admire. They are unbidden, ready for partial or wholehearted acceptance (or refusal). I do not fabricate the goods of my life out of whole cloth, nor do I create them by a brute choice. That they are goods is something I can grant. I cannot force their goodness to happen.

In *The Sickness Unto Death,* Kierkegaard has his pseudonym Anti-Climacus lay out a daunting schema for selfhood. The self, we are told, is a "relation which relates to itself, and in that relating to itself relates to something else".[37] The self is not just a passive conjunction or correlation – say of mind and body. It is an active, dynamic relationship. It is not a substantial center but a relational ensemble of sub-factors – my desires or projects, for instance – that are in intimate processes of negotiating, assessing, and realizing.

This ensemble is a relation, first, between three sets of opposed self-factors, labeled with metaphysical austerity: freedom and necessity, eternity and temporality, infinite and finite. If I am aligned with "infinity" I will expose myself to the call of "infinite things," things that can be boundless, like courage or patience. I will also expose myself to its opposite, to the call of "finite things": this pet, this task, needs attention. The pair "freedom-necessity" can be heard as a person's enjoying activities that spring free of social constraints, versus undergoing the necessities of life with others. Obligations bind, pleasure and delight set free. I am free in submission to a God who grants me independence; am bound in relation to my neighbor to whom I am bound, commanded, to love. Of course, these self-factors vary in plasticity and intensity through the time and unfolding of any phase of a life.

Each of these *relata* can be interpreted as a need, project, or desire. A need for immersion in time is opposed to a need to escape the burdens of temporality. These paired "self-factors" have their correlative goods. My need for detachment or freedom is a need for the good of detachment or freedom. My need for immersion with others and in tasks is a pursuit of the good of immersion, say in the dependences of family life. These goods are spun together in webs or ensembles.

Evaluation and negotiation

These self-relations are not given complete and assembled. They are always open to revision and assessment internal to their unfolding, part of their unfolding. They are self-relating, and their mode of relation is evaluative. Kant saw the essence of our humanity in our capacity to step back to add an "I think" to any state of consciousness – to be a consciousness relating to itself, as it were. Kierkegaard sees the essence of my humanity as a capacity to step back and ask, "Am I really this?" Thus do I value and evaluate a need, desire, project, or correlative good. The process of acknowledging, disowning, promoting, or dismissing strands of self is undertaken tacitly or explicitly by other members of the self-ensemble that I am. Regulation is internal, and the role of regulator, shifting.[38] I am a being who evaluates and negotiates my becoming in the world.

Thus I am not a rigid structure, but flexibly tiered. To see my career life, love life, athletic life, religious life, art life, family life, bar life, or couch life as loosely interwoven is to see an ensemble of goods interwoven, each capable of evaluating the importance of the others. Strength of self is the strength of the meshing and raveling of unfolding fibers, ever spinning threads that enter fabrics, never-yet complete. Loss of self is the dispersion or disappearance of some array of goods I desire (or demands that call me), or the dispersion of my capacity to assess or negotiate the array of goods, demands, and desires – for, I no longer relate to those relations. That the set of paired relata in fact relates to itself, just is "the self." Self-reflexive negotiation and evaluation going on in the environs of my bodily location is what it means for me to be a self.

Authenticity

The raveled realizations of these paired arrays of commitments or desires are open to evaluation and revision as a self-ensemble improvises its way into a future it will call its own. An authentic self underway, in motion, is fairly constantly under negotiation and revision.[39] This is the familiar process of weighing alternatives: one's family needs more time; one's career can be cut back; one has been lax in attention to relatives; one needs to resurrect one's early life as a musician. Humans are a disquieting issue for themselves. Authenticity comes into play as persons care for, take a stand on, what they are about and what they will be. Will they be true to the identity roughly shaped by those stands and cares? My friend is vulnerable to the conflicting demands of being a sister, a pilot, a cancer survivor.

As a person evaluates whether she has been or will be true to herself, she asks whether she has been in line with the self that over time she has articulated and become for herself (and others). This is no easy assignment. Will she fall prey to self-righteousness or self-deception? Does she feel a (true or false) glimmer of satisfaction in the turns her life takes? Perhaps she blushes with shame in the suspicion that she has betrayed the self she would be. She would not enjoy narrating that self. She might vacillate, especially in midnight hours, between negative and positive self-assessments.

There is no room here for a "super-self" – an executive self that conducts the negotiations and evaluations. Evaluations and negotiations happen in the locale of my corporality, of my arms akimbo, legs tensed, brow furrowed in concentration or worry. My finite needs qualify (and assess) my infinite hope; my momentary anger qualifies (and assesses) my lasting compassion. There is no digging deeper than the ensemble of relations that reaches out expressively to others. Like a jazz ensemble that can relate to itself without an independent conductor to negotiate its progress, so the ensemble-that-is-myself relates to itself – minus an executive "director in residence."[40]

But if this is correct, what are we to make of Kierkegaard's claim that the relational self relates to "another" in whom it finds itself "established"?[41] Doesn't this make me beholden to a director, or to God?

Grounding power, abyss

The ensemble of relations finds itself grounded transparently in another, or "the power that established it." Is the self now submerged in reverential deference? A no-nonsense reading would have Kierkegaard appealing frankly to God as the power that grounds the self, thus rescuing it from an abyss of flailing relations. This power will be the source of all goods, thus itself the Supreme Good. Anti-Climacus sometimes speaks of God, but also adopts a more religiously non-committal stance. In the penultimate paragraph of *The Sickness Unto Death*, he speaks only of an "establishing power."[42]

Dependence on God

There is a lucid and doctrinally Christian way of interpreting the "establishing power" on which a self is dependent. I will put that obvious interpretation on hold in order to expose a dependence felt intimately without necessarily being felt in overtly theological terms. This brings to the fore a proto-Christian, experiential substrate on which subsequent theological thinking can be based, and keeps wide open the roughly anthropological frame I have been developing so far.[43] Kierkegaard read Schleimacher in his formative years, so it could be, as George Pattison has it, that "the Christian and doctrinal material is the most adequate way of saying what's going on in our relation to that power."[44] Without delving deeper into Kierkegaard's historical context, let me quote Pattison once more: "for those in the stream of Schleiermacherian thought (and I think Kierkegaard was), the choice is not: do I have to be a fundamentalist believer or a secularist, but: how can I best articulate this mysterious moment in which I realize my life is given to me, as if from another."[45] That moment would be a moment in which, even fleetingly, I sense that my self-relations are secure, that my life, however fleetingly, is well-grounded, "transparently grounded in another."

Thus I aim to inhabit a space between a dogmatic and loud unhumble assertion that "everything rests on God" (a sort of raw fundamentalist stance) and a militantly secularist dogmatically unhumble view that since God is a mirage, Kierkegaard's appeal to a grounding power is a mirage, to be passed over in contempt. I think that this space between pre-theological experience interpreted philosophically and theological interpretations is inhabitable and facilitates both non-theological and theological discussion. One can, I hope, then make sense of Kierkegaard and a sort of theism whether or not one buys into theism, and make sense of a too-rapid dismissals of theism, whether or not one buys into anti-theism. This open space should welcome theologians of many stripes, non-theologians of various sorts, and even anti-theologians. So let me ask, "Why would I – why would anyone – be driven to ground human existence 'transparently' in an 'establishing power'?"

** ** **

There is a natural tendency to seek layers under layers, grounds under grounds, reasons beneath everything. This is a form of what Kant calls a "need of reason" – and perhaps a need that can never be satisfied.[46] Yet we shudder at the prospect of a dizzying regress. We want reason to bring closure, finality. Hence we seek Ultimate Power (underneath powers), Final Good (underneath goods). But why abandon the itch of reason? Why are ultimate Good, Power, or God themselves exempt from grounding – apart from our stipulation that they are, by definition, exempt?

The appeal to God as the self's establishing power might be no more than an arbitrary posit, a matter of falling back on an authoritative Father or Power that is by definition beyond challenge or review. Does this last-ditch appeal post up a fact of the matter open to elaboration and justification? Do I give reasons for holding it? Let's say instead that appeal to a grounding power is an exclamation, or an emphatic (but tenuous) address to the dead – an apostrophe. The subtext or counter current in this call to something absent is an exasperated concession, and grateful attestation, that there is something – a power – that holds me! I exclaim: my handhold holds. This is what Merleau-Ponty beautifully characterizes as "regaining the grace of our first certainties in the doubt which rings them round."[47]

I can't assert or posit anything explicit because I have absolutely no idea what such an establishing power would really be like. And perhaps invoking a power is the end of the line, because such a power is not anything that could be known to be real or unreal. (Does it make sense to ask, generally, if ghosts really exist? – I do not mean that feeling such power is feeling the presence of a ghost.) Conceding that I find rest, that I am held in an establishing power, I stammer something I cannot assert as a clear and simple fact to be tested in the public arena. I face my ignorance, I see I'm left empty-handed, I've not found a regression-stopping absolute that can be posted as a discovery. I face my ignorance, I see I'm left empty-handed, I've not found a regression-stopping absolute. My will is stalled, idled. Nevertheless, in the instance I invoke here, I do not look into a frightening abyss; I find rest patient in an establishing power.

Here we see two senses of "grounding" that can overlap or pull apart.[48] When I ask for grounds for a belief, I ask for a ground-as-reason. When I am overwhelmed by rampant contingency or the absence of a publically certified pillar of existential assurance – then, I seek ground-as-assurance: a handhold. If reasons run out, and I am to elude despair in that moment, I need – and can be graced by (so I argue) – ground-as-rest, as assurance, as respite from despair or a debilitating absurd. The knight of faith from *Fear and Trembling* who looks for all the world like a shopkeeper (or tax-collector, or postman) feels grounded (not in the sense of having reasons).[49] I feel "secure" in my wonder at the smile of a child (without having reasons). Socrates is enraptured by Diotima (without giving reasons).

Finite knowledge and awe

Tracking the world to know it better is not the same as being captured, enraptured, simply struck by it – perhaps even being terrified by its shear existence. Wittgenstein said with characteristic bluntness: "For me the facts are unimportant. But what men mean when they say that 'The world is there' lies close to my heart."[50] He reports "the experience of seeing the world as a miracle" ("Lecture on Ethics"[51]) and "astonishment that anything exists" ("Talks with Wittgenstein"[52]). With regard to an establishing power of the sort Anti-Climacus alludes to, the facts of the matter might be massively unimportant, and unimportant because any interest in them is ill conceived. In the matter of being struck by the existence of the world, or being struck by the wonder and fragility of a self relating to itself (and to others and goods), without a director, more or less suspended over an abyss (as it can seem), then – Sorry! – there just are no further facts of the matter to track.

What strikes me is existence itself, the world as a whole, the wonder of raveled personal existence, the smile of a child, or infectious classroom mirth. Then I'm not struck with "facts of the matter" but with minor or major miracles. Aspects of a world before me elicit awe or mirth and stop the inquisitive self in its tracks (at least for the moment). This is an encounter with something absolute, in that I enjoy a delight or wonder that demands no deeper grounding than itself. And it is not an encounter with an entity or thing that might (in another world, at another time) be available for bare knowledge. This experience displaces assertable, disinterested knowledge as the sole operative revelation of the world. To invoke "grounding power" here – a power permeating mirth, smiles, or wonder – leaves aside detached, observational knowledge. Yet to abandon such dispassionate knowing is not necessarily to be left staring into an abyss. It may be less a signal of despair than a moment of rest, a heartening moment of faith.

Final faith

We yearn for moments of mutual affinity and passable understanding, of feeling at home, even without the promise of absolute grounds providing indubitable knowledge. The capacity for attaining such moments of affinity and understanding does not rest on any one authority, economy of power, set of rules, or system of essences or universals. Stanley Cavell speaks to our proceeding without despair, despite lacking "an absolute." It is:

> a matter of our sharing routes of interest and feeling, modes of response, senses of humor and of significance and of fulfillment, of what is outrageous, of what is similar to what else, what a rebuke, what forgiveness ... all the whirl of organism Wittgenstein calls 'forms of life.' Human speech and activity, sanity and community, rest upon nothing more, but nothing less, than this. It is a vision as simple as it is difficult, and as difficult as it is (and because it is) terrifying.[53]

This is a form of faith, or hope, to be taken up in fear and trembling, but finally affording joy and delight. It is living in "communicative mutuality" in awareness that abandonment, loneliness, communicative misfires, and outright evil, although surely afoot, do not exhaust our ways of becoming. Of course, communicative mutuality can fall dead in its tracks. In that case, despair of the world ever working out is painfully apparent. This is the inverse of the "happy fact that the world is working out and that we are made for it."

In registering a welcome world without knowable, absolute grounds, I acknowledge what we might call a paradox, enigma, or mystery – a world that still shimmers happily despite the absence of final knowledge of a foundation. We are neither foundationalists nor fundametalists. Final faith as final assurance despite cause for despair replaces final knowledge. To be abandoned by impersonal knowledge is not to be hopelessly abandoned. The place of unknowing is the place where I sense that existence is affirmable, worthy of celebration. "Here was serious mirth in progress." This moment confirms Cavell's "utter faith" [my emphasis] in a "public victory of sweet and shared words – mirth over the happy fact that the world is working out and that we are made for it." Is this Kierkegaardian faith?

A picture of faith as "grounding power" – that power just being the sense that the world is welcoming – is implicit in the image of the jaunty shopkeeper lookalike, the knight of faith in *Fear and Trembling* who, strolling home for dinner, takes delight in all that strikes his eye.[54] Johannes de silentio, in *Fear and Trembling's* "Preamble from the Heart," avers that he is "secure to take pleasure in [the world]"[55] – he is "living joyfully and happily."[56] (Of course, there may be a modulation in this tone in Kierkegaard's late discourses; there certainly is in his "Attack Literature.")

This view of faith as a silent, implicit power underlying living securely, happily – a mood ever lacking explicit epistemological grounds (say, explanatory reasons) – can be reconstructed from several Kierkegaardian texts.[57] We don't find it laid out in a single place with the clarity today's professional philosophers would desire. Like a good dramatist, he leaves his performance with questions still abuzz. We're left wrestling with questions of faith and despair, and the sense that ease with the unfinished, unanswered, is delivered only through a patience that is ours to assume. Kierkegaard won't give answers on a platter. We get the raucous upending of platters. Irony and indirect communication, his typical modes of address, are upendings of so-called definitive interpretations of "establishing power" – or of anything else.

Philosophical accounts typically promise reasons for accepting one position or interpretation rather than another. Kierkegaard is cagey and elusive here. He refuses to write a treatise in defense of his appeal to "establishing power" or of his sketches of the contours of faith as assurance. To provide explication or defense would give pride of place to academic or forensic reasoning, which would bury the phenomena in question, opening the door to infinite digression. Anti-Climacus has a wonderful satire on offering three reasons for believing that one is in love. This makes love not a wonder or mystery but part of a forensic or tavern dispute, as if one were giving three reasons for voting for new taxes or ordering Bud Lite.[58] Giving three reasons for the proposition that I am at this moment in love with this child, or with God (or in fear of God), at that moment vaults me out of love (or terror or wonder) – into reasoning.

Faith as acknowledging establishing power

"Grounding power" may be a marker for the displacement of dispassionate knowledge and reason-giving, even as these become displaced in moments of falling in love. If this displacement does not catapult me into despair, one reason might be that I sense that an assuring demeanor mysteriously envelopes me. If I still find myself perched at the edge of an abyss, I do not fall. Enveloping assurance is not an intellectually explicit ground offered argumentatively. Rather, it points quixotically to the power of grounds to ground, or to the radiant goodness of goods, or to the power of a relation to relate to itself, ever lacking explicit ground or authority. In a quasi-comic-pathetic-existential desperation, I might register this non-despair, this affirmation of the goodness of goods, with the magical gesture of capitalization.[59] I appeal to "the Power that Grounds me," or "the Absolute in which I find my Being." As the rose radiates its beauty without a Why, so I am grounded without a Why.

I make this bewildered gesture toward a grounding power – no doubt masking some of my anxious bewilderment – without for a moment thinking that I am asserting a claim for dispassionate debate regarding an eternal Something. I don't assert as a claim to debate a power lying behind the beauty of this rose – a beauty that sweeps all need for reasons or metaphysics brusquely away. Nor do I loudly assert as a claim to debate a power lying behind the absolute security I feel in beholding this rose, or this child's smile, or this heart warming mirth – beauties and securities that sweep all need for reasons or metaphysics brusquely away.

Nevertheless I might ackwardly stammer something about the power of beauty, its power to establish my becoming, to fuel and raise up my soul. We recall Merleau-Ponty's witness, the moment of "regaining the grace of our first certainties in the doubt which rings them round" – our first certainty here being not just that the ground beneath our feet will not fail, but the unfailing certainty or security of beauty in a child's smile. We add Gillian Rose: "You must be able to say you don't know. Agnosticism is the only true religion because to have faith is not to give up knowledge, but to know where the limit of knowledge is."[60] Any mention of "establishing power" in this context remains a confession of ignorance about how to explicate ultimate power (the power of love or beauty to bind) – even as hopeful confidence, security, or trust in the world abides. As with Socrates' quixotic ignorance, there is nothing ill advised in affirming and welcoming wonders afloat, despite and alongside utter ignorance.[61]

Socrates is ignorant, we might say, about what lies behind his giving credence to Diotima, as she speaks about love. He floats the wonder of her song and we listen, enraptured.[62] Diotima cross-examines Socrates, but Socrates does not cross-examine her. He is taken. The apt response to whatever evokes wonder or awe, if those states are to be valued and sustained, is not to revert immediately to formulating objective knowledge aimed to capture or explain them, in the interest of increased mastery. With time, it may or may not become appropriate to seek a why for one's wonder. But if wonder (and allied states) are to live in their immediacy, then the apt response is to live out one's ignorance and wonder – and to abide in patience, gratitude, and humility. To be "held," "captured," "grounded," or "enraptured" is beyond dispassionate knowledge. – But to the soul and heart, it brings things as close as can be.

** ** **

Kierkegaard repays attention in any number of ways. He can bring us to academic issues, but he wants more of us than that. Philosophy, and writing more generally, can, but shouldn't, conform to mediocrity. It should unsettle a reader in a way conducive to a better, richer life. I set out to place Kierkegaard's importance among other thinkers, especially in the twentieth century, and within current explorations of the self, accepting his view that exposure to better, more acute reflection, can clean out the dregs from a self or soul, not least our own, as we read. He leads us by lyrical evocation to respond from the heart – even as his dialectical, conceptual clarifications clear passages to our necessary interests and passions.

Immersion in Kierkegaard's writing can bring arresting discoveries quite apart from a report on what, in a pedestrian or perfunctory way, he might be said to have said. Hamlet, Lear, and Quixote, through their lived words, actions, and sufferings, teach us to surpass ourselves by refining and tempering imagination – to see better what we have been and what we might be, in one or another aspect of our tangled or orderly lives. Philosophical writing can lead us through argument but also through image and metaphor. Kierkegaard can – and does – lead in this way, giving new images, scenarios, and formulae for grasping our fluid existence with others among ideals that call us out from a miserable or mediocre or passable self to a better self we still might be.

Notes

1 Unamuno recalls: "[I]f I began to learn Danish by translating ... Ibsen's *Brand*, it was the works of Kierkegaard which led me to congratulate myself for having learned [the language]," Miguel de Unamuno, *Our Lord Don Quixote: The Life of Don Quixote and Sancho, with Related Essays*, trans. Anthony Kerrigan (Princeton: Princeton University Press, 1967), p. 476n. 22. Also see Habib C. Malik, *Receiving Søren Kierkegaard: The Early Impact and Transition of His Thought* (Washington, DC: The Catholic University of America Press, 1997), pp. 284–5. I thank Eric Ziolkowski for his help tracking this down.

2 At a late 1990s Kierkegaard Conference at St. Olaf College, a Kierkegaard scholar and student of Wittgenstein, Paul Homer, reported that Wittgenstein wrote to David Swenson, then in the middle of translating *Works of Love* into English, wanting to see the translation as soon as possible. He complained that he could not grasp the argument in German, and hoped the English would help. Later, he wrote Swenson that even in English, he found the argument impossible. That did not shake his judgment that Kierkegaard was a genius.

3 Ludwig Wittgenstein, *Culture and Value*, trans. Peter Winch (Chicago: Chicago University Press, 1980).

4 See Kinya Masugata, "A Short History of Kierkegaard's Reception in Japan," in *Kierkegaard and Japanese Thought*, James Giles, (ed.) (New York: Palgrave Macmillan, 2008), pp. 31–52.

5 Stanley Cavell, *Little Did I Know: Excerpts from Memory* (Palo Alto: Stanford University Press, 2010), p. 326.

6 Kierkegaard scholars visited Iran (2006 or 2007), invited by West-leaning Iranian academics. They admired Kierkegaard for championing religious individuality against a theocratic state.

7 *The Living Thoughts of Kierkegaard*, ed. W. H. Auden (New York: Random House, 1952), is one of the first English language Kierkegaard anthologies. Robert Bretall's widely used *A Kierkegaard Anthology*, Robert Bretall, (ed.) (Princeton: Princeton University Press, 1946), preceded it by six years.

8 Most "Introductions to Existentialism" in America in the 1960s began with a distinction between religious and atheistic existentialism: Buber, Kierkegaard, and Dostoevsky were listed as religious; Heidegger, Nietzsche, and Sartre, as atheistic. By the 1980s, "existentialism" came to mean Sartre and Camus, and "theistic existentialism" began to sound oxymoronic. George Pattison brings back the religious wing in *Anxious Angels: A Retrospective View of Religious Existentialism* (New York: Palgrave Macmillan, 1999).

9 See George Pattison, "Existence, Anxiety, and the Moment of Vision: Fundamental Ontology and Existentiell Faith Revisited," in *After the Postsecular and the Postmodern: New Essays in Continental Philosophy of Religion*, Anthony Paul Smith and Daniel Whistler, (eds) (Newcastle: Cambridge Scholars Publishing, 2010), pp. 128–51.

10 See Matsugata, "A Short History."

11 George Pattison points out (private correspondence) that Leon Chestov's book *Kierkegaard et la philosophie existentielle*, (Paris: J. Vrin) appeared in 1936, "though he'd been lecturing on Kierkegaard at the Sorbonne since earlier in the decade)." And he calls attention to *An Atheism that is not Humanist*, Stephabos Geroulanos. Stanford (2010) for coverage of this period. See also, fn 12 and 13, below, and Jon Stewart, "France: Kierkegaard as a Forerunner of Existentialism and Poststructuralism" in *Kierkegaard's International Reception*: Tome 1, *Northern and Western Europe*, ed. Jon Stewart, (ed.), Aldershot: Ashgate 2009, 421–59, esp. 427– 8.

12 Recent volumes that explore this multi-faceted ferment include Samuel Moyne, *Origins of the Other: Emmanuel Levinas between Revelation and Ethics* (Ithaca, NY: Cornell University Press, 2005); Ethan Kleinberg, *Generation Existential: Heidegger's Philosophy in*

France, 1927–1961 (Ithaca, NY: Cornell University Press, 2005); and Peter Eli Gordon, *Continental Divide: Heidegger, Cassirer, Davos* (Cambridge, MA: Harvard University Press, 2010). Julia Kristeva focuses on Arendt in the 1950s and 1960s in her *Hannah Arendt*, trans. Ross Guberman (New York: Columbia University Press, 2001).

13 Jean Wahl's *Le malheur de la conscience dans la philosophie de Hegel* (1929), and *Études kierkegaardiennes* (1938) are seminal publications that both capture and shape the discussions in Paris between wars.

14 In France, 2010–11, there were major celebrations of the work of American philosophers with impeccable "analytic" credentials: Stanley Cavell, Cora Diamond, and Thompson Clark, to name three. In the United States, French, Italian, and South American scholars give papers that move seamlessly through Kierkegaard, Cavell, Habermas, and Wittgenstein (for example). This establishes an intrest in analytic philosophy on the Continent, just as there is a powerful interest in Continental philosophy in North America.

15 See Gordon, *Continental Divide*, Moyne, *Origin of the Other,* and Kleinberg, *Generation Existential.*

16 See Ray Monk, *Ludwig Wittgenstein: The Duty of Genius* (New York: Penguin, 1990); Victor J. Krebs, "'Around the Axis of Our Real Need': On the Ethical Point of Wittgenstein's Philosophy," *European Journal of Philosophy* 9:3 (2001), pp. 344–74; and J. Mark Lazenby, *The Early Wittgenstein on Religion* (New York: Continuum, 2006).

17 Wittgenstein, *Culture and Value.*

18 Ludwig Wittgenstein, "A Lecture on Ethics," *The Philosophical Review* 74:1 (1965), pp. 3–12; Matthew Pianalto, "Speaking for Oneself: Wittgenstein on Ethics," *Inquiry* 54:3 (2011), pp. 252–76.

19 Cavell pairs Kierkegaard's *Postscript* with Wittgenstein's *Investigations* in Stanley Cavell, "Existentialism and Analytic Philosophy," *Daedalus* 93:3 (1964), pp. 946–74, reprinted in Stanley Cavell, *Themes out of School: Effects and Causes* (Chicago: University of Chicago Press, 1984), pp. 195–234. See also Stephen Mulhall, *Inheritance and Originality: Wittgenstein, Heidegger, Kierkegaard* (Oxford: Oxford University Press, 2001); Hilary Putnam, *Renewing Philosophy*, (Cambridge, MA: Harvard University Press, 1992); George Pattison, *The Later Heidegger* (New York: Routledge, 2000); and George Pattison, *The Philosophy of Kierkegaard* (Kingston and Montreal: McGill-Queens University Press, 2005). The divide disappears in a recent study of Levinas: see

Bob Plant, *Wittgenstein and Levinas: Ethical and Religious Thought* (New York: Routledge, 2005).

20 By the 1990s it was clear that Richard Rorty, Robert Brandom, Jürgen Habermas, and Martha Nussbaum – to name a few – were also doing philosophy that defied the continental-analytic divide. Also, see Anthony Rudd, *Expressing the World: Skepticism, Wittgenstein, and Heidegger* (Chicago: Open Court, 2003).

21 See Charles Taylor, "Responsibility for Self," in *The Identities of Persons*, Amélie Oksenberg Rorty, (ed.) (Berkeley: University of California Press, 1976), pp. 281–99, reprinted in Charles Taylor, *Philosophy and the Human Sciences, Philosophical Papers 2* (Cambridge: Cambridge University Press, 1985), under the title "Self-Interpreting Animals" ; Harry G. Frankfurt, "Freedom of the Will and the Concept of a Person," *The Journal of Philosophy* 68:1 (1971), pp. 5–20, reprinted in Harry G. Frankfurt, *The Importance of What We Care About* (Cambridge: Cambridge University Press, 1988), pp. 11–25. For a later summation and expansion of the discussion, see John Davenport, *Will as Commitment and Resolve: An Existential Account of Creativity, Love, Virtue, and Happiness* (New York: Fordham University Press, 2007).

22 I link Taylor and Frankfurt (and Bernard Williams) to Kierkegaard in my *Knights of Faith and Resignation: Reading Kierkegaard's* Fear and Trembling (New York: SUNY Press, 1991).

23 For recent work on self and agency from an Australian conference, 2006, see *Practical Identity and Narrative Agency*, Kim Atkins and Catriona Mackenzie, (eds) (New York: Routledge, 2008). And see the important work of Patrick Stokes, *Kierkegaard's Mirrors: Interest, Self, and Moral Vision* (New York: Palgrave Macmillan, 2010).

24 See Taylor, "Responsibility for Self," on the self's necessary relation to more-than-utilitarian goods.

25 See Chantal Bax, "The Fibre, the Thread, and the Weaving of Life: Wittgenstein and Nancy on Community," *Telos* 145 (2008), pp. 103–17.

26 Søren Kierkegaard, *Concluding Unscientific Postscript*, vol. 1, trans. and ed. Howard V. Hong and Edna H. Hong (Princeton: Princeton University Press, 1992), p. 237. I discuss this passage in my "Transfigurations: The Mysterious Agency of Death," in *Kierkegaard and Death*, Patrick Stokes and Adam J. Buben, (eds) (Bloomington: Indiana University Press, 2011). And more generally, see my *On Søren Kierkegaard: Dialogue, Polemics, Lost Intimacy, and Time* (Burlington, VT: Ashgate, 2007).

27 A more refined account of a Kierkegaardian self-ensemble would have "flow" not a matter of passion but of "*interesse*" or "interest." The flow would be two-way: toward the explicit object of interest, and simultaneously flexed back toward the implicit then-operative-self. For these fine points, see Patrick Stokes, *Kierkegaard's Mirrors;* and my review of this work, in *Søren Kierkegaard Newsletter* 56 (2010), pp. 25–31. See John Davenport's exhaustive treatment of these issues centering on passion and autonomy in Davenport, *Will As Commitment and Resolve.*

28 See my "Hidden Inwardness as Interpersonal," in *Why Kierkegaard Matters: A Festschrift in Honor of Robert L. Perkins*, Marc A. Jolley, (ed.) (Macon, GA: Mercer University Press, 2010), and my discussion of subjectivity as a responsiveness to ideals in my *On Søren Kierkegaard*, p. 63.

29 See my "Style, Genre, and Pseudonymity," in *The Oxford Handbook to Kierkegaard*, John Lippitt and George Pattison, (eds) (Oxford: Oxford University Press, forthcoming 2012), where I discuss the multiple identities Kierkegaard assumes in his writing.

30 Note the conference on "Narrative, Identity, and the Kierkegaardian Self," University of Hertfordshire, November 2011.

31 Perhaps Plato wished merely to have his own poetry replace the commonplace, inferior poetry entrenched in his time.

32 Stanley Cavell, *A Pitch of Philosophy: Autobiographical Exercises* (Cambridge, MA: Harvard University Press, 1994).

33 We might say that community is not an imposition on individuals, not a dominant source of power or authority that strips individuals of expressiveness, but is rather an ambience that makes individual expression possible by offering possibilities of expression.

34 See my *On Søren Kierkegaard*, p. 63.

35 Søren Kierkegaard, *Either/Or*, vol. 2, trans. and ed. Howard V. Hong and Edna H. Hong (Princeton: Princeton University Press, 1987), p. 491; see also my discussion in "Self-Choice or Self-Reception: Judge Wilhelm's Admonition," in *Selves in Discord and Resolve: Kierkegaard's Moral-Religious Psychology from* Either/Or *to* Sickness Unto Death (New York: Routledge, 1996), pp. 11–26.

36 The young man in *Repetition* hopes that he will get back his love, just as Job got back his world. See Søren Kierkegaard, *Philosophical Crumbs* and *Repetition*, trans. M. G. Piety and Edward F. Mooney, (ed.) (Oxford: Oxford World's Classics, 2009).

37 Søren Kierkegaard, *The Sickness Unto Death*, trans. Alastair

Hannay (New York: Penguin, 1989), p. 43. Here are the essentials, excerpted from two pages of thick prose, pp. 43–4: "The self is a relation which relates to itself… . A human being is a synthesis of the infinite and the finite, of the temporal and the eternal, of freedom and necessity… . [The] human self … in relating to itself relates to something else… . [I]n relating to itself and in wanting to be itself, the self is grounded transparently in the power that established it."

38 On tacit and explicit evaluation, see Stokes, *Kierkegaard's Mirrors*, and my review.

39 John Davenport writes, "Personal authenticity is often taken to signify simply being true to yourself in the sense of 'following your heart,' for example in not selling out your deepest interests for temporary advantages such as monetary gain… . If the 'self' to which one remains true involves commitment to moral principles or ideals of excellence, then it can mean something very close to 'integrity' in the sense of loyalty to one's principles and ideals," John Davenport, "Frankfurt and Kierkegaard on B. S., Wantonness, and Aestheticism: A Phenomenology of Inauthenticity," in *Living Reasonably, Loving Well: Conversing with Frankfurt and Kierkegaard*, Myron Penner and Søren Landkildehus, (eds) (forthcoming). See my "Authenticity in Kierkegaard," in *Authenticity*, ed. Taylor Carman, *Oxford Philosophical Concepts* (Oxford, Oxford University Press, forthcoming 2012).

40 See my discussion of the self as a musical sextet, in "Music of the Spheres: Kierkegaardian Selves and Transformations," in *Selves in Discord and Resolve: Kierkegaard's Moral-Religious Psychology from* Either/Or *to* Sickness Unto Death (New York: Routledge, 1996), pp. 89–104.

41 After claiming that "*the self is a relation which relates to itself,*" Anti-Climacus adds, "the self is grounded transparently in the power that established it." Toward the end (but before the final paragraphs) we have: "Faith is: that the self in being itself and in wanting to be itself is grounded transparently in God," Kierkegaard, *The Sickness Unto Death*, p. 114.

42 The text's next to last sentence has the self rest not in God but transparently in "the power which established it," ibid., p. 165.

43 See Peter Dula, *Cavell, Companionship, and Christian Theology* (Oxford: Oxford University Press, 2011), esp. the Conclusion, and Part 2, beginning with Chapter 5: "*The Claim of Reason's* Apophatic Anthropology."

44 Do we need, in interpreting Sickness, to move to the theistic level of our relation to Another," or can we rest content with a "proto-Christian"

reading of "the establishing power" that grounds us? Pattison suggests, in personal correspondence, that the Christian and doctrinal material in *Sickness* is the most adequate way of saying what's going on in our relation to (the more theistically neutral) "establishing power." That is, the theistic reading – based on the specifically Christian and doctrinal material of Part B of Sickness not "already implicit in the more neutral idea of a power that posits us" but instead, that "the more neutral idea" can be better filled out in the Christian idiom than in any other.

45 Pattison, personal correspondence. See his important discussions in *Kierkegaard and 19th Century Theology*, forthcoming, Cambridge.

46 In the second *Critique*, Kant comments on "the expectation of being able some day to … derive everything from one principle – the undeniable need of human reason, which finds complete satisfaction only in a complete systematic unity of its cognitions" *Critique of Practical Reason, Kants gesammelte Schriften, Akademie* (ed.) (Berlin, 1902–), vol. 5, p. 91.

47 See Kelly Jolley's discussion of Merleau-Ponty on "first certainties" at http://kellydeanjolley.com/2011/09/11/ reading-rm-11-the-grace-of-our-first-certainties.

48 A discussion with Rick Furtak helped me emphasize the difference between grounding as giving reasons and grounding as existential assurance – the capacity to go on, not be stuck or overwhelmed in the face of the end of reasons. We need to attend, I think, to *the principle of insufficient reason* – a notion more placid than "the absurd" but still of rich importance. It is, of course, the counterweight to Leibniz's principle of sufficient reason.

49 Although I've often written elsewhere of "the shopkeeper knight of faith," this should really be considered shorthand. Alastair Hannay reminds me that the text reads, "you might think he was a *kræmmersjel* (mercenary soul)" which is not to say that he actually is one – a mercenary soul or shopman. Hannay also notes that these unassuming and unlikely knights might also show up, in "Preamble from the Heart," as "a tax-gatherer, quill-pusher or clerk, a postman, a restaurateur, a capitalist, and in a way even a girl of 16." He goes on, "These are ascriptions or types that might come to the observer's mind, not actual characterizations. '*Kræmmersjel*' is often (though not necessarily) derogative, as, e.g. 'huckster', with 'petty' as part of the connotation." The upshot is that perhaps this "mercenary soul," this figure who calls to mind a shopkeeper, should be designated, for shorthand, a "shopkeeper lookalike." And Hannay adds, "Part of the point is surely that you just can't tell where this unlikely knight of faith gets his assurance from." (Personal correspondence).

50 Friedrich Waismann, "Notes on Talks with Wittgenstein," *The Philosophical Review* 74:1 (1965), pp. 12–16.

51 Wittgenstein, "A Lecture on Ethics," p. 11.

52 Waismann, "Notes on Talks with Wittgenstein," p. 12.

53 Stanely Cavell, "The Availability of Wittgenstein's Later Philosophy," in *Must We Mean What We Say?*, Updated Edition (Cambridge: Cambridge University Press, 2002), pp. 44–72, p. 52. Arguing for a convergence between Cavell and Kierkegaard on authority and grounds would take another paper.

54 The best discussion of the tax man, and how his simple faith can sustain his joy and delight amidst a world of cruelty, boredom, and sin, is Sheridan Hough, "What the Faithful Tax Collector Saw (Against the Understanding)," in *Without Authority*, Robert L. Perkins, (ed.), vol. 18 of *International Kierkegaard Commentary* (Macon, GA: Mercer University Press, 2006), pp. 295–312.

55 Søren Kierkegaard, *Fear and Trembling*, trans. Alastair Hannay (New York: Penguin, 1985), p. 70.

56 Ibid., p. 79. See my discussion, *Knights of Faith and Resignation*, pp. 58f.

57 See my reconstructions in *Knights of Faith and Resignation* and in *On Søren Kierkegaard*.

58 See Kierkegaard, *The Sickness Unto Death*, p. 136.

59 Climacus writes a 600-page tome titled *Concluding Unscholarly Postscript to Philosophical Crumbs, a Mimic-Pathetic-Existential Contribution*. There's something aptly Kierkegaardian about imagining ourselves comically-pathetically flailing desperately to make sense.

60 Rose is commenting on Simone Weil's remark that (as Rose paraphrases), "agnosticism is the most truly religious position." See "Interview with Gillian Rose," Edited and Introduced Vincent Lloyd, *Theory, Culture and Society* 25:7–8 (2008).

61 See Krebs, "Around the Axis of Our Real Need."

62 In *On Søren Kierkegaard*, Chapter 2, I discuss wonders-beyond-reason that Socrates floats (e.g. that a good man cannot be harmed, or that he owes insight into love to the mysterious Diotima). In another context, I approach similar issues by referring to the difference between hearing the Kantian "thing-in-itself" as an Entity beyond "things for our knowledge," and hearing it as precisely *not* a thing, but an admission that however much we know of things in general, or this thing in particular, new aspects may – and will

– dawn. Acknowledging that ineliminable possibility of new dawns is not to imagine an extra thing in the world "behind" the thing that appears. It is to imagine a fount, even a sacred fount, that feeds appearance with ever-new aspects. I find clear analogies between this quasi-Kantian position and what can be said about "establishing power" and faith. See my "'Concord River': Living Transcendentally on Currents of Time," forthcoming.

3

On Style and Pseudonymity

Pseudonyms

What does it mean to sign one's name, or withdraw it, at the close of a piece of writing? Librarians dedicate a yard of shelf space to an author they name "Kierkegaard," but opening the books shelved there, we find that they are written by a motley crew sporting names like "Johannes Climacus," "Johannes de silentio," "Vigilius Haufniensus," and many others. We could find the anonymous "A," the enigmatic "Anti-Climacus," one "Constantine Constantius," and so forth. Few in Copenhagen were fooled by these pseudonyms, nor are we fooled today. So why indulge Kierkegaard's hide-and-seek? Is there a literary, moral, or religious rationale to this amusing veiling, unveiling? Are these phantom authors, instead, mere flourish, like a book's front illustration or back cover blurb?[1]

Pseudonyms *are*, to be sure, an attention-grabbing flourish but that's hardly the end of the story. These flourishes make us ask what it means to be an author, what in a book's impact is an impact of its author, and what "essential" moral or religious truth (if any) authors and books can convey. At the very least, the pseudonymic flourish directs us *away* from pondering the street conversations, polemics, or broken engagements of an eccentric resident of 1840s and 1850s Copenhagen. Yes, there is a tax-paying citizen found walking about town, possessed of an acerbic wit, fine gastronomic tastes, and a monstrous intelligence. Yet immediately before us is not citizen-Kierkegaard but Johannes de silentio (or Johannes Climacus), who buffers the citizen from our gaze.

We wonder about Homer's link to the *Odyssey*, Plato's link to Socratic dialogues, an unknowable poet's link to the biblical Book of Job, Shakespeare's link to an actor-director named *Hamlet*. But this wonder can disappear. Captured by the world of Socrates, Homer, Job, or Hamlet, the question of authorship can vanish. Our attention is absorbed by the old nurse who recognizes Odysseus' scar, or by Socrates incautiously requesting free meals as punishment, or by the Whirlwind's display of vultures feasting on human blood, or by Hamlet's deft staging of a play before the murderous King (and his wife). Wonder about who writes the story of the nurse, or of Socrates, or of vultures, for the moment disappears. The part played by writer-Kierkegaard (not exactly the citizen) in literary production, his importance and authority, might intrigue us. Yet immersed in the portrait of the taxpaying knight of faith, the wonder about who writes *Fear and Trembling* easily disappears.

On the other hand, it also can become urgent to know who writes what. As we ponder a text, its pseudonym can become a key to interpretation. For if we declare that Johannes de silentio (of *Fear and Trembling*) is an autonomous author, then *his* accounts of faith are not necessarily Kierkegaard's. And if Johannes Climacus (of *Concluding Unscientific Postscript*) is not "Kierkegaard-the-writer," then the *Postscript* distinction between religiousness A and religiousness B is not necessarily a Kierkegaardian distinction. On the other hand, we might revert to the stance of the good librarian. All works shelved under "Kierkegaard" are the work of a single writer, and the pseudonyms, no more than a cocky flourish.

We might consider, as a third option: just bypass any concern with authorship. Texts are primary and always trump (more or less superfluous) issues of authorship. We take up the account of faith in *Fear and Trembling* and set it beside the account in *Postscript*, and set both beside accounts in the *Discourses*. We develop a deep appreciation of these texts without caring who wrote them. If each washed up in a bottle by the sea, lacking an author's signature, we would still have in hand texts worthy of a lifetime's attention. Like the Dead Sea scrolls, the writing would be primary. Say I learned that a committee of 20, with shifting membership, worked diligently over centuries to compile and revise the *Book of Job*. My admiration for the text will be neither diminished nor enhanced.

Of course Job belongs originally to an oral tradition, where authors are typically unknown, and singers of stories are constantly revising "the text" in endless recountings over time. Yet at some point, oral traditions begin to compete with literary ones. The literary challenge brings with it signed authorships. With the emergence of writers and signed works, as readers we discover that we have what amounts to a metaphysical need for identifiable authors. Kant posits an inescapable need of reason (or need for reasons) that merges with a need to know origins.[2] We crave knowledge of fathers and mothers, of first causes, of first settlers of the land. We want narratives to be truthful, and at some point we link this to a need for truthful narrators. It is not enough that in the beginning was waste and welter; we crave the good God who creates a viable world from welter and waste. Creation (so we think) requires a creator.[3] We posit authors even when we know absolutely nothing, biographically speaking, about them. Homer must be more than a librarian's filing device. We'd be crushed if "Kierkegaard" turned out to be a storytelling troupe.

Our biographical instincts point to Copenhagen, journal records on file, a weathered headstone with chiseled words provided by the author himself. Yet our philosophical instincts aren't easily quelled. Perhaps Kierkegaard is a citizen and also a storytelling troupe or its theatrical director. We have the stage names of his players: among others, "Inter et Inter" and "Vigilius Haufniensis" (Watchman of Copenhagen, whose Freiburg reincarnation kept anxious watch over Being).[4] The plot thickens when we realize that granting a metaphysical or literary multitude at work, this creative ensemble pens a part for an author named "Kierkegaard." Then he can seem single, legion, and even self-creating. "S. Kierkegaard" and others are stage names the ensemble puts forth.[5]

A creative genius named Kierkegaard creates an ensemble only a few of whom will answer to the name "Kierkegaard." Yet without the skill and talent of a pseudonymous (and veronymous) ensemble, we'd lack any figure history would remember as "Kierkegaard." In *Fear and Trembling*, de silentio says that the person of faith "gives birth to his own father."[6] Could the ensemble "give birth to its own father"? The span of books that librarians innocently (and properly) shelve under "Kierkegaard" is a city of troubles and wonders, a hydra headed set of biographical, literary, and philosophical enigmas.

Self: Single or legion

Melville wrote to his neighbor Hawthorne, "This is a long letter, but you are not at all bound to answer it. Possibly, if you do answer it, and direct it to Herman Melville, you will mis-send it – for the very fingers that now guide this pen are not precisely the same that just took it up and put it on this paper."[7] Melville suffers a lack of felt-identity through time. It disturbs him. He writes: "Lord, when shall we be done changing?" (ibid.) Heraclitus wrote that one couldn't step in the same river twice. Melville seems to doubt, that he, or anyone else, can encounter the same Melville twice. When Melville gets immersed in Ahab, Ishmael, or Starbuck, one by one he becomes the players in this performance, and so vanishes as an enduring, authoritative presence.

Does Kierkegaard become a new author each time he starts a new book (under a new pseudonym, or non-pseudonym) – the new author only problematically related to predecessors and successors? But surely Kierkegaard-the-writer is an inescapable presence in European, American, Asian and other cultural histories. His monumental status as the source of an *oeuvre* remains. Here are four lines of sight on "Kierkegaard" that don't easily converge.

"Kierkegaard" appears 1) as a familiar object of biographies of the Copenhagen citizen and writer. But perhaps instead he will appear 2) as a useless phantom: like Melville, he disappears or evaporates behind texts. More metaphysically, "Kierkegaard" might appear 3) as an implied author, as a posited transcendental subject that unifies an array of texts, functioning not unlike "Homer"; he would be a Kant-like "transcendental unity of authorial production" presupposed in reading *Postscript* or *Fear and Trembling*. Finally, far less metaphysically, "Kierkegaard" appears 4) as a cultural figure without whom we would have far less grasp of Heidegger, Rilke, Ortega, Barth, Auden, or the Kyoto School. Lacking Kierkegaard, none of these would exist exactly as we know them. Spans of the familiar texture of twentieth century thought would be altered.

Hamlet

Harold Bloom holds that Shakespeare's consummate invention is Hamlet, who embodies – he says, "invents" – our modern notion of the human.[8] Although there is no shrine to mark the bones of an historical Prince of Denmark, worthy of biographies, Prince Hamlet, Shakespeare's invention, has an incredibly powerful poetic and cultural actuality, as Bloom avers. Johannes de silentio and Johannes Climacus will never be subjects of biographies, but they have a powerful poetic and culture presence, in undergraduate classes – a presence reinforced through the artistry of Ibsen, Kafka, Walker Percy, Derrida, Ingmar Bergman, and endless others.

Hamlet's play within the play, "Mousetrap," will flourish in the flow of cultural history, as will de silentio's multiple Abraham scenarios. Hamlet directs that play before his mother and the king to test them. Climacus casts Socrates in a solo dance before God to test our credulity.[9] He gives lines to a figure named "Kierkegaard" in *Postscript's* "A Contemporary Effort."[10] "S. Kierkegaard" makes a late intervention at the close of *Postscript*.[11] This extraordinary nesting of texts within texts, authors within authors outshines even the endlessly inventive Hamlet – Hamlet does not insert "Will Shakespeare" in his play before the king, nor let "Shakespeare" comment *sotto voce* from the stage on Hamlet's inventiveness.[12]

A Copenhagen citizen and literary genius adopts an authorial strategy, darting forward and back as "Kierkegaard," and as this pseudonym or that. He seduces, then abandons, his readers, playing a kind of fun and dangerous hide and seek. The problem of the Kierkegaardian authorship is ultimately our own. We have an obsessive desire for the real, single Kierkegaard: Will he please stand up!

Sublime unsettling

What can we make of these antic authorial proliferations and imbrications? As it dodges stable representation, the sublime unsettling that we call "Kierkegaard's works" nevertheless has a halting, mobile, ever changing sense. A carnival's confusion makes some sort of sense, even though it can overwhelm in its spectacle, noise, disorientation, chaos, and color.[13] Call that moment of excitement and fear the "carnivalesque" sublime.[14] It shimmers a many-sided kind of sense that emerges as we escape the immediate crush and glitter of arcades.

As we escape (if we do), the flickering sense we can carry away is not like a well-focused snapshot or clearly drawn map. It comes despite unsettled disorder, as a sigh of relief – as we achieve safe distance. A taste for the everyday is revived. We might relish a nostalgic calm, having ridden a large wave without mishap.

And we suppress the intimation that at any moment a swirl can reappear. The sea has its rogue waves, but for the moment, the last word is not sound signifying nothing.

Who determines identity?

Tax collectors know how to nail down a tax liable resident of Copenhagen, and librarians know how to shelve an author whose books arrive in the mail. When it comes to full authorial identity, however, they don't have a clue. They duck all interest in Johannes Climacus, humorist and author of *Concluding Unscholarly Postscript,* for he has no tax-liable, shelf-location status. Nevertheless, Climacus demands that *we* determine an identity for him as source of a book or two whose shelf location is "Kierkegaard."

Do we hold a pseudonym responsible for what's said in his book? Kierkegaard-the-writer might or might not be responsible for the opinions of Climacus, who in turn might or might not be responsible for what he says about Johannes de silentio. Is writer-Kierkegaard responsible for opinions inserted at the end of *Postscript*, signed "S. Kierkegaard"? Is Climacus responsible for letting S. Kierkegaard glue unnumbered pages to the end of his tome? Each instance of alleged responsibility cries for testing, one by one, and the jury may remain hung. Do the opinions of S. Kierkegaard from the end of *Postscript* trump opinions voiced from the body of *Postscript*? Why accept remarks that purport to give a retrospective assessment of a *Postscript* authored by Climacus?

If I *avow* that I believe in God, or that I believe love should hold sway here, or that from now on I will support my son, then (in the right settings), my saying so to some open extent will make it so. My avowals work on the model of a promise, of a performative. In apt settings, my saying "I promise" makes a promise happen, changes the world. A judge saying "you can go free" makes me free in the very saying. My identity is based partially on my avowals ("I am – I will be – a good parent!") and partially on how others take me (they may well reject my self-avowals). And importantly, my avowals of care and commitment can be embodied non-linguistically in gesture and responsiveness as I lovingly play with a grandchild. My identity in that setting is locked into how I avow, express, or enact, my care.

In *The Point of View of my Work as an Author*, Kierkegaard avows that he has always been a religious author.[15] Does his saying so make it so? The jury is out. "S. Kierkegaard" declares that he takes responsibility for Climacus' *Postscript*. Can he usurp responsibility from Climacus by mere declaration? The implied author of the Kierkegaardian *oeuvre* transfers authorial powers to Climacus. Sometime later "S. Kierkegaard' seems to renege. Does "S. Kierkegaard" have the authority to strip Climacus of authorship? He says he is the "author, as people would call it," of eight major works from *Either/Or* through *Postscript*.[16] Does his saying so make it so? Perhaps no one has authority to strip Climacus of his authorship – once granted.

In Melville's great book, Ahab has authority to cast judgment on Starbuck. In *Postscript*, Climacus casts judgment on de silentio.[17] Although Ahab can't cast judgment on Melville, the infinitely clever Climacus casts judgment on Kierkegaard, feigning annoyance that someone in Copenhagen is stealing his lines and publishing his ideas in books with titles like *Either/Or* and *Fear and Trembling*.[18] Ahab can't comment on Melville, and Hamlet can't comment on Shakespeare. Climacus, however, can come alive and talk back, a version of Pygmalion, who makes a statue that comes to life. Kierkegaard dreams up Climacus who is dreamily amused at the dreamer who dreams him.

Veronyms, pseudonyms

It's natural to think that texts signed "Søren Kierkegaard" minimize doubts about authorial responsibility. Those signatures ought to point to "the true Kierkegaard," apart from the masks. Yet some years after Søren's death, his brother Peter suggested, in effect, that works signed by Søren should be treated as if written by a pseudonym[19] Peter wanted to have a high opinion of his brother. He also wanted to reject his brother's well-circulated polemics against the Danish church hierarchy and against a godless Danish society. Peter was a high-ranking bishop in the Danish State Church, the very church Søren relentlessly ridiculed. As his brother was dying, Peter might have sought to forgive, but didn't. Years later he had every reason to wish that his brother's attacks on the Church did not represent Søren's real views. Perhaps his brother's now famous polemics were just another mask.[20] Then Peter could despise the mask and embrace the brother.

Peter's hypothesis has some plausibility. "Kierkegaard" might be just another pseudonym. An only implied author of an *oeuvre* has some of the irreality of a pseudonym. Peter's flesh and blood brother walked the streets, attended church, and paid taxes. Peter's brother stands to Climacus and the author of the excoriating "attack literature" as a flesh and blood Copenhagen judge might stand to "Judge William." The gap between "Judge William" and any factual Judge might be as large as the gap between a "Kierkegaard" (whose books librarians shelve), and a resident of Copenhagen whose brother was Peter.

In the long run, Peter is almost right. It is the implied author of the *oeuvre*, rather than any particular resident of Copenhagen, who will (or will not) have made an indelible mark on the times and beyond. Peter's younger brother can be freed from the irascible critic we call Kierkegaard just as Shakespeare can be freed from the agony and madness of King Lear. Or so it seems. Against Peter's view, Climacus and the author of the "Attack Literature" are Kierkegaard, in the way Lear and Hamlet are Shakespeare. The Shakespeare who did or didn't pay his taxes is of no more interest than the Kierkegaard who did or did not put his brother to shame, but of enormous interest are Shakespeare taken as Lear and Hamlet, and Kierkegaard, as Climacus and de silentio.

Difficult reality

Have we volatilized Kierkegaard? Does Kierkegaard perform a kind of self-volatilization? If Melville has authority to say to Hawthorne that his identity seems volatilized, who is the Melville who can thus undo himself? If he is volatile, he has no position or authority from which to speak of his undoing. Without a position, he can't write, "the very fingers that now guide this pen are not precisely the same that just took it up and put it on this paper." Perhaps Kierkegaard can't fashion himself as ephemeral, shifting with each new voice, lacking a stable identity. He surely changes, yet he must just as assuredly *not* change (too radically).

If an author is like a speaker, she must have enough permanence to promise, avow, take something as her own, and enough permanence to hold her future self responsible for her present or past declarations. Otherwise, no declarations or promises can be made. (Yet Hamlet can promise!) Melville's Copenhagen counterpart writes a carnival of creations that seems to volatilize its director and producer and performer – yet logically that venture can't quite succeed.

The conundrum is rooted in what Cora Diamond aptly calls "difficult reality."[21] We must hold steady two (or more) conflicting views. Sitting up from the steady side of the bed, we know that Kierkegaard knows that it is the same "he" who sips coffee, who gives lines to Climacus, who sincerely writes signed religious discourses – who takes back Climacus' status as author, who gives Johannes de silentio such a loud and raucous voice. Sitting up from that assuredly non-metaphysical, practical, and everyday side of the bed, however, does not foreclose our sitting up from the unsteady side. As in an all-too-real dream, we fall into the mix, glitter and darkness of the *oeuvre*, wherein the author and others (including myself as awakening reader) float eerily – float within an elusive, ghost-like multitude. There is no "right side" from which to sit up. Reality is difficult.

The existential-literary worries about permanence that Kierkegaard and Melville present are not to be dismissed as frivolous, ill-founded, or hysterical. We must resist the temptation to conclude that on pain of contradiction, one or the other of these standpoints must be rejected. We are simultaneously old and young, happy and sad, single and legion. We are, and inhabit, a rather anomalous reality that suspends tensions not easily resolvable, and are sometimes irresolvable.

A young woman holds the hope of the world in her smile; we see simultaneously the hope of the world shattered in her smile, for she has but minutes to live. A young writer holds the hope of a strong and resilient identity in his pen; we see simultaneously that this hope is shattered as his pen moves in ways that are self-volatilizing. The writer both laments and celebrates puzzles and anxieties about who he really is, and by implication, about who anyone really is. And as I read with empathy, indeed, I celebrate and lament the puzzles of who I am at last. Reality resists a comforting seamlessness.

Genres

Kierkegaard pens his way into history as master of an incredibly varied number of genres. These should catch our attention even more than his neon-lit pseudonyms. He resists, even scorns, a standard philosophical or theological prose. He is in turn a dreamer, fabulist, and diarist; a publicist, dramatist, and dialectician; a sermonizer, satirist, and lyricist; a conjurer of pseudonyms, an ironist, humorist, and poet; a polemicist and aphorist. And he invents works that defy all known genres – that are one of a kind: we are offered a so-called "book" of nothing but prefaces.[22] Perhaps the key to Kierkegaard's multiple identities is not the varied signatures. Mixed genres signal mixed identities. Johannes de silentio calls *Fear and Trembling* a "dialectical lyric." What sort of genre is *that*? Climacus identifies the genre of *Postscript* as "unscholarly" – in the manner of a "postscript" to some "philosophical crumbs." And the genre is further specified as a "mimic-pathetic-dialectic compilation," and an "existential contribution." We can only applaud such framing clarity!

We've asked how authorial prerogative pervades a text (or doesn't). Now we ask how genre exerts its prerogatives (or doesn't). Genre provides a subtle, intimate frame to lead us to appropriate ways of reading. We read a discourse in one way, a set of aphorisms in another, and a book of nothing but prefaces in yet another. Issues of authorial identity shift to issues of genre identity, and issues of multiple authors retreat as we take up issues of multiple genres. *Fear and Trembling*, for instance, is claimed by but a single pseudonym, but the genres within that slim text are amazingly varied. The panoply includes the carnivalesque and bawdy, the fairy tale or fable, the satirical, burlesque, or farcical, the tragic, the labyrinthine unfathomable, the grotesque and the sublime, the dialectical and lyrical, the fantastical and dreamlike, the antinomian, apophatic, and eucatastrophical (an unexpected finish that's marvelously good).

Local history gets written up in one genre (we might call it factual), and local poetry gets written up in another. The genre of Judge William's letters differs from the genre of a sermonic discourse. The implied author of Johannes de silentio's "Speech in Praise of Abraham" is slightly different from the implied author of the earlier section, "Attunement." Judge William may not speak from the factual, but he is surely not speaking from the neighborhood of Batman or Snow White. Poetic actuality is as varied as factual actuality. Beyond the familiar (and flawed) fact-fiction duplet, taking up a multiplicity of genres can be taking up multiple metaphysical possibilities. Authors of the non-factual aren't thereby captive of the fictional. Are my dreams my fictions or my intimate facts? Hamlet is neither "*merely* fictional" nor "poetic." Our sensibilities outstrip our lexicons.

Dialectical writing (say, *Philosophical Crumbs* or *Unscholarly Postscript)* implies an author in philosophical space – not exactly poetical or fictional space. The genre of *The Point of View of my Work as an Author* is contested: it's too simple to say we have a factual Copenhagen resident reporting the facts about a writer who is also a local resident. We've said Kierkegaard can write as a dreamer or fabulist, diarist or publicist, dramatist or dialectician, sermonizer, satirist, and more. There are not just one or two metaphysical slots (say the poetical-fictional and literal-factual) within which to sort this marvelous array.[23]

Looking at the variety of writing spaces might be like looking at a variety of places where action and reception occur: spaces of confession, for exhortation, of song, for exposition, of thanksgiving, of critique, of history lessons, of story-telling, of quiet listening – and so forth. Genres would pair up with sorts and styles of action and reception. The spaces where Kierkegaard writes then proliferate as varied as these spaces are. At these sites of action and reception and communicative exchange are the items just listed (thanksgiving and story-telling, for instance) and also oratory, monstrosity, circus, the ridiculous-academic and the political harangue – in endless variety, all in a carnival whirl.

Change and changelessness

An outpouring of genres, an ongoing motley of the carnivalesque and more didactic or prayerful writings, carries an existential lesson, a determined refusal to stop time. The onrush of genres marks an exhilarating embrace of temporality. This is an embrace of the endlessly surprising – the newness, sufferings, and restorations of time. Melville cries out to Hawthorne, "Lord, when shall we be done changing?" He's desperate as he is gripped by Ahab, then Ishmael, and loses his center, just as Kierkegaard is gripped by Johannes de silentio, then Climacus, and so opens the issue of an ever-changing center. As if frightened by ephemerality, Melville hopes that Hawthorne's friendship will be saving. "Knowing you persuades me more than the Bible of our immortality."[24] In contrast, Kierkegaard is exhilarated. Change is a bracing condition to live out and replicate in literature.

Opposed to the sense of endless change is the presumption of a minimal stability.[25] Melville did not create Ishmael, Ahab, or Starbuck to make readers wonder *where*, or *who*, or whether he, Melville exists now and tomorrow. But I suspect Kierkegaard created Climacus and Anti-Climacus (and a dozen other figures) to disrupt stability, to vex readers. The texts of the *oeuvre* set us wondering *where* (and *whether*) a character or writer was and will be; and where and whether I, as a reader, exist and will be. To exist and own a life parallels performing a character and owning the performance – enacted here or there – and to be invested in how that performed life fared yesterday, and fares now, and will fare tomorrow. Thus a now-familiar tension: it matters where, when, and how a writer and reader stand, changing yet changeless.

Writers give their work a kind of imperishable existence or immortality.[26] Death and resurrection are in play as tax-liable Kierkegaard dies, and implied-author Kierkegaard, a cultural presence, gradually rise up from the grave. As we read, we find an author alive post-burial. There is yet another way to think from the far side of the grave. Kierkegaard writes looking back on past thoughts and intuitions that were his and are now past, left behind by time. It's as if he places himself beyond the grave, and looks back. The true poet, we may think, is engaged in "posthumous production." Kierkegaard gives as a subtitle to one of his treatises, "A Posthumous Work of a Solitary Human Being."[27]

Posthumous work is work of one who has died and is now alive, resurrected, beyond bones marked by a headstone. Any praising or deflationary biography addressing the mortal taxpayer and flawed suitor becomes superfluous on this view. "The freedom of literature – its true immortality – is its absolute distance from the factual."[28] And flight from the factual is *not* flight to the fictional. As I dream of tomorrow, recollect my early childhood, or get my life in view as if it were done, I think neither fact nor fiction. And a text's immortality also means that readers are equal over time in addressing it. No nineteenth century Danish writer has privilege in fixing the meaning of a part or the whole of the authorship. Kierkegaard is dead, and hence disabled from giving the "incontrovertible last word on Kierkegaardian authorship."[29, 30] And insofar as he is alive, he gives multiple, unsettling answers.

Whirl and sudden center

Subjects reside in inter-subjective relations, not in isolated Cartesian mental substances or Cartesian-Sartrean centers of choice and action. They reside, as Kierkegaard stages things, often in a street theater or carnivalesque whirl. That's the way it can feel from the inside as we face the array of "Kierkegaardian" texts, and the way it may feel as we enter any one text. No doubt there are days when our own lives have the excitement and anxiety of whirl – no reassuring anchor of identity to grip. All that notwithstanding, subjectivity and inter-subjectivity can appear not only from the inside in the midst of moments of whirl, but also from some relatively more distant vantage of composure.

Stepping back, say in retrospect, I may reflect that the carnival scene that sweeps me up is put together by the vision, execution, and managerial skills of CEO Jones, CEO Kierkegaard. He is its heart and soul, what holds it together. So although Kierkegaard-Jones is from one angle just another subject in inter-subjective space, from another he is boss, inspiration, and source of power – however artfully he may hide this fact, and deflect attention away from himself toward the multitude performing and caught up in the whirl.

Similarly, I can be caught up in the whirl, and seem to myself to be as centerless as my surround. But the spell can be broken. Suddenly a small child darts toward the Ferris wheel. Without losing a beat, I grab her hand. I may not have been aware of a center for myself apart from the engulfing whirl. But after my action, I know there was a "me" at the ready, prepared to take charge, alert to practical emergency, ready to act from a singular center, from an identity, a strong integrity.

Being a self in a mobile world presents a "difficult reality" for philosophy. There are tensions between at least two senses of our existence. We have subliminal confidence (usually) that a centered self is at the ready. It will spring into action and forestall doubts. Yet we admit that we may lose even the confidence of a self at the ready. This may occur because of inattention, carelessness, or despair. But also, more sanguinely, a dependable identity can be swept away in a fluid mood of love, in a rising arc of music or poetry or dance, in being swept out of ourselves by majestic seas or landscapes, or swept up in the crush of Mardi Gras. Difficult realities make for difficult philosophy.

Kierkegaard was polemical and cagey enough to revel in the changing shadows of a self and in the difficulties others would have in finding him. And he was sharp enough to see a moral and religious advantage in elusiveness. He continually intimates that only where radical openness to change is present – that is, only where a solid self *can't* be pinned down – can there be hope of real transfiguration. The apparent "solid self," often enough, is only a social shell, a convenient surface for others, lacking a personal heart.

Melville avowed that knowing Hawthorne persuaded him of "our immortality." Kierkegaard saw writing itself working toward an eternal transfiguration. In a moment of prophecy, he declares that *Fear and Trembling* will make his name immortal. And if he were persuaded of immortality, it would not be (as with Melville) through a glimpse of undying friendship. He craved, we suppose, the glimpse of a God who would acknowledge his authorship, and furthermore, place him beyond all change and corruption.

Communications

Kierkegaard writes in his journals, "Real ethico-religious communication is as if vanished from the world."[31] In the *Postscript* he writes, "In its inexhaustible artistry, such a form of [ethico-religious] communication ... renders the existing subject's own [inexhaustible] relation to the idea."[32] I take these words to mean that an ethical-religious status or posture or bearing can be communicated by mentors, writing, or events in a medium of infinite artistry, and be received by a subject whose relation to a proper ethico-religious aspiration ["the idea"] will itself be a medium of infinite artistry, an ongoing and inexhaustible receiving and making-real.

We crave the specificity of a particular life that, in its vivid detail, can exemplify one that could be ours. Kierkegaard brings moral knowledge and its art, the lively artistry of the soul, down to earth, letting it speak in its varied plenitude, in its alluring, halting, terrifying energies. Having pseudonyms present various viewpoints and embody various stances encourages our free responsiveness across a range of affect. We can take Kierkegaard's works (the pseudonymous ones, at the very least) to be works of art that address us. They appeal to and activate our interpretative sensibilities, and nicely detour around an argumentative essay's explicit propositional outcomes, or a preacher's imperious or intimidating (or quite gentle) exhortations.

These works of art (as I'll call them) have pedagogical aims. Their aim, for instance, might be to show how an Abrahamic stance, or a Socratic or Christian one, might animate one's life. Accordingly, Kierkegaard artistically displays, or enacts, the "dialectical lyric" of a Johannes de silentio (as he mulls through multiple versions of the Abraham story in *Fear and Trembling*). He artistically sketches out the "comic-pathetic- dialectic" of a Johannes Climacus in the *Postscript*, a figure who might as well be a voluble Socrates. We see thinking on the go, improvising, exploratory, as art can be mobile, improvisatory, exploratory – sketching a possibility of action or understanding, but not spelling it out in the way a treatise or lecture in morality would. We can ask what happens or is communicated as one is overtaken by a work of art, or overtaken by a pseudonymous work, or some portion of it? This brings us to Kierkegaard's contrast between direct and indirect communication – what I prefer to call the contrast between objective and subjective communication.

Objective and subjective communication

"Information-only" communication contrasts with subjective communication – communication of affect or virtue or "existential status." When I take in an "objective communication," I take in information, doctrine, or creed, delivered in explicit propositions or argument. On the other hand, when I take in a "subjective communication" I take in an affect, virtue, or status (I'm a new man!) – I take in an existential orientation, mood, or disposition. A mentor, piece of literature, or an event can present an occasion of transforming reception. We might receive generosity or courage, cunning or playfulness, honesty or outrage, imaginative freedom, combative intellect, or surpassing kindness. If these lodge in the soul, it is not as new information.

Religious or ethical writing, and religious or ethical acting, found in exemplary lives, and in stage, cinematic, or street performance, or in liturgical ceremonies, can have deeply transformative, non-propositional impact.[33] Kierkegaard correctly stresses the importance in a life of the transfer of "existential," or "subjective" significance. But he fails to see that communication of "facts-only" can be indirect, and that the communication of affect or virtue can be direct. His oppositional "direct/indirect" can't do the job he wants done.

If I read a medical journal's account of pulmonary embolism, the medical writer intends to transfer bare bones, objective-only content. Under Kierkegaard's rubrics, this is direct communication. But for me, a lay reader, the delivery is indirect, for I must detour through dictionaries and other articles to get the simple facts straight. (Of course, this is not what Kierkegaard means by "indirection," but that's my point: what he has in mind does not coincide with our ordinary intuitions about "indirection.")

Coming at this awkward rubric from the other side, some of what Kierkegaard labels "indirect communication" – the transfer of subjective affect or virtue (say) rather than objective-only content – has an unequivocally direct impact. If I express my rage by yelling "No!" in your hearing (or express my joy by yelling "Yes!"), an existential or subjectively experienced fear or alarm, or an existential delight or affirmation, will arc from my voiced-body and enter yours – directly. Thus Kierkegaard's contrast must travel under new names. A relay of something objective can happen indirectly; and a relay of something subjective can happen directly.

Simultaneously subjective-objective

Utterances are not definitively one or the other, subjective or objective. Some are neither (say a policeman's asking me to pull over). Many are both. If I yell "Watch out for the truck!" I convey objective information: the truck approaching presents an objective danger. I also want my words to startle you, to arrest your motion, to transfer passion or fear that (I hope) will be like a physical push to get you out of the way. I need both subjectivity and objectivity to be directly conveyed in my "Watch out!" In my intensely vocalized "Yes!" I convey something subjective – that I'm utterly enchanted. But I'm enchanted about an objective fact, a "bare fact," if you will: we share a magical view of surf through the Pacific mist. My "Watch out!" or "Yes!" release affect and subjectivity aimed in your direction in the hope that my subjectivity is imparted to you. That imparting can be as immediate and as direct as a blow to the chest or a touch of a hand. What gets imparted is not just objective information but my passion, my orientation, perhaps even my freedom. My *"Yes!"* is my release, my freedom, my unabashed delight that if successfully imparted invites you to share in this unrestrained delight.

Paraphrase

Propositional or information-transfer can easily be paraphrased. "It's raining in California" might be paraphrased, "if you go to California, you'll discover a downpour." On the other hand, the expression of mood, affect, or freedom, resists paraphrase. The launch of affect or mood is not the launch of a string of words to interpret with other words. When we hear Lear's anguished "No! No! No! No!" the bulk of what's conveyed is a kind of desperate agony and anger.

You can't paraphrase a "No!" If you hear it you're moved. King Lear transmits not a proposition, but some mix of despair, rage, deep refusal, desperation. The affect is a "what" that requires a proper "how." The rage can't be voiced casually, flippantly, in a monotone. He must cry, cry out – "No! No! No!" *How* that cry arrives, inflected at its apt degree of passion, will make all the difference in what arrives. Voiced properly, we have nothing like data for a log. Imagine the bland entry: "Tuesday, 12:01 pm. King said 'No' five times. Bad weather."

A cry reduced to data is no longer a cry. Everything subjective about Lear arrives in an anguished "No!" Everything subjective about Molly Bloom arrives in an ecstatic "Yes!" No fact or piece of creed, no "objectivity-only" expresses her ecstasy or his anguish. And these passions are imparted to me, rend my heart, opening the felt possibility of a passion that might just be mine – *is*, for the moment, mine.

Any single utterance can simultaneously transfer a mix of objective content and subjective disposition. And the objective-subjective contrast does not exhaust the types of interpersonal communication. If I am a policeman I may order you to stop. That will not be an ethical-religious communication, but more like grabbing your arm. As a cop, your action matters to me, and you should heed my imperative. But I have no aim to alter your ethical-religious constitution.

There need be nothing indirect about our commonplace capacities to share a sense of confidence, a mood of terror, a spirit of playfulness, a passion for truth. Yet it's not easy to understand how these conveyances work. You communicate your phone number. If asked *how* I got it, I say, "you spoke clearly, I wrote it down." End of story! Socrates imparts his allure – I'm shattered. Asked *how* I got seduced, I stumble: "That turn of phrase ... *you* know, that gentle wit, his touch, his intelligence!" – I'm inarticulate and blush.

Socratic subjective communication

In *Postscript*, Climacus ponders how Socrates can teach while withholding objective content. Something gets transferred from mentor to student, but it's hard to pin down exactly what. Let's say that to be won over by Socrates is to fall in love as he asks questions, to fall in love with his orientation toward inquiry. Socrates does not pass on a doctrine or creed to shout from the rooftops. We receive (through Plato's rendition) a transfer of allure. Socrates is a master at drawing us into his net (which is not teaching us the truth of a proposition). And the impact of his allure can be as direct as a lover's touch, or the intimate gaze of his eyes – just ask Alcibiades, who falls directly, madly, in love.

When Kierkegaard addresses me in his discourses, "My dear reader ..." he is directly inviting an intimacy, directly transferring his subjective openness in a way he hopes we will accept. When Dostoevsky has Christ kiss the Grand Inquisitor on the lips, the intimacy and subjective impact is deep and striking – even as we struggle with the hermeneutical question of what, objectively speaking, that kiss is supposed to mean (is it acquiescence, approval, forgiveness, resignation, pity ... ?).

We will quickly sound foolish trying to say what (objectively) it is, exactly, in the person who steals our heart, that dispossesses the mind, that allows the theft. Take Socrates. Is it the look in his eye, the slight hesitancy in his rough speech, a melting in his shoulders as they turn slightly to one side? Is it the sensation that he sees through me, and is close enough to touch me? In the case of Kierkegaard, is it his sparkling wit, his intimate address, his sense of the great pain of love and devotion, his capacity to have Christ walk hand in hand with Socrates?[34]

Theatre and freedom

Perhaps what steals our hearts is Kierkegaard's exuberant launching of street theatre – a young swain in love with a princess, an ex-alcoholic seeing a friend (a suicide) drawn from the Seine, a barefoot dancing Socrates, a mother weaning her child with Abraham's knife over her shoulder. Sometimes Kierkegaard's array of books, each book an array of unexpected drama, can operate like a theater-troupe in waiting. Now one ensemble of actors steps forward, now another, pseudonym by pseudonym, signed work by signed work, this section of *Either/Or*, now that section of *Either/Or*. Now we see the knight of faith as a dancer – now, the knight as a woman knitting – now, the quixotic knight as a jaunty burgher whistling all the way home. This artistic troupe can be shifting and elusive in its address, but at the level of individual subjective impact, it can be as direct as can be. Improvising political street theatre, antic troupes in a beleaguered and melancholy city can communicate politics (or an ethico-religious truth, as in a medieval mystery play) without placards or requisite chants from the crowd or mandatory parades or riotous sweeps into battle (or rushes to conversion). One by one our hearts can be affected. How the transfer of political or ethico-religious affect will play out in our subsequent thought and comportment is an open question.

Kierkegaard and Socrates leave us in a space of responsive freedom. Our ethico-religious imaginations have been invaded by a wondrous, even sublime, allure that leaves us ripe for change or consolidation. And a wide range of objective uncertainty or ignorance accompanies this "subjectivity transfer." Socrates says with a wink, "I know nothing!" (yet speaks on); Johannes de silentio says with a wink, "I am silent!" (yet writes on). With a wink (after 500 pages of tome-like disquisition) Climacus writes "I take it all back" (yet leaves us a jewel).

Finding a life

If one aim of spiritual or moral communication is ministering to others in their existential need, then Kierkegaard insists that renewed examination of old creeds or propositions, or the conveyance of new ones, is way off the mark. What is needed is change of affect, orientation, virtue, or enablement. Kierkegaard's great insight is that we don't always need more discussion of facts or revision of theories. Our need is to find a life, say of Socrates or Christ, of devoted knitting or dancing, of inspired writing or talking, of holy walking or comforting, a life that exemplifies what's best – morally, spiritually, religiously. This happens as an exemplar's power enters our lives, or as the artistry of the written word enters our lives, or as the allure of street theatre enters our lives – to be taken up and expressed in whatever way seems fitting (or not) – from my point of view, in a life that is mine.

Kierkegaard's use of pseudonyms opens our frustrations, apprehensions, curiosities, alert interests. There is more to this than being coy, exhibitionist or secretive, more than being perverse or provocative, teasing, wicked, or deceptive, more than being playful, jesting, experimental or evasive. We're forced to figure what's going on, to at least partially resolve the whirl, to gather our imaginative capacities and focus them on the matter at hand, the difficult reality impinging. Perhaps entering the field of pseudonyms and varied genres creates the tension between representation and what exceeds and defies representation so familiar in encountering the sublime. And the sublime, in eluding our grasp, sets us free.

Pseudonyms create an aperture for freedom, for realization of an interpretative existence that sloughs off the automation of direct data absorption or creedal transfer. Like a good metaphor, the shocking interruption of a pseudonym spawns an abundance of thought, feeling and images. I experience my mind-body-soul at sea, thrown into the labyrinth of freedom – not just told about it.

Without a proper distance between a pseudonym and its creator, a reader will mistake Kierkegaard for an authority on some matter of fact or doctrine, an authority charged with communicating in objective address – with all urgency. However, Kierkegaard's task is to awaken *our* subjectivity. Accordingly, he must partially veil or disguise his seriousness, for authorities can intimidate or overpower, as well as inspire and command. Yielding to his charisma, our freedom is at risk.[35] Socrates must hide to protect his students from too easy a seduction, and of the wrong sort. Kierkegaard must hide so that his reader may come to "exist in the truth." [36] No authority, but a pseudonym speaks. With that, anxiety is conferred, but also essential freedom.

Freedom

In *Postscript*, Climacus tells us, "The secret of communication [or imparting] specifically hinges on setting the other free."[37] In line with this, Climacus appends to the very end of the *Postscript* a revocation of all he's so far asserted. In the tome's "final explanation" to make matters worse, under the signature "Kierkegaard," an author of that name distances himself from the entirety of the pseudonymous works (including *Postscript*). Creating distance between texts and authors reduces their looming authority. The printed word is released to speak on its own, a word addressed *from* a subjectivity *to* a subjectivity, who in turn can speak (or remain silent). Veiling a word's authority promotes a reader's freedom from an author's pressure or coercion. Kierkegaard is not a policeman shouting "stop!" The space between reader and text is aesthetically maintained. As Climacus puts it,

> Wherever the subjective is of importance. ... communication is a work of art; it is doubly reflected, and its first form is the subtlety that the subjective individuals must be held devoutly apart from one another and must not be left coagulating together in objectivity.[38]

We don't parrot slogans. Artistry protects subjective freedom to enable another to become ethical, Socratic, or Christian. If Kierkegaard's only thrown a bone to a bored intelligentsia who coagulate in a crowd chanting objectivities, then he'd rather take the book back.

Exemplars and artistry

If I teach "Thou shall have no disciples" in such a way that disciples gather around, or if I teach "The unexamined life is not worth living" as a random truth for mindless duplication on exams, then I have failed to communicate an appropriate concern. The outcome, as Climacus would say, is comic. I will not have exemplified the relevant truth in the telling. To fail in this regard is to have failed to convey decisive subjectivity, a capacity for living in a certain way. "The thinker must present the human ideal ... as an ethical requirement, as a challenge to the recipient to exist in it."[39] With regard to the human ideal, "the simple as well as the wise must be so obliging as to exist in it." [40]

Showing or exemplifying truth is distinct from stating truth. If an ethical or religious individual wishes to convey the truth she inhabits, she must avoid the appearance and the reality of reducing it to a telling or a statement, even a roundabout telling. Socrates would dodge telling if he thought his interlocutors were just looking for a slogan or principle to run with. If a Christian should communicate compassion, that can't be by saying "be compassionate," or "I'm compassionate, follow me." Perhaps an "existence communication" of compassion is most salient in silence, taking no part in what William James calls the chatter of the boundlessly loquacious mind.[41] Kierkegaard fears for our souls because he knows our susceptibility to street gossip, celebrity and political chatter, to academic vanguardism, news-speak and newspeak. Ethico-religious communication is "vanished from the world."

Teaching subjectivity and freedom

Socrates can turn a soul, unleash a life. There is no simple statement that says how he or a Christ or an ethico-religious teacher might turn a soul, how they impart necessary passion. "I only wish," Socrates confesses in the *Symposium*, "that wisdom were the kind of thing that flowed from the vessel that was full to the one that was empty."[42] An exemplar's life administers independence even as it bequeaths a pattern and swerves away from doctrine – of rights or sin, of rituals for birth, marriage, or death, of catechism or creed. Accepting the allure of a Socrates is a commitment to him and to the path he lights up. But the path he lights up will be (and become) my own. As Climacus puts it,

> no one is so resigned as God; because he communicates creatively in such a way that in creating he *gives* independence vis-à-vis himself. The most resigned a human being can be is to acknowledge the given independence in every human being, and to the best of one's ability do everything in order truly to help someone retain it.[43]

The independence necessary between persons and the divine is maintained by the artistry of the divine, who on pain of stealing freedom withdraws as creator from creation. Just so, the independence (and dependence) necessary between persons is maintained by a reciprocal respect, artistry, and reserve or withdrawal.

Pseudonymity, genre, communication

In Kierkegaard's practice, the matters of pseudonymity, genre, and communication are interlocked, joined in the service of bringing an ethico-religious individual to life, joined in the service of increased freedom from a stifling onslaught of false authority, pervasive gossip and sloganeering, of objective-only measures of truth rather than measure of truth that radiates from exceptional artistic, dialectical, ethical, religious persons like Socrates. His is the vocation of an ethico-religious individual, which centrally involves communicating an identity, a life. Kierkegaard said at the end of his life that his task had always been Socratic. The best way to frame his proliferation of style, genre, artful communication, and pseudonymity, is through the light of the Socratic: dialectic and eros in the service of goodness, beauty, and the divine.

The subjective thinker is not a scientist-scholar; he is an artist. To exist is an art. The subjective thinker is esthetic enough for his life to have esthetic content, ethical enough to regulate it, dialectical enough in thinking to master it. [44]

The subjective *thinker's form* … is his *style* … His form must first and last be related to existence, and in this regard he must have at his disposal the poetic, the ethical, the dialectical, the religious.[45]

Notes

1 Parts of this chapter lean heavily on previous studies: *On Søren Kierkegaard: Dialogue, Polemics, Lost Intimacy, and Time.* (Burlington, VT: Ashgate 2007, Chapter 11) and "What is a Kierkegaardian Author?", *Philosophy and Social Criticism*, 35, no. 7.

2 "[T]he expectation of being able someday to … derive everything from one principle – the undeniable need of human reason, which finds complete satisfaction only in a complete systematic unity of its cognitions," see Immanuel Kant, *Critique of Practical Reason, Kants gesammelte Schriften, Akademie,* (ed.) Vol. 5 (Berlin: De Gruyter, 1902), p. 91.

3 The Hebrew *tohu wabohu* is given as "welter and waste" (rather than "formless void") in Robert Alter, *Genesis*, trans and commentary (New York: W. W. Norton, 1997).

4 Vigilius Haufniensis is the pseudonymous author of *The Concept of Anxiety*. His vigil (or anxious watch) foretells Heidegger's "watch over being." Heidegger's *Augenblick* is also taken from *Anxiety*.

5   For a path-breaking study, see Joseph Westfall Joseph, *The Kierkegaardian Author: Authorship and Performance in Kierkegaard's Literary and Dramatic Criticism* (Berlin: De Gruyter, 2007).

6   *Fear and Trembling*, Hongs trans., 27

7   Melville, Herman, *Tales, Poems, and Other Writings*, ed., intro. John Bryant (New York: Modern Library Melville, 2001), p. 44.

8   Bloom, 2003: p. 8.

9   *Concluding Unscientific Postscript*, Hongs, V. 1: 89. See Climacus dances with death in Preface of *Crumbs* (2009), last sentence.

10 *CUP* 1, p. 251.

11 *CUP* 1, pp. 617–23. The final inserted sheets, initialed "S.K.," are unpaginated.

12 Climacus lets himself explain the authorship of which he is a member (as if Hamlet's play, Mousetrap, were to explain the play *Hamlet*, or perhaps, all of Shakespeare).

13 *Fear and Trembling* is a sublime spectacle that parallels the new Tivoli Gardens (Mooney, 2007, Chapter 8).

14 Bakhtin, 1984: p. 107.

15 *The Point of View of my Work as an Author*, (Hongs trans. 41–2).

16 *CUP* 1, 623 ff.

17 *CUP* 1, 261f.

18 Plato is the classic precursor here: he authors Socrates, yet Socrates speaks Plato's lines and even upstages him, just as Climacus can upstage Kierkegaard, ribbing him.

19 Hannay, Alastair, *Kierkegaard, a Biography* (Cambridge: Cambridge University Press, 2001) pp. 422–3.

20 I reject the premise that the variety of masks Kierkegaard presents betray a penchant for deception – Edward F. Mooney (2007, Chapter 5).

21 On "difficult reality" see Stanley Cavell, Cora Diamond, Cora, et al *Philosophy and Animal Life* (New York: Columbia University Press, 2008).

22 Søren Kierkegaard, *Prefaces and Writing Sampler*, trans. Todd W. Nichol, Princeton (1998).

23 The burlesque is suggested as a Kierkegaardian genre in Mark D. Jordan, "The Modernity of Christian Theology or Writing Kierkegaard Again for the First Time," *Modern Theology*, Vol. 27: 3, 442–51.

Polonius reports the variety of genres in a Kierkegaardian spirit when he promises "the best actors in the world / either for tragedy, comedy, history, pastoral / pastoral-comical, historical-pastoral, tragical-historical / tragical-comical-historical-pastoral / scene individable, or poem unlimited." (*Hamlet*, Act 2, Sc. 2, 405; see Harold Bloom, *Hamlet, Poem Unlimited* (New York: Penguin 2003). On the carnivalesque as a genre, see Mikhail Bakhtin (1984). *Problems of Dostoevsky's Poetics* (Minneapolis: University of Minnesota Press).

24 Melville, 2001: p. 44.

25 Existential stages combine the stability of a stage with the instability of stage-shift. Because each stage-heading oversees many genres, however, stability is diluted.

26 Westfall, 2007: p. 51.

27 Søren Kierkegaard, *Without Authority*, trans. Howard V. Hong and Edna H. Hong, Princeton, 1997, p. 51.

28 Westfall, 2007: p. 135.

29 Westfall, 2007: p. 77.

30 As a visitor to Copenhagen, I want to meet Kierkegaard to get him to sign my copy of *Concluding Unscholarly Postscript*. I ring his bell. Noting the tome and divining my purpose, he says, "I'm sorry, there is no Johannes Climacus at this address – you've been misinformed." I try to match wits. "Ah! But Mr. Climacus has added a few pages at the end – they declare that S. Kierkegaard, not Climacus, is the author!' He retorts, "Young man, I wouldn't believe everything you read in books, especially in books that are dialectical and unscholarly, written by fanciful and humorous authors, full of dubious mental exercises and imaginative travels! Neither S. Kierkegaard nor Climacus reside here!" Although Kierkegaard is clearly cagey and elusive, I reject the premise that he is therefore deceptive.

31 *Journals and Papers* 1, 656.

32 *CUP* 1, 80

33 See Aumann, Antony, "Kierkegaard on Indirect Communication, the Crowd, and a Monstrous Illusion," in R.L. Perkins (ed.), *International Kierkegaard Commentary: Point of View* (Macon, GA: Mercer University Press, 2010), pp. 295–324.

34 I propose that Kierkegaard accords Christ and Socrates a collaborative identity in (Mooney, 2007, Chapter 3).

35 Climacus brings out the contrast between Socrates' outwardly unfavorable appearance and his inner beauty. Through the repellent effect exerted by the contrast, the learner understands that he has

essentially to do with *himself*: Inwardness or wholeheartedness is not fusion with a common truth but a separation in which each exists in the truth.

36 If I tell you that I've just become a grandfather, I may find myself overtaken by the wonder and fear crystallized in the advent of a child, the fragile abundance of its coming to pass – of my passing, and of the passing of a world that both pulls me forward and leaves me behind. More dramatic is the pathos of Socratic encounter, the passion of Lear's cries, the subtle irony of pseudonyms, are relatively dramatic cases of subjective (or existential) communication. They are also instances of the connection between encounter with the sublime and the freedom of the interpreter. Yet the sublime can appear in the relatively pedestrian. Mentioning I've become a grandfather is one of those moments of sharing and everyday transfer of subtle affect, mood, passion, and orientation that make up rich and fragile lives. For a good discussion, see Aumann, "Kierkegaard on Indirect Communication, the Crowd, and a Monstrous Illusion."

37 *CUP* 1, p. 74.

38 *CUP* 1, p. 79.

39 *CUP*, p. 358.

40 *CUP*, p. 367.

41 James, William, *The Varieties of Religious Experience, Centenary Edition* (New York: *Routledge*, 2002), p. 62. See also *Varieties of Religion Today: William James Revisited* (Cambridge, MA: Harvard University Press, Charles Taylor, 2002), p. 52; and Mooney, 2007, Chapter 13.

42 *The Symposium of Plato, The Shelley Translation,* ed. and intro. by David O. O'Connor (South Bend Indiana: St. Augustine's Press, 2002), p. 175d. This translation captures the visceral immediateness of being touched by "wisdom-in-Socrates": "It would be well, Agathon, if wisdom were of such a nature that when we touched each other it would overflow of its own accord ..." Grant that wisdom *is in fact conveyed* in the way a lover's touch conveys love. As I read this passage, that doesn't mean it will *simply flow* of its own accord, like water gravitationally pulled. The flowing touch will be much more subtle, delicate and complicated, like conveying extreme delicacy in musical phrasing, requiring interpretative delivery and attuned interpretative reception.

43 *CUP* 1, p. 260.

44 *CUP* 1, p. 351.

45 *CUP* 1, p. 357

4

A Faith that Defies Self-Deception[1]

It is quite common, if erroneous, to assume that a person of faith must be a person in self-deception. From the outside, it can seem that faith is a kind of protective shield against harsh realities. Given our exposure to cruelty and suffering, what would be more natural than to adopt a belief that would act as a shield? If my self-esteem suffers at the thought that I cheated my neighbor, I can shield myself from this hurt by working up the belief (self-deceptively) that I did *not* really cheat him. If the span of history seems to flaunt one evil after another, I shield myself from the agony this occasions by working up the belief that God did *not* really cheat us, that He will make things right, or they've been right all along, that the world *isn't* rotten to the core.

There is a surface plausibility to this view that the genesis of faith lies in self-deception, and so cannot be authentic. Despite appearances, however, it can't be the whole story. I'll argue that in Kierkegaard's *Fear and Trembling* we have a dramatic reversal of this position. Within the covers of that startling book, we discover that faith is designed so that it *can't* be self-deceptive. On the contrary, we discover that the trust and openness of faith is an inoculation *against* self-deception. The *openness* guarantees that harsh or rotten realities are *not* covered up, and that faith's *trust* is a *stance,* not a *belief.* If it's not a belief, I can't be deceived about it. This is faith's two-pronged defiance of self-deception.

The pseudonymous author of *Fear and Trembling,* Johannes *de silentio,* does not linger discussing what beliefs or tenets about God are essential to faith. The book's "dialectical" sections pit ethics (which incudes many beliefs), against God's command to Abraham, that he offer up Isaac as a sacrifice. But even here, the issue seems to be less about *belief* than about how one can *trust* ethics, and *trust* God, when these trusts collide (as they seem to in God demand). If Abraham suffers a collision of trusts, the question is how he weathers that collision, how he proceeds without revolt against one or the other, against God or against Ethics. The question is not about propositions but whether he can *live from a stance* that *mitigates or displaces despair.* Can he live from open trust, from a steady faith. A love toward, or trust in, the world or the divine or one's neighbor is not a tenet or belief. It is not a bundle of affirmed propositions but a constellation of affirmative passions and dispositions that are one's poise in the face of unaccommodating harsh, sometimes brutally unspeakable, realities.

Keeping faith in the face of unmistakable desolation is compatible with being quite *agnostic* about what propositions might (or might not) *ground* one's steady assurance. The bottom line in the conduct of life may be primitive assurances rather than foundational tenets.[2] Of course, a faithful stance is not beyond critique. It may be ill advised, foolish, infantile or self-destructive. But a stance is not shattered or defeated in the way an assertion is. A person does not fall apart the way a proposition does. A stance is *there*: it either works to inform my living with grace, or doesn't. Snow is *there*, it either works to grace the limbs of my trees or it doesn't. Snow can't deceive itself as it falls with grace, nor can a stance deceive itself as it informs my living with grace. I live from faith I don't. Only if I attempt to *ground* my faith in a tenet do I ponder beliefs about which I could deceive myself (or not). And (so I'd argue) there is no requirement that I ground every stance from which I live in an explicit propositional belief. Life would stop dead in its tracks if that requirement were in force.

"Once There Was a Man"

Faith sprawls throughout Kierkegaard's corpus, early to late. I stick to *Fear and Trembling,* a text that is lyrical and dialectical, full of polemics and improvisations. There we find three inhabitants to reckon with: Abraham, the *father* of faith; an anonymous *mother* of faith smuggled in as Abraham's counterpart; and an utterly worldly chap as unlikely and unassuming as a tax-collector or a shopkeeper would be.[3] The figure who might be a shop man is a domesticated, citified Abraham, a father without fangs. The mother is Abraham as maternal, a soft source of nurture, meditative, tender, and private, not whistling jauntily down the street.

The mother and "shopkeeper" exemplify a miniature sublime on the scale of an everyday roast lamb, green peas, and a baby's soft coo. De silentio speaks of the knight of faith finding "the sublime in the pedestrian."[4] Thus the sublime is the wondrously unexpected and tremulous but found in the everyday, not only high in the heavens or in raging seas. Both mother and shopkeeper play *simple* virtue against Abraham's heroics. This says that it's a *mistake* to model faith on the *outwardness* of grand heroics. When the matter is not wondrous but monstrous, the fear is scaled down; only minor tremors of disquietude speak out. Terror ceases to be the preferred vehicle of instruction. Nursing mothers and burghers on the way home teach, by embodying the trusting openness of faith.

In the persons of the mother, "shopkeeper," and Abraham, we have three improvisations on faith.[5] This makes for contingency of meaning or interpretation. Grant that each exemplifies a trusting openness. What do we make of their obvious differences? There's a contingency that surrounds who is a *person* of faith, and also, around who is the *author* of these sketches of faith. Is it Kierkegaard speaking, or is it *silentio*? And if the latter, why trust a writer whose code name is "silence," who is loud about silence and faith, and who frankly confides that he *can't understand* it?

The text lacks a stable figure of faith, a stable author, and in addition, lacks a stable register, style, or tonality. Style and genre set the aims and moods of writing. Lyric is one mode of writing, and dialectic, another; yet we're told on *Fear and Trembling*'s title page that we hold a "Dialectical Lyric." We also have burlesque, fairy tale, and fable; satire, farce, and tragedy; the grotesque and the sublime. We have the antinomian and apophatic and what has been dubbed the eucatastrophical (a tale with an unexpected finish that's marvelously good).[6] There are scenes that approach slapstick: Johannes mentions the possibilities of killing Isaac at home to avoid the bother of a climb; of having a parishioner run out after the sermon, knife in hand, to corner his own son; of having the strolling burgher stop to watch rats, or of having his wife serve him lamb. And more serious than slapstick, but eccentric and unfathomable, *de silentio* gives us four serene captions under the opening quartet of terrifying Abraham portraits. What genre or mood are *they* meant to enact? Abraham holds a knife. The captions have a mother weaning her child. Soon we realize that this is a improvisatory installation without center. How can this four-movement *divertimento* give us a clue about faith?

Especially at the start, anything like fear and trembling is subdued or sidelined. It's as if we're meant to bracket such intensity, leave it at the door. Perhaps its impact, if permitted, would disable our reflective capacities. The *Preface* doesn't prepare us for a killing scenario, and the opening "*Attunement*" (meant to set a mood for thinking), let's us mull wistfully or daydream. There's a pervasive tone of fantasy and "what if" afoot. "What *if* we take Abraham (or the nursing mother, or the figure who could be a shop owner), to be a figure of faith?" *Fear and Trembling* begins as if a fairy tale were being dreamily recalled: "*Once there was a man...*" And the would-be fairy tale is about a man who had a *daydream*, who remembered "a beautiful childhood tale."[7] This is decidedly *not* the tonality of reporting or critiquing would-be child-sacrifice, about which there is absolutely *nothing* dreamy nostalgic, or beautiful. It's as if Johannes wants to suspend any frame that delivers stark, bare bones realities. Even a monstrous Abraham, the father with knife in hand, might be a diversion from the truth, for that knife *blinds*, doesn't it? Think of Chagall's dreamy version of the scene – so unlike Caravaggio's full-force rendering. Chagall has Abraham almost whimsically floating, among stars, angels, and lambs.

Improvisation and fantasy are the other side of Kierkegaard's aversion to doctrinal disputation and academic commentary or contention. Look again at the titles of the two books universally taken as the core of his theology and philosophy: *Philosophical Fragments* and *Unscientific Postscript* may not strike one as punchy at first. But those are only discrete tags, not full titles. The little book usually translated *Fragments* is best rendered in full as *Philosophical Crumbs, or Scraps of Philosophy*. Its follow up – a *600 page afterthought*, postscript or appendix – is best rendered, in full, as *Concluding Unscholarly Postscript to Philosophical Crumbs: A Mimic-Pathetic-Dialectic Compilation – an Existential Contribution*. Sober scholarship? Hardly. A Serious Contribution to Philosophy or Theology? Perhaps it's improvisational kitsch, but if not, the *Postscript* especially is surely the most comical para-philosophy ever. It belongs to no genre, is infinite in scope, and infinitely becoming.

Let's say that we've more or less established that *Fear and Trembling* is a text of diverse and indeterminate tonal register, genre, and authorship that gives us not just Abraham on Moriah, but a mixed crew of faith's exemplars. If we grant all this, why should we think that *Fear and Trembling* is a guide to a stable conception of faith?

Here are three answers. First, we are shown over and over what faith is *not*. This clears the board for what faith might be. Second, by rummaging through candidates that turn out not to pass muster, we get habituated to *precisely the difficulty* of faith, of tracking it and of *living* by it, through trial and error. The difficulty and temptations of the terrain are replicated, testing our acuity and resolve. Third, there is what we could call the "positive theme," that faith is *trusting openness* modulated as *giving up* (or resignation) and *getting back* (the world or love or faith as a gift). Let me pause on the second sort of teaching the book affords: the way we are led through the difficulties of tracking faith.

Working through the conundrums of the text, seeing how faith as open trust permeates the comportment of Abraham, of the mother, of the burger, is seeing how faith might permeate any number of lives. The indeterminacy of faith is the indeterminacy and contingent variation in lives that can be animated by faith. We learn what faith is while avoiding theological thesis and antithesis. Tracking *de silentio's* multiple images and styles and figures merely recapitulates given experience in the world at the level of text. By practicing the knack of tracking faith's varied embodiments, in mothers and women rocking silently as they knit, grooves are laid down in the heart and mind that deepen our capacity to follow the dispersion of faith through any number of persons, and to avoid identifying faith with church-goers or creedal confession. A knack for following the text becomes a knack for seeing faith outside the text. It is a knack for keeping faithfully trusting and open in the interpretation of life experience and its ambiguities as they flow into the present.

Insofar as we give ourselves to indeterminacies in this way, we inoculate ourselves against the strident singleness of vision so characteristic of self-deception. The self-deceiver needs to bolster self-esteem and reduce complexity. We'll feel better about ourselves (we think) if we simplify and purify our sense of the world, burying the distasteful or cruel things elsewhere. Faith is an *expansion* of virtue – self-deception, a lethal *contraction*. I'll return to this.

Descent and rebirth

Here are two enigmatic, tone-setting pronouncements: "*Only one who descends to the underworld saves the loved one.*" But we might ask why the lover and beloved are charged with descending into the nether regions? Is all love an infernal *ordeal*? Here is a second pronouncement: *[T]he one who works will give birth to his own father.* This echoes the psychological truth that in acknowledging our ancestors, inheriting them properly, starting with my father, is work, spiritual labor. Linking the two gives us a compound enigma: a descent in the name of love into the nether regions of unclarity is a prerequisite to fixing one's paternity, and hence, one's birth, or rebirth. Go down, then come up, reborn.

Fear and Trembling is a kind of motley or medley; a quilt or collage, many panels and squares stitched loosely together, scene after scene; a carnival and horror show, a Chagall-like *dreamy* sort of art.[8] Abraham first appears in "*a beautiful dream*" of an old man remembering a childhood story. Giving up waking life for a dream – and then getting waking life back, dream included – is entering the giving up and getting back of faith. Cycling in and out of imagination can be radically transformative. We redo our past by such cycles, and so redo our present as an offspring of the past. As in a dream, oracle, or prophecy, *de silentio* whispers that the faithful *give birth to their fathers.*[9] Such is the power of imaginative transformations. In a simple biological sense mothers give birth to their children from the womb, and in a more complex imagi-native sense they give birth to an infant's growing independence in weaning. If we are beings toward death, as Heidegger learns from Kierkegaard, we are equally beings from birth, as Arendt learns from Kierkegaard. Birthing ourselves is modeled on birthing our children. We are mother and father to ourselves, giving (imaginative) birth to our fathers and mothers in practices of self-nourishment and earning inheritance or legacy.

Levinas sees only the monstrosity of Moriah with its apparent invitation to killing. He misses these quiet images of faith as natality or birth.[10] A mother weaning, or a shopkeeper watching rats scamper under gutter planks, are images of a tender attention to, and acceptance of, life.[11] The denial of the maternal in philosophical thinking is pervasive. To account for its repression would be a long story, but a colleague puts the issue this way: "As philosophers, we have engaged in self-deception in order not to "messy" the waters of philosophical investigation by recognizing the voice of the maternal. Doing so would complicate an otherwise tidy, 'single-vision' view of the world." And she adds, "Leaving out the maternal closes off a morally essential reality."[12]

In addition to a view of natality, de silentio's writing provides numerous other glancing perspectives: a critique of bourgeois market society (*Preface*); a critique of direct communication (*Epigraph*); a critique of religion as bible-based hero-worship (*Speech in Praise of Abraham*); an attack on rule-based and bureaucratic conventional morality (*Problema*); an appreciation of domesticity (mothers weaning, shopkeepers strolling home for dinner, knitters by the fire – sovereigns not wanted). In addition, the little tome provides a slightly pornographic peephole into dream-like blood-and-violence, as well as a critique of the Spectacular City.[13] It provides a range of polyphony (the voice of terror, of praise, of detached analysis), and a startlingly imaginative array of thematic variations on the theme: Abe might have dallied there, rushed there, stabbed himself, asked God to do it, refused outright, done it in despair, or in deception. All this, in a little non-book by a non-author.[14]

It's remarkable that Don Quixote can belong in this varied troop of knights of faith – perhaps de silentio's inspiration![15] The merchant-like fellow will not *immediately* bring to mind the mad Spanish knight, but imagination can mark links. Quixote was living Christianly and erratically in a world that took him to be mad; yet he was more Christian than they. The apparent merchant is living Christianly but not erratically, not madly; yet he is more Christian than they. How? Well, he refuses the ethics of convention that guarantees that a wife shall not leave her husband without dinner. He will be free of resentment should the meal not be there; he'll feel perfectly at ease. There is a notable delight and a freedom from presumption or moralism. He shows delightful assurance paired with cognitive, moral, and spiritual humility. All this makes this sane fellow a likely knight of faith.

The pattern of faith in *Fear and Trembling* is an assured stance amidst threatening contingency. Now we can add that this faith is lived out in *giving up and getting back*, being quieted then receiving, suffering then celebrating, moment by moment over time.[16] Is this what the poet Yehuda Amichai has in mind in his title *Open Closed Open*? Abraham opens to God, closes down in fright, hand closed on the knife, then opens to a transformed world as the angel speaks. The nursing mother opens her breast to her infant, closes it off in blackening the breast, then opens the infant to a new, more independent world. The shop man opens to the world, imagining even a roast head of lamb awaiting him at home, finds that possibility perhaps closed, gets his world back, as fresh as before. Job is wonderfully open, then horribly closed in his anger and grief, then wonderfully silenced, opened, by the gift of new worlds. Faith is this pattern of giving up Isaac and getting him back.

Covering suspicions

Self-deception is defense against threats to moral self-image or integrity. Say you lie to a thief to protect your daughter. That's deception, but you're not deceiving *yourself*. If you utter what – to your friends – is transparently a lie, you might admit it, inwardly. That would not be self-deception, either. In self-deception, I want to *hide my lying from myself*, and hide from myself the threatening facts that *need* to be hidden to protect my moral self-image. As Melville has it, "[W]hen a man suspects any wrong, it sometimes happens that if he be already involved in the matter, he insensibly strives to cover up his suspicions even from himself."[17] In faith I hide nothing from myself. That's how it defies self-deception.

Let me pause for a moment to consider how self-deception is possible. Sartre and others have wondered about this. If I do the deceiving, I must know I'm deceiving; but if I successfully deceive myself, I can't know I've deceived myself.[18] Which is it? Do I know or not know what I'm doing? Well, when I skillfully apply my brakes, I knowingly, skillfully, act, yet I don't have to advance, or have, any belief about what I know. If someone asks, "Do you know how to brake?" it suffices to say, "I do it all the time." The proof is in a way of acting ("braking"), not in holding a belief or in knowing that something is so. I can know how to deceive (how to keep a straight face when lying, say) without knowing about what goes into doing this successfully. The paradox of knowing and not knowing is only apparent. "Knowing" can mean that I know how to do something skillfully, say how to negotiate complex situations where cognitive uptake is essential. Just as I know how to correct my imbalance, as I'm about to slip on ice, so I know how to correct psychic imbalance as something transpires that wounds my self-image. In this sense, I can know how to hide hurtful things from myself, and how to hide that process of hiding from myself. The net result is that I can avow sincerely in some circumstances that I am not hiding things from myself when in fact I am doing precisely that. Children of five or six can be enormously skillful in evading damage to their self-image–"Mom, I didn't steal the cookies from Jane!" (said in worked-up but "real" sincerity).

I tell myself a lie (knowingly-unknowingly making myself unknowing) in order to restore balance to my reigning self-conception. Self-deception works "out of sight" in the way catching one's balance works out of sight. It's a kind of "learned instinct" to recapture one's balance, whether on ice or when one has "slipped up" in maintaining the moral ground one hopes to flawlessly tread. Yet we also have instincts that oppose the mechanisms of self-deception. With luck and companionable mentors and friends, we learn to catch those moments when our first impulse is to cover up. But often the instinct of wanting to be better than we are wins out, and we kid ourselves, shamelessly.

As we drive home, I mention that I feel sorry about your daughter's "bad luck" in an advanced geometry class. You protect your self-image by passing off what you know full well is her poor performance by protesting that she didn't perform that poorly – and by venturing that her bad grade will almost certainly be overlooked by the teacher in the long run. You skillfully give a tilt to whatever evidence and interpretation can boost your self-image as a successful parent of a successful child – and you cover up the rest with aplomb and finesse. You sense my mild skepticism, and so work harder to make your character – and hers – spotless. She didn't do *that* poorly, you repeat, raising your voice in irritation.

You close yourself to hard truths, to full realities, to painful ambiguities, persuading yourself that contingencies are in your control when they aren't. You are without faith, for faith is living without despair and transparently, hiding nothing from yourself, in circumstances that threaten your sense of moral viability.

Imagine that the weaning mother is self-deceptive, without faith. She has (let's imagine) an investment in thinking of herself as never causing worry or pain to her child. Even as she blackens her breast she tells herself that her infant "won't notice a thing" – a tremor in her hand betrays the contrary: she fears she'll hurt her infant, depriving it of succor. A concerned friend tactfully asks about her trembling hand. She hides the truth from herself, saying she shakes from too much caffeine. She's without faith, she can't brook contingency. Imagine that the shopkeeper is self-deceptive, without faith. He strides home, at peace with the world, relishing in anticipation the meal his wife has prepared: a head of lamb with spiced apples to the side. Somehow he's not utterly sure. Perhaps she stopped on the way home from the butcher to help an ailing friend, who just that day has taken a turn for the worse. When he gets there, she won't have arrived. But he's invested in believing that his wife will never fail him. He tells himself insistently – *too* insistently – that the meal will be there. He quickens his stride (though if he were asked, he'd *deny* it). He's without faith; he can't brook contingency.

This imagined duo, mother and shopkeeper, are faithless because they know implicitly that contingency can befoul their dearest wish (that their child not be harmed, that their wife's meal be waiting). And they manage to deny to themselves such contingency. Their bodies show fear and trembling not simply because of objective circumstance but in subtle half-awareness that they are in the risky project of lying to themselves in hope of self-protection. These pictures of their *unfaith* show how self-deception is a refusal of faith. Conversely, living faithfully with uncertainty and contingency is perforce the absence of self-deception.

Fear and Trembling displays a faithful responsiveness to contingency in meaning, interpretation, mood, situation, and selfhood. It's a linguistic assemblage meant to subvert the natural desire to avoid or deny the multifold uncertainties that constitute rich life. To live faith's wild, tender, and pedestrian unfurling is to open to contingency. Love, wonder, and grief are responsive to fragility. To protect my investments in power and efficacy, I may come to deny the uncertain and fragile, against which I am ultimately powerless. I bury this denial from myself in order to shore up commitments to things I control: critique, discipline, technique, or efficacy. But then I forfeit those humane responses – love, wonder, grief – that presuppose vulnerability. To relentlessly assert prerogatives of the mastering, executive self strips the world of the background against which humane response shimmers.

Affliction and reception

Neither shopkeeper nor mother are self-centeredly wrestling with a problem, gathering their resources to master it. The world presents issues: the child must be weaned, set free; the shop man must have nourishment before the sun sets. But the mother, we surmise, realizes that how the weaning goes is not totally in her control. If she is of faith she awaits her time, the child's time, and doesn't cast blame if her timing is off. The shopkeeper, we surmise, realizes that how his dinner goes is not totally in his control. If he is of faith, he awaits his time, and will accept the world come what may. Rats scamper under gutter boards or not; the table is set or not.

The infant speaks its comfort (or discomfort) to the listening mother. The evening meal declares its presence (or absence) to the attentive shopkeeper. Both nursing mother and strolling burgher listen willingly, patiently to an outer, intimate world. Those of little faith try to wrestle the world to make it answer their needs and aspirations. Those of faith realize that some veiled contingencies may eventuate, and they will be patient – not attack the veiling or contingency to eliminate it.[19] The minute either of them attempt to wrestle ambiguity or contingency to the mat, they will have lost faith.

When I turn to technique to skirt or subvert obstacles that confront me, I become, for the moment, a technocrat, not a person of faith. Yet love, death, grief, shame, or birth are matters to which we are existentially subject, and not at all amenable to diminishment, enhancement, or administration by technique, by tools I might wield, or by tools others might offer me: "Don't cry, take a walk, you'll get over it, trust in the Lord, don't probe, answers are at hand, be a grownup." All too readily, we are offered psychological, doctrinal, rabbinical, or ministerial nostrums, tools to lean on and apply. But these are not ultimately effective – *nothing is* – and they are often little more than superficial and condescending diversions.

Death, love, and grief are not problems to solve with appropriate tools, nor will knowing more about them help to manage or corral them. Knowing more about delights (in love) or aches (in grief, death, or love) only deepens our appreciation of their elusiveness, their bottomless mystery – veiled and shifting, alluring and repelling. Enigmas don't retreat but expand and fan out as we dwell on, as we experientially undergo, the multifold meanings of grief, innocent delight, vulnerability and love.

As thinkers who by profession are trained to attack and subdue the ambiguous and problematic, we take offense at those regions where faith is at home, and seek to drain any need or trace of it. Pervasive commitments to rational progress, whether Hegelian, Analytic, or Marxian, aim to disenfranchise and bury quietude or inexpugnable darkness. We wield dialectics meant to subdue. But ultimate vulnerability and contingency disarm us – and not always when we're in the vicinity of faith. When this disarming is devastating, we have what Simone Weil calls affliction.

Afflictions are contingencies that are disturbing, harmful, painful – that we *suffer*. She writes, "To acknowledge affliction means saying to oneself: 'I may lose at any moment, through the play of circumstances over which I have no control, anything whatsoever I possess, including those things which are so intimately mine that I consider them as being myself.'"[20] And Stanley Cavell sees that the loss of self might be a condition of gaining a self. As he puts it, "[The] possessing of a self is not – is the reverse of–possessive; ... it is the exercise not of power but of reception."[21] Faith is a mood, stance, or condition under which a self is received, with full knowledge that at any moment it might be taken, that contingency could destroy it, that one could have to "give up" or relinquish the self. But the trusting openness of reception allows a getting back.

Faith is first a trusting openness. It can now be further specified as a *giving up* (as in Job or Abraham or a weaning mother) and a *getting back*, a receptivity, openness, to a return of the world, the son, the nursing infant. Giving up and getting back is the double movement of faith in *Fear and Trembling*.[22] Self-deception is willfully, strategically, engineering a clean bill of moral health, which means willfully dismissing the verdicts of our own experience.

We would masterfully take possession of the self we would be. But that mastery is denied us. To avoid self-deception, to abide in faith, the trick is to remain open to the world despite the contrary desire to master it, to close in on it, take possession of it. Yet affliction speaks only to a vulnerable, less than lordly self, only to a soul, and only less than a lordly, masterly soul can muster true response.

Faith is at risk from several corners, not least our fear of the evident fragility of life. Love and faith reside amidst acknowledged vulnerability to contingency. They are an undergoing that is neither uniform nor transparent but eccentrically, enigmatically, open closed open, without rules for when to hold or when to let go – when to relinquish, when to welcome, arms open.

Double vision

I've said we deceive ourselves in order to crudely simplify and violently purify our virtue – which makes of our virtue a vice. Faith, in contrast, is a subtle two-fold (or multifold) vision or mood, a yielding relinquishment of will-to-power, a willingness to await reception, and a ready responsiveness to what may be given. Faith is a giving up and getting back that *sustains without simplification* what emerges as a veiled and vulnerable complication and expansion of virtue.

Self-deception is a killing *contraction* of virtue. Single vision is subject to "hypo-nomia," a compulsive adherence to narrow rules, to artificially constrictive and inflexible norms. Its rigid focus blocks out a saving modulation that could be provided by an openness to complex and multivalent circumstance. Such openness shows up in acknowledgment of contrary-tilting norms embedded in one's circumstance. Kindness can conflict with truth, mercy with justice, strength with humility, and so on. Rather than shutting it down, an expansive virtue listens to increasing complexity. Kierkegaard is right to link faith to objective uncertainty, to a self striving in darkness to become itself, to the possibility that ordinary ethics, as simple commonplace rules, might have to be suspended. And Kierkegaard is right to highlight the terror that accompanies radical suspension of rules in the name of deeper connections to difficult realities.

When we simplify in order to preserve a single constricted and violently "purified" virtue, we sacrifice what does not fit, creating, as I mentioned, from virtue what is surely a vice.[23] Sometimes the self kills itself, sacrifices itself, in the name of a radically "purifying" *nomos*. A soldier commits suicide because he can't live up to the categorical and pure demand that because others in his unit died for him, he must die for them. His survival profanes the nobility of their sacrifice, and so he must not survive. A celebrity singer, in her own eyes only a would-be beauty, takes her life because she lets her vision of superlative beauty become isolated from all other value, and demands categorically that she be an instance of "pure beauty." She excludes herself from being *ordinarily* beautiful, or simply *attractive*.

Sometimes the narrow self of constricted vision kills others, sacrificing them as scapegoats in the name of "purifying" the social landscape by installing a restrictive ideal or archetype: the pure Aryan, the pure Christian, the pure male, the male who must despise any hint of heterodox sexuality (it's all brotherhood and guns), the pure female, who must be sexy, striking, and pose. Many, if not all, of our ideals or aspirations can slip in a moment from legitimacy to poison: "No one's better than anyone else!" "You're mine, my dear!" "Anything less than winning is losing!" "The unexamined life is not worth living!"

A colleague reminds me how it can be that neither "know thyself" nor faith's "allegiance to openness" are exempt from poisonous descent: "Couldn't faith's 'I hide nothing from myself' be denatured into a perverse nepsis, a remorseless, light-glaring-in-the-face interrogation of the self, distorted and distorting?"[24] Knowing oneself, or wanting to be faithfully open, requires a certain gentleness towards oneself. He adds,

> It strikes me that living by faith ... is so to live that faithfulness itself is rarely dwelt upon and certainly does not become overtly programmatic in the faithful person's life. Faith-fulness is an unforced, active, inward and sympathetic attention to what is uncertain and contingent, even while it is acknowledged to be uncertain and contingent. But it is not, or not often, attentive to itself. (Perhaps this is, phenomenologically, part of the experience of faith as a gift, a theological (and not a cardinal) virtue.)

I find this very helpful.

If self-deception closes off morally essential realities, faith opens *to* them – ever more opens to ever *more of* them. It is the opposite of an embrace of a dogma. Love, too, opens endlessly, shifting between relinquishment and embrace. Although I can't make the case here, I'll stand by the equation: what goes for faith goes for love. And what goes for Kierkegaardian faith is the utter absence, the ultimate impossibility, of anything like self-deception. Whether mortals can attain (receive) such faithfulness or love, and what the odds are, is quite another matter.

Notes

1 This chapter evolved from a paper read at Tel Aviv University, November 9, 2011. I thank my hosts there for their generous invitation, and my audiences for fruitful discussion.

2 At some point reasons for what we do, or for what stance we assume, run out. This is the anti-foundationalism of both Wittgenstein and pragmatism. The moment reasons run out can be one of despair and skepticism, or of trust that we can nevertheless go on, and the world, with us.

3 The man "looks for all the world like a shopkeeper" but in fact is not one, though he "might as well be." *Fear and Trembling*, trans. by Howard V. Hong and Edna H. Hong (Princeton: Princeton University Press 1983), p. 39. *Fear and Trembling*, trans. Alastair Hannay (Harmondsworth: Penguin Books 1985), p. 68

4 *Fear and Trembling* p. 39, Hannay, p. 69.

5 Another figure of faith is a woman knitting; Agnes (in the third *Problema*) also wrestles with faith.

6 John Davenport picks up Tolkien's discussion of the eucatastrophical and deploys it in "Faith as Eschatological Trust in *Fear and Trembling*," *Ethics, Love, and Faith in Kierkegaard: A Philosophical Engagement*, Edward F Mooney, (ed.) (Indiana University Press, 2008), pp. 196–233.

7 I follow Hannay's translation, rendering the title of this opening section, "*Stimung*," as "attunement."

8 For *Fear and Trembling* as depicting spectacle and carnival that diverts us from faith, see my *On Søren Kierkegaard: Dialogue, Polemics, Lost Intimacy, and Time* (Ashgate, 2007, Chapter 8).

9 No doubt this echoes Eckhart. I discuss de silentio's allusion to giving birth to one's father, of being mother to one's father, and hence to oneself, in *Knights of Faith and Resignation: Reading Kierkegaard's "Fear and Trembling"* (SUNY, 1996), p. 40. In the Book of Job, Elihu tells us that in spiritual matters we are instructed by dreams, suffering, and songs in the night. To have access to "dreams, suffering, and songs in the night" is a condition of access to faith and its gifts.

10 See my discussion of Pattison on natality, Chapter 10, "When is Death?" a version of "The Intimate Agency of Death," *Kierkegaard and Death*, Patrick Stokes and Adam Buben, (eds) (Indiana University Press, 2011), pp. 136–8.

11 I pass on a caution first raised by Patrick Stokes (in personal correspondence). "I think we [must] face the question of how some of *de Silentio*'s rather domestic pictures of modern knights of faith cohere with Kierkegaard's later writings, particularly the 1855 writings. Is there a problem with the fact that late Kierkegaard insists that to be Christian is to suffer and be prepared to be put to death?" Surely there is a problem reconciling various perspectives on faith that Kierkegaard presents in the corpus as a whole. It is sufficient to say that the accounts of *Fear and Trembling* define a major strand in Kierkegaard's understanding.

12 Jennifer Lemma, in correspondence, adds "There is an innate philosophical value to Kierkegaard's faith as it pertains to the population of women who are mothers and because of this, it deserves to be recognized as an integral part of ethical, philosophical discourse."

13 See Note 8, above.

14 I consider what lies behind philosophy's neglect of the feminine and maternal in "Gender, Philosophy, and the Novel," *Metaphilosophy*, July/October 1987.

15 See Ziolkowski's chapter on Cervantes in *The Literary Kierkegaard* (Northwestern, 2011).

16 See my extended discussion of this "double movement" in *Knights of Faith*, op. cit.

17 *Moby Dick*, Penguin Anniversary edition, Chapter 20, p. 106.

18 See Herbert Fingarette's classic analysis, updated: *Self-Deception: With a New Chapter* (University of California Press, 1969), 2000.

19 See Sheridan Hough on how the "shop man" lives with contingency: "Silence, 'Composure in Existence,' and the Promise of Faith's Joy,"

in Marc A. Jolly, (ed.) *Why Kierkegaard Matters* (Macon, GA: Mercer University Press, 2010).

20 Simone Weil, *The Simone Weil Reader* (New York: McKay, 1977), p. 332.

21 Cavell, "Thinking of Emerson," *The Senses of Walden*, expanded edition (North Point Press, 1981), p. 135.

22 Mooney, *Knights of Faith*, Chapters 3–6.

23 Some of these formulations follow the reflections of Andy Martin, in "Winehouse, Breivik and Deadly Ideals," *The Opinionator, New York Times* July 26, 2011, written only days after the Oslo massacres. Of course not all self-deception leads to violence; and not every attempt to save face is an instance of self-deception. Furthermore, I have kept close to faith as we find it in *Fear and Trembling*; Kierkegaard changes his tune later in life (see Note 11, above). And there are numerous interpretations of faith in general circulation that in no way block, and no doubt encourage, the possibilities of self-deception.

24 Kelly Jolley (in correspondence).

5

On Reflexivity, Vision, and "The" Self

When we hear that the knight of faith is at home in the finite, walking more or less undetected through town with the gait of a contented burgher, or when we hear of an unassuming moral kindness in a next door neighbor helping a child across the street, moral and even moral-religious responsiveness can seem easy, a kind of untroubled, seamless fit-to-world. Of course, that's a kind of ideal. It may be achieved in part, now and then, in exemplary action, but it's a norm notable for its failure to be realized over any sustained period of time. The ideal shimmers in reveries of easy shopkeeper knights, or contented knitting ones. How could it have emerged from an unsentimental appraisal of others and their worlds, full as they are of hard-heartedness and cruelty?

If we can effortlessly answer, and fall painfully short of, the moral demands of others and the world, how can that be? Patrick Stokes sets a stage for the answer with a proposal focused on moral perception. Such perception is a marinate of imagination and cognition. It saturates the moral response that is perception's culmination or *telos*.[1] A person achieves a crystallized self that is energized by robust moral vision and responsiveness. We might call that amalgam a person's sensibility. We could say, then, that one achieves personhood – moral personhood, but also religious personhood – only with the achievement of a sensibility in which perception and imagination uncover moral sufferings, bringing them forward *to us* in their immediacy, and delivering their claims with an urgency to which we aptly respond.

Kierkegaard's texts convey unsurpassed genius in displaying (or theorizing) moral-religious fit to world, and in displaying the many innocent and nefarious ways we inevitably fall short of such fit. "Through the use of literary and indirect modes of communication," Stokes writes, "Kierkegaard presents a more fully developed description of moral experience than any other "philosophical" writer of his era."[2] Is there a structure underlying his many descriptions of moral experience? An answer will travel the feel and contours of selfhood, from its minimal functioning to its culmination in that sort of self we can praise and admire.[3] Stokes looks back on the project this way:

> We have developed, in a sense, a prolegomena to a Kierkegaardian theory of moral peceptualism ... which has as its *telos* the immediate coextensiveness of vision, volition, and action... . It is in the moments that characteristically ... intervene between perception and action, the moments of indecision, hesitation, and ... failure to perceive our own implicatedness in that which we see, that the morally 'fallen' character of human agency is to be located. It is within this space, within a framework laid out by Kierkegaard the philosopher in the service of Kierkegaard the theologian, that Kierkegaard the psychologist diagnoses the evasions and self-deceptions endemic to human beings.[4]

My presence in perception

What is it to recognize "our own implicatedness" in the moral worlds we inhabit? Typically, we learn to inhabit a moral world by imaginatively and empathetically inhabiting the worlds of others. I put myself in the shoes of another. But that's only part of the story. I have to know what it's like to be in my own shoes, and furthermore, I have to recognize (however tacitly) that in fact I am standing in my shoes, even as I (more explicitly) stand in yours. To relate properly to another I must already be properly related to myself. In the idiom of *Sickness Unto Death*, I must already be a "relation relating (properly) to itself". If I'm momentarily stunned by grief, or greatly distracted, "beside myself" in despair, I might be at a loss as to how to be in my *own* shoes, or at a loss as to whether I *had* any to stand in. In that case, I'd be in no shape to stand in the shoes of another. I could not, for the moment, be fully implicated even in my own moral world, let alone yours.

My niece needs comfort and rescue as she totters high in the tree she's inadvisably climbed. My shoes no longer cover the feet of an athlete – I tacitly recognize that fact of my person. I won't climb up to lead her down. My explicit awareness flows to and from the needs of my imperiled niece. Yet I must have a coordinate and inevitably tacit awareness of myself, a species of shadowed self-recognition caught in something like a silent warning, "You're no longer an athlete!" Tacit self-recognition is implicit, and absolutely important, in reliable and explicit recognition of others. Take an edgy Kierkegaardian "joke" in which the mirror in which I should normally see myself utterly fails.

A barefoot peasant, so the story goes, comes into the city to buy a pair of shoes – and to down a drink, and another (and another), to celebrate.[5] In a stupor, he passes out in the middle of the street – then finds himself startled rudely by an impatient cab driver. He should get out of the way or his legs will get run over by the carriage. The poor man looks out at the unfamiliar shoes and stockings, and waves the driver on, explaining that there is no problem, the legs to be broken are not *his*.

The peasant can be faulted for not caring a whit for his neighbor's legs. But more to the point, he's in an infinitely comic mis-relation to his own body. Identity is not entirely social. Beyond rank, class, and identities of record, we are something to ourselves. We should – but so often don't – recognize that elusive "something" that we are to ourselves – to our limbs and bodily strengths or weaknesses, but also to our own loves and fears and aspirations.

Kierkegaard's concept of *interesse* (or "interest") exposes the relatedness that constitutes the multifold self (or selves) that we are. We are an unfolding backward- and forward-looking weave with a present temporal center, a relation that relates to itself in self-recognition and evaluation. In the slim book *Johannes Climacus*, we find *interesse* to be a tacit, non-focal self-awareness (or relatedness) – while explicit, focal awareness is directed elsewhere. It is a key to passion, subjectivity, and consciousness, and also to vocation and imagination. It makes possible choice, self-recognition, despair, and more.

Interesse is a "between" ("inter") holding apart and together (at one pole) the *target* of attention (the *what*), and (at the opposite pole) the implicit manner of attending that brings the target into focus (the *how*). Because I am implicated in a "manner of attending" (as well as in whatever I respond *to*) I am implicated in the moral world I perceive. Attention, "interesse," is a "between sort of being."

Tacit moral self

My immediate consciousness of slipping on ice gets articulated by wildly flailing arms. This immediate awareness of being off balance, and of needing the corrective that flailing provides, has a powerful and tacit counterpart that is *not* immediately conscious. I relate to my fundamental need (seldom forefront in consciousness) to prevent violent falls, to preserve bodily integrity. I am directly aware of flailing but not, at that moment, directly aware of a counterpart harm-prevention need or commitment. Yet a "between sort of being" seamlessly holds these two levels of awareness together (and apart). *Intereesse* is an "interested connective" between a *tacit* self-making vector of fundamental need (with its *telos,* "preserve thyself!" and its attendant "it's *you* that's falling") and an *explicit* awareness-responsiveness (with its *telos,* "flail until steady!").

In *The Concept of Mind*, Gilbert Ryle spoke of the systematic elusiveness of the "I" that lies behind any explicit awareness of "I" – that *has* that explicit awareness, as it were. I failingly seek the "I" that declares "I choose myself," or says "I see I'm late," or "What do I *really* think of myself?"[6] Reliable response to the "otherness" of ice is coordinate with reliable tacit recognition of myself as one who shuns concussions. Of course some time *after* the flailing, I might *then* bring the counterpart need to explicit attention – perhaps chastising myself for being deaf to the danger of slick streets. Then I will be *focally* aware of chagrin, regret, embarrassment, and self-chastisement. The counterpart, *unarticulated* "self-recognition" might be acknowledging a need to explain myself to myself after moments of crisis have passed.

Interesse has a regulative function and can *fail* as a good "between sort of being."[7] We know that the ice dancer in the midst of her routine is aware of her body in flow, even though her body is not an explicit, focalized object of consciousness. Were our dancer to think too explicitly, focally, about aspects of *how* her body skims, or how the *crowd* sees her float, she would tilt toward a *mis*-relation to her flowing, and *that* sort of awareness leads to falls.

We know that the lover is somehow inchoately aware of herself in love – she delights in the warm glow all about. Nevertheless, it would be disastrous for her to attend *explicitly* to aspects of her being in love, as she meets her lover for coffee, for example. She might reflect lovingly on her love in solitary reverie, but too explicit a focus on being in love, when she is not solitary, can derail her grace in balancing her cappuccino or in negotiating her discussion of *Middlemarch*. In *Works of Love*, Kierkegaard gives new meaning to the blindness of love. He writes that love is like an arrow in flight; but if it thinks about itself flying, or looks at how its flying measures up, it will fall like a stone.[8] Leaping a gap between promontories, one looks down – and instantly plummets.

Of course the impulse is irresistible to look at one's flight. In retrospect, the lover stands back to observe. But this non-amorous, reflective project has dangers quite apart from short-circuiting love. Say one could live with setting love aside, and decided to embark on an investigation of one's consciousness for its own sake, come what may. One might look at the doubleness of consciousness with a fully objective stare. But then, as Johannes Climacus writes, "As soon as I as spirit become two, I am *eo ipso* three."[9] Looking objectively at myself as a threefold, I'd then become fourfold; staring at *that*, a fivefold, and so on in a dizzying regression.

Can I block this tilt toward infinite regress? I might let the standpoint from which I appear explicitly tripartite to exist only under a tacit restraint. I harbor an implicit promise that for my thenoperative self, a three-fold split is enough. "Enough is enough, go no further!" declares my shadowed self. It's enough to see that I'm tripartite, and at times it's too much to see even *that*. This capacity to call a halt to reflection is perfectly familiar. If I must suddenly respond to a child in need, all objectively reflective projects are suspended. First-personally, I am an ongoing perception-responseme, unified in a temporally and spatially unsegmented flash of protection and helpfulness.[10]

Tacit unexplicated self-recognition and concern for oneself self are essential to immediate engagements of agency, passion, responsiveness, cogitation, or perception. Consciousness is based on an "interested relatedness" to pre-consciousness. Action underway is always based on an "interested relatedness" to a darkness that in that moment it cannot and dare not know. This is a limit to explicit cognition. Love and other passionate responses – even a passion for objectivity in all things, flowers in an "interested relatedness" to what it can and cannot know.

Perception, principle, irony

Dancing or regaining balance displays the subtle relatedness of a shadowed-but-essential self-recognition, on the one hand, and on the other, overt, immediate response. Imagination plays a part, too, a "reality-oriented" imagination that intensifies, sharpens, refines my dynamic links to world and others. This is far from a fantasy-oriented, childish escape from the world and its demands.[11] As it refines, imagination "brings forth."[12] Imagination is *instar omnium*, the "faculty of all faculties" (as Kierkegaard has it). Imagination, at an implicit pole of consciousness, foretells dire consequences if I do not regain my balance. Imagination is at work as I strain for a better perception of dangerous surfaces ahead: that might be black ice, so I alter my course. This needn't be much temporal sequence. I might see, and change course simultaneously, much as a quarterback sees an opportunity and responds to it synchronically. But where in all this does specifically moral imagination, moral vision, or moral claim or response fit in? We can take our bearings from an exemplary act of simple kindness, or more ambitiously, from the sublime movements of knitting or shop-keeping knights of faith. The responsive flow of moral adepts turns out to be surprisingly similar to the responsive flow of a fluid dancer. Let's remember that Johannes de silentio's dancing knight of faith does not stumble.

This insight can startle! If the moral is at issue, we habitually presuppose disquisitions on the morally good will, or debates about principles of practical wisdom or about utilitarian outcomes. We presuppose, not fluid dance, but moral struggle, quandary, or defeat. We drift toward genealogies of how specific configurations of moral imagination evolve and take hold, and we move toward attendant worries about "moral relativism." But none of this is has been dominant in our discussions so far.

Kierkegaard sets to one side most of what passes for contemporary moral theory. He begins with an immediacy of meaning this side of principle, maxim, theory or critique. "The lily in the field" (or in a dung heap) provides moral instruction, but through an immediacy of meaning. Kierkegaard trusts we will get drift, as he elaborates the image of the lily, without backtracking to explain the place of moral purity in Western European cultures. He evokes the lily and the birds confident that a minimal moral meaning is accessible. The biblical lily is already partially embedded in the milieu he and his audience share. His task is to refine or deepen local moral imagination, and to give moral adumbrations.

Principles or maxims are left to the margins. He assumes (and we assume with him) minimal acquaintance with the goodness of charity, and badness of cruelty. We trust we (his audience) can provide uncontested examples of cruelty or charity. To contest the purity of lilies or the repulsiveness of dung would be churlish or petty. Of course many moral visions are contested. Kierkegaard (and his surrogates) revel in imagining alternative ways of life, set out, for example, as stages or spheres of existence. But such displays rest on prior consensus about brute cruelty or stunning goodness. In any case, these are not developed to promote a moral theory in the manner of Kant, Mill, or Hume.

Neglect of principle or theory is not the root of moral indifference; shoring up principle can be fruitless. Take a disturbing yet familiar scenario.[13] One neighbor "sees" or "knows" what must be morally done yet is unmoved. A second neighbor "sees" or "knows" what must be morally done exactly as the first, and simultaneously responds. A frightened child needs help crossing the street. With impeccable moral perception, you see the child in need, see that that situation is *yours,* and deliver apt moral response instantaneously: your sight of the child and reaching for its hand fold into a single response. With what is apparently impeccable moral perception – *objectively* impeccable perception – I, too, see the child in need, know I should respond, and don't. I don't take the situation as *mine. Your* objective sight of the child includes seeing yourself subjectively implicated in it. The perception and reaching for its hand meld into a single response. Disgracefully, *I* stand idly by, or walk on, inexcusably. These cases

– not disputes over principles – define the arena of Kierkegaard's moral attention.

I have described the familiar case of moral indifference, but things could be worse. I could objectively see that the child has a moral need but (probably tacitly) delight in not answering it. More demonically, I could see the child's need, know I should rescue it, and instead push it violently into traffic. Some moral breakdown can exhibit a person with an objectively impeccable moral eye (he misses nothing) with a subjectively evil or demonic disregard. Hannibal Lecter (in *Silence of the Lambs*) is remarkable for his fine-tuned moral discernments (he knows what people *care* about) and for his gargantuan implication in evil. He has an insatiable and discriminating taste for the horrific perverse.

When perception and its coordinate tacit self-assumptions are moral through and through, impeccable perception flexes back to implicate the morally good-enough self that I am – and that I recognize that I am. Yet as we've seen, my objectively adequately moral perception of a needy child might implicate me in any number of less-than-optimal relations to the child.

I needn't be perverse. I might be attuned as "a dispassionate objective viewer." My operative self (at the moment) would then be someone who notes down a "child-in-need event" – say, as part of an anthropological survey. I take an only academic interest in needy children. A richer response flexes back to implicate a richer self (and a tacit richer self tacitly "projects" a richer response). As a better operative self, I know where I stand, my limbs move effortlessly to help. Moral perception, response, and person are of a piece, like the dancer's graceful flow across ice.

Interesse holds the duplexity of immediate and not-so-immediate consciousness together. Jonathan Lear recognizes this duplexity as the space of irony, and claims, correctly, I believe, that we could be neither good nor evil without it. I see the needy child. Irony opens a gap between at least two possible identity-establishing responses: the quick helping hand, the indifferent glance. Living in irony is living in double consciousness underlying the possibility of alternative responsiveness. When explicit and implicit consciousness are geared to the good, we have exemplary moral agents. In what *is*, I see exactly what *should* be – and *act* as I should. Yet sometimes through bad luck even the exemplary agent can fail. My child is about to step into the street, I feel faint, grasp for a steadying pole, and fail to grasp her. My reality (I miss her arm) is severed from my moral aspiration (to have grabbed her). When gaps between reality and aspiration obtrude, the necessity of *interesse* linking better perception to better tacit self-configurations is only accentuated.

Lovers and neighbors

Kierkegaard's *Works of Love* provides a rich field to elaborate the ideas of moral perception and vision developed so far. There he brings self-recognition and imaginative perception of others to bear on love of neighbor. In discussing neighbor and preferential love, Kierkegaard lets love of one's wife stand in as a preferential love. One's wife is not a generic neighbor, but a special "you," one whom a husband ardently prefers. Yet in promoting the priority of gospel neighbor love, Kierkegaard declares, almost perversely, that "your wife must be first and foremost to you the neighbor; that she is your wife is then a more precise specification of your particular relation to each other."[14]

In fact, however, it is not necessarily perverse to get neighbor love in place with regard to one we prefer, say a wife, and to have a romantic, preferential love between wife and husband flower though in some sense second in line. Although conceptually the contrast between preferential love and neighbor love is oppositional, that needn't be so in concrete cases.

The oppositional contrast, however, is important to establish. Let me illustrate a parallel contrast between two sorts of respect (rather than love), by an author who takes Kierkegaard very seriously. Here the question, for Ibsen, is not whether neighbor love and preferential love can collaborate, but whether respect owed any human being (something like neighbor love) can co-habit with respect for the positional duties of a wife and mother (where the roles of wife and mother are occupied by someone in a relationship that began as one of preferential love).

In *A Doll's House*, Ibsen has Helmer say to Nora, "First and foremost are your duties as a wife and mother!" In firm rejection of this declaration, Nora says, "I no longer think that: first and foremost I am a human being!" Nora might have said, "I am to be loved first and foremost as a person, second, as wife and mother."

(And some years earlier, in exasperation, Nora might well have cried out, "If only God would *command* that my *person* comes first!")

Now in the drama's present moment, Nora either renounces her status as wife and mother, or (more likely) renounces the priority of the duties attached to those roles. She has every right to claim recognition as a person first and foremost, whatever other roles she inhabits. Can we translate her plea into the terms of love? Helmer may (or may not) love Nora preferentially. Does he feel her special allure as his wife and mother of his children? But regardless of his preference or aversion to Nora as wife and mother, he must accord her first and foremost a neighbor love.

Whatever else is owed to the person next to you (the neighbor), at the least you must love the neighbor, where "love" means (at the least), regarding them as persons – as objects of singular worth in God's eyes. Now it's obvious that we never confront another solely as a person. He or she will be a store clerk, a wife or fellow-sailor, a favorite uncle or friend. But these titles mark a "more precise qualification" of just being human – being "the neighbor." If Nora's humanity is recognized, it will saturate any other status she might have – say "womanhood," or "mother" or "homemaker." If we *hear* her desperation, then for her to have existed only under the duties of "wife" or "mother" would mean not to have existed at all – any other duty-fulfilling piece of physiology could serve as well. But she is a person, and this particular person, with a proper name.

Ideally, husbands see wives as persons – and wives. Imagination enables such dual, or triple, perception. One sees "person/wife/graceful dance partner" in a triple single flash (whether or not such perception is largely tacit). And imagination can revise self-perception. Nora learns to imagine herself as other than a doll in a doll's house, a new-found perception allowing her to declare herself first and foremost "a human being." And her struggles let us see why the idiom of command appears. Nora's husband is blind enough to need a command to straighten him out (though there is little chance he would hear it). And his case is not the exception.

I may need a sharp and emphatic command when I face those for whom I have no preferential attraction, whom I would prefer *not* to love, those I find *without* allure, for whom I perhaps have even an aversion. I need such a command when I pass by members of an anonymous crowd, to whom I could easily think I owed nothing. And I need such a command when I pass by the deserving but anonymous dead – think of those listed on a war memorial.

Can I have a preferential love here? To love another as human (or "neighbor") when I feel nothing immediately, or only aversion, seems to map out a perfectionist demand. But the demand (or command) is no less intelligible or admirable for that. The gospel command, "Love Thy Neighbor," is a counterweight to our natural inclination to love only those who stand in preferential relations to us. If I am a *mensch*, however, I will see as persons both those *in* favor and *out* of favor, and perhaps some who are neither in nor out.

Nora has moved out of her husband's favor, but she remains a person, or in Kierkegaard's idiom, a neighbor. Does Nora have the right to be heard? If I am beholden to see those both in and out of favor as persons, I can ask why others aren't likewise beholden. So I might ask to be loved (or regarded) first and foremost as a human being, or I might ask that the gospel command to render neighbor love be placed first and foremost. I might enter such a plea in order to counteract the all-too-human tendency to see me first as preferred because I am rich (or poor), black (or white), female (or male), student (or teacher), gay (or straight), mother (or daughter), old (or young). The harried mother of teenagers pleads, "Just treat me like a human being! Like anyone else on the block!" In a theological idiom, we are commanded to love the person (not just the attire or role in which they now appear).

Others and particularity

Let me briskly raise issues I've left somewhat open. Tacit self-recognition *requires* the face of others. At the limit, as Kierkegaard has it, we live under the gaze of God.[15] Might I also live under the gaze of my cat, or my son – each face resonating with a tacit self that is operative at the moment? Second, the opposition between objective and subjective regard is often misconstrued. We can do science, where we seek objectivity above all, without jettisoning the self's subjectivity.[16] I tacitly bask subjectively in myself as a lover of astronomy and of stars even as my focalized attention is on objective targets that I accord the most objective attention imaginable. Third, there is the issue of subjectivity and choice. Isn't it time to jettison the Sartrean distortion of Judge Wilhelm's injunction to *choose* oneself – as if self-choice meant looking at mug-shots of possible future selves I might be (or become) and then choosing ... well, that one as myself? Can whatever does the choosing (under this conception) be anything we can respect at all? It looks like a non-self is all that's left to do the choosing. Perhaps responsibility for self is less a choice than a strong yet tacit sense of the moral seriousness of the journey toward whomever, in time, I will have become, and whomever, in the past, I have been, and whomever I am in the present.[17] Fourth, there is a difference between tacit regard for myself and self-centeredness. Finding you in the scope of my moral vision, I regard you wholeheartedly. That is, I tacitly recognize that it is indeed *I* who is wholeheartedly present to you. But to have a focused regard for *you* is quite other than being focused, selfishly, wholly on me. Fifth, *interesse* is more a *structural* feature of the self than a passion.[18] Passion can be episodic, go astray, and be self-disruptive, whereas *interesse* is best construed as a formal linkage always present in holding together varied "factors" or "elements" among the, dispositions and passions, but also avowed role identifications, and so forth. Passion can be a driving force for the good, but also, a dissipating free-floating swoon or a destructive onslaught of irrational anger; or at another extreme, the place of passion can be an empty shell, excessively detached, a kind of dispassion, or cynical indifference. So structurally, whether proper or improper, passion needs a self-reflective link to a tacit sense of self. In both excess and deficit, *interesse* has a separate and essential role as a bridge between immediacy of expression and deeper regions of self from which expression springs.

Let me comment briefly on the idea of moral perception as primarily ocular, a matter of sight – insight or outscape. Patrick Stokes, like Iris Murdoch or Sabina Lovibond, explores moral vision, and here he quotes Eckhart: in relation to God, one will "see God's image in all things." In the same sentence, Eckhart says that all things *taste* of God.[19] This raises a large question about privileging vision over other modes of perception in a "theory of moral perceptualism." Can we have transforming and self-constituting taste, touch, or smell? Political society can have moral *stench*, self-recognition can be a matter of being in touch. We speak of the touch of love. We can thirst after God, and smell the divine in the lily. Our sense of being grounded, morally or religiously, might be like the proprioceptive sense of the position of our limbs and of where we stand – a perception that is non-visual, even non-passional, and perhaps even like Kant's *sensus communis*. Moral perception, or perception of the divine, we might think, can be tracked through several modes of perception.

The ideality and generality of being human co-exist in imagination with concrete particularity. In good enough moral perception, I strip off neither your particularity, nor your ideality. I love (and prefer) your special way with children and plants, even as I see that like all mortals you will suffer loneliness and death, and that claims to love will arise from these very general features of your person. Schopenhauer addresses persons not as "dear Reader" but as "fellow sufferers." Preferential love is non-general, not for "humanity in general." It is for particulars rather than for mothers or neighbors or mortals or victims *en masse*.

Here are some final thoughts on the aim of joining preferential love with love of neighbor. If moral vision allows me to see you both as friend and as mortal, this vision flexes back to implicate my tacit moral stance: surely I am not a self who loves only what I prefer. Could I prefer mortals? Do I prefer humanity? As opposed to what? At my best, perhaps I am a self who can answer a command to love even those who are objects of reservation, or my aversion. Of course in the best of cases, self-reflexive non-preferential love for neighbors (or persons generally) completes itself in relation to particular neighbors or persons, one by one – she with a dog in tow, he with a cap askew, she with a severe bearing. Or in a more heartbreaking case, I see the emaciated ill-clad child before me both as a particular starving child with an adorable smile and as one of thousands who are victim to genocide. [20]

The universal thus shimmers in the particular. Seeing the lily, I see purity and the hand of the divine. Seeing the hand of the divine does not compete with seeing a lily, any more than seeing a starving child competes with seeing global disaster. Just so, my attention to your particular startling beauty (and my preference for it) is compatible with simultaneous wonder that such persons exist at all – just as *persons* – beyond startling beauty (or lack of it); and I startle with wonder that *you* are one among them. All this is even compatible, I'd think, with wonder at whatever hand has come to add to the earth such bloom.

Notes

1 Patrick Stokes, *Kierkegaard's Mirrors: Interest, Self and Moral Vision* (Palgrave Macmillan: Houndsmills, Basingstoke, 2010).

2 Stokes, p. 7.

3 Much of this essay is derived from an earlier study of Stokes's book, published in *The Kierkegaard Newsletter,* 56, November 2010.

4 Stokes, 180

5 *Sickness Unto Death* (Hongs trans., Princeton), p.53.

6 Stokes speaks of the tacit connection between *subsurface* vectors and more explicit and directly conscious ones as "non-thetic" relatedness to oneself. Stokes, pp. 126–30.

7 Stokes, p. 59.

8 Stokes, p. 144.

9 Stokes, p. 45; *Johannes Climacus, Omni Dubitandous Est*, p. 169.

10 Stokes, p. 144.

11 Stokes, p. 78f.

12 Stokes, p. 6.

13 This example is Stokes's beginning and ending scenario.

14 Stokes, p. 136.

15 Stokes, p. 108.

16 Stokes, Chapter 10.

17 Stokes, p. 167. We act forward but understand only backward.

18 Stokes, p. 165.

19 Stokes, p. 127.

20 Stokes, p. 140–1.

6

On Faith, the Maternal, and Postmodernism

We know our futures from our adopted pasts. The Ur-text for continental philosophy of religion is penned by the elusive Johannes de silentio, sometime freelancer in the employ of Søren Kierkegaard, in 1843 in the Danish market town, Copenhagen. Surprisingly, the first really *intelligible* figure of faith in *Fear and Trembling* is not the grotesque, or shall we say, monstrous father who binds Isaac at God's command, but an unassuming mother weaning her child. De silentio announces that his approach will employ resources both "dialectical" and "lyrical," both philosophical and poetic. In the event, however, even these measures do not make Abraham a figure he can understand. At issue, of course, is faith, and Abraham is the father of faith.

Why does a mother of faith, a weaning mother, make such a startling early appearance – as if *she* is the key to the tale? Abraham is opaque, elusive, a nightmarish apparition. The weaning mother seems transparently familiar. After the weaning mother, the second ordinary figure of faith is an unassuming shopkeeper – simple, like a tax collector, nothing like the fearful Abraham. Later, our transparent figures of faith will include a silent woman knitting by the window.

Johannes de silentio, the elusive author, writes through the elusive Søren Kierkegaard, who is midwife to Heidegger, then to Levinas, Derrida, Kristeva, and Caputo – figures without whom we have nothing like continental philosophy of religion. *Fear and Trembling* is mother and father to continental philosophy of religion, its Ur-text and womb. But what is Continental philosophy of religion after all?

In a nutshell, the Continental movement is marked by labor under the shadow of Nietzsche's death of God, under the associated threats and realities of loss of unified authors, selves, texts, and ethics, and under the loss of confidence in epistemology, ontology, and representation. All of this labor can be filed under the headings of absurdity, impossibility, and *aporia*. Take it on faith, all of this arrives newborn and wailing in the labored but joyous deliveries of *Fear and Trembling*.

I turn to Derrida and Kristeva as writers born with assistance from Johannes de silentio. Derrida's *The Gift of Death* is *Fear and Trembling's* offspring, despite its wayward reading of Abraham.[1] Kristeva also is an offspring. She can guide our understanding of natality – of the significance of de silentio's lyrical evocation of a weaning mother. Kristeva keeps Kierkegaard in the wings, a Cordelia in her silence.

**   **

We can work forward and backward in establishing these genealogical connections. The cultural DNA is transmitted forward from *Fear and Trembling* via Heidegger and Levinas and then on to Derrida, Caputo, and Kristeva. Equally, the descendants of *Fear and Trembling* are identified as such because we look backward, altering the past through present acts of adoption and care-taking.[2]

A courtroom judge brings a neglected point of law, long dormant, into present and future prominence, thus changing the significance of the past as well as the future. He declares it decisive, letting it become powerful by present adoption. Just so, I invite you, with no legal but perhaps some tribal authority, to find this little non-book by a non-author to be henceforth a common ancestor for continental philosophers of religion. In adopting *Fear and Trembling* as an Ur-text, we welcome as a progenitor a motley of figures, heroic and anti-heroic, paternal and maternal – a shifty-but-marvelous cast of players in a piece of theater still infinitely interpretable.

The "Book" – lyrically considered

Fear and Trembling is a basket of false starts and marginalia, of fantasy, fairy tale, and farce. It undermines any pretense to displaying a unified or stable text, author, or self. Also absent is a sense-making God. In the early "Attunement", Abraham's four ascents of Moriah depict failures of faith.[3] Each failed attempt at portraiture has a caption beneath its frame that sketches a mother weaning her child. It is as if *her* trial were a variation on the trial of the father – as if the uncanny Abraham is weaning Isaac, or an uncanny God is weaning Abraham. The mother is the first unproblematic, canny portrait of faith – a mother of faith. The second portrait is of the equally overlooked tax collector, that unassuming, nonchalant churchgoer who strides home from work. He imagines a fine head of lamb prepared by his wife. He notes, bemused, a scurry of rats under a board over the gutter. He finds the sublime in the lowly, every day, and pedestrian.[4] And where Abraham fails every test of representation, these knights of faith pass with flying colors.

Why must representation of Abraham fail? Simple objects (trees, flagpoles) are easily represented; faith and knights of faith are not. De silentio offers credible portraits of tax-collectors, mothers, knitters, and young men caught in unrequited love. Abraham defies description because he is no simple person or object or concept. He leaves us speechless the way a *spectacle* or the *sublime* leaves us stammering. The sublime or the spectacular can be *defined* as that which in its arresting significance nevertheless defies adequate description.[5] Abraham is like a wild storm that just can't be caught in a simple, single snapshot.

As a "freelance" reporter, Johannes is "de silentio," is silenced, because the spectacular and the sublime are silencing. If he approaches Abraham along the route of the spectacular or sublime – which he mistakenly does – he will be confined to silence about faith. He only half believes his important *aperçu*, that there's another route to take. Faith can be embodied by a weaning mother or a jaunty tax-collector – ordinary and unspectacular humans, far from Abraham's monstrosity. De Silentio becomes unsilent as he tells of these "ordinary" knights of faith, and lets the diction of faith move away from the spectacular to dance steps or leaps, to giving up and getting back an object of love, to walking jauntily home. His ordinary knights give us simple actions and sufferings that speak of grace, courage, trust, and delight in the simple shimmers of a life. They are what they are, not what they represent or try to dramatize on the stage of the Terrible and Holy. What they are can be described. Dance embodies faith. It is not a true or false proposition, or explication. A knight dances, just as Socrates dances solo before the Divine in the *Postscript*. Dancers are articulate through bodily gestures that "speak" – not *about* anything. They bespeak what they are.[6] We are there to behold, but we behold the simple, not the spectacular or monstrous or wild sublime.

The tax man and weaning mothers are as inconspicuous in their faith as Abraham is conspicuous. No drama! But the drama of Abraham is mesmerizing, even as every representation of him fails. Johannes is ingenious and outrageous in depicting him fail: he runs up the mountain too fast, he stays home too long, he decides he'll avoid the journey and raise the knife at home, he decides he'd rather kill himself, he passes the knife to God, saying, in effect, if you want Isaac, YOU kill him, he decides he misunderstood, that his God could never ask such a thing, he raises the knife but feigns being a murderer (not a man of faith), he raises the knife but sinks in despair, unwilling to forgive God for asking.[7]

In contrast, more squire than knight, the jaunty burgher shows us faith's double movements, resigning the world, then receiving it back as gift. But there is no terrifying near-murder on Moriah. We see the "movements" first in terms of a walker, and then of a dancer, whose lifts and falls become leaps up (in resignation), and sure landings (in faith). Dancer and burgher are at home, always on the *way* home, bodies ever in motion, like the quiet good woman stitching: no drama.

We want the glorious, impossible spectacle of Abraham, not the simplicity of de silentio's mothers, knitters, burghers, or dancers. We are tornado chasers. Tivoli Gardens opened in Copenhagen the year *Fear and Trembling* appeared – one of the first theme parks in the world. Abraham can be the main attraction, a grotesque, viewed for a price on the grounds of the ongoing carnival. Faith is a carnival distraction, a spectacle to gawk at and applaud.[8]

Lyric poetics

This Ur-text is neither theology nor scholarship but art: poetry, collage, many panels and squares and portraits stitched loosely together; theater, scene after scene loosely stitched. It is carnival and circus, a poetics of life and death – and is *dreamy* art. The Abraham portraits are moments in "a beautiful dream" of an old man who remembers. Remembering dreams is a key to faith – giving up waking life for a dream, and getting waking life back, dream included. We're told dreamily, as an aside, that in such remembrance the faithful give birth to their own father. The faithful wield powers of the maternal, are immersed in natality, in motherly openness to a possible intervention of gratuitous good, as birth, and rebirth, and birth through one's father.[9] This quiet story of faith is missed by Levinas, who sees only the monstrosity of Moriah, and an invitation to killing or violence. The quiet story is the weaning of a child who lives to give birth to its father in a faithful stride, at home in the world, watching rats scamper under the gutter planks, accepting them heartily as a gift of life.

Kierkegaard lets the story provide other critical lessons of interest to continental philosophers of religion. The little non-book gives a critique of bourgeois market society (Preface); a critique of direct communication (Epigraph); a critique of religion as bible-based hero-worship (Speech in Praise); an attack on rule-based and bureaucratic conventional morality (Problema); an appreciation of domesticity (mothers weaning, shopkeepers strolling home for dinner, knitters by the fire) – No aspiring Sovereigns need apply.

Furthermore, it provides a pornographic peephole into dream-like blood and violence; a critique of the Spectacular City; a range of polyphony (the voice of terror, of praise, of detached analysis); a display of thematic variations (Abe might have dallied, rushed, stabbed himself, asked God to do it, refused, done it in despair, in deception).

Finally, this little non-book by a non-author gives us a striking panoply of genres: the carnivalesque and bawdy; the fairy tale or fable; the satirical or farcical; the tragic; the labyrinthine unfathomable; the grotesque, the sublime; the dialectical, the lyrical; the fantastical and dreamlike; the antinomian and apophatic; the eucatastrophical (an unexpected finish that's marvelously good).

Hamlet, about to catch the conscience of king and queen, gets a preview from Polonius of the little play about to be performed. We are now about to watch the play performed by Kierkegaard-de silentio. We should be prepared to witness *"… the best actors in the world, either for tragedy, comedy, history, pastoral, pastoral-comical, historical-pastoral, tragical-historical, tragical-comical-historical-pastoral, scene individable, or poem unlimited."*

Derrida's daring misreading

Derrida devotes a chapter and more to the Abraham-Isaac scenario in *The Gift of Death*.[10] In other works, he mirrors Johannes de silentio's extravagant experiments with style and genre, adding his own striking improvisations. Both thinkers, it seems, prefer literary seduction and ornamentation to abstract demonstration; they prefer philosophical tease and exploration. They both abjure the classic Cartesian quest for certain knowledge and come to stress the responsibility of singular agency over the acquisition of objective knowledge. Kierkegaard's "Truth is Subjectivity" is better rendered "Truth is Responsibility," a *troubled* responsibility. But, Derrida parts ways with Kierkegaard – whether knowingly or from inattention to the text, I cannot say.

As Derrida would have it, the troubled responsibility in *Fear and Trembling* is the troubled knowledge that I sacrifice *many* in taking up responsibility for *some* – that I sacrifice Isaac in being answerable to God, or that in sacrificing Isaac I compromise myself and my answerability to Sarah. Silentio is focused on Abraham's troubled responsibility, and also on the faith prerequisite to spiritual survival. Can Abraham weather this agony of crossed responsibilities? Can his trust or faith survive an even higher-order "impossibility" or "absurdity"? His faith is that God will *give Isaac back*. (That God has demanded Isaac is never in question.)

Faith is to weather a storm of intermixed joy and terror – joy in the expectation of Isaac's return, and terror in the expectation that Isaac will be lost. Abraham's faith is akin to a faith God must harbor. He can order Isaac to be sacrificed and – quite incredibly – have faith that Abraham will keep loving Isaac and keep loving God. Superimposed on this is the faith that He can order Isaac up and expect Abraham still to believe in the promise that he will father a people through Isaac. God serves Abraham a concatenation of impossibilities – and must have faith that Abraham will joyfully, fearfully, impossibly, weather them.

In *The Gift of Death*, Derrida takes the Abraham-Isaac scenario to exemplify what he take to be a quite universal, and terrible, boundlessness of responsibility. In answering God, Abraham sacrifices Isaac. So much is incontestable. But then Derrida launches this fact into a universal principle – every responsible response wreaks endless irresponsible harm. He illustrates: in answering the needs of my daughter, I irresponsibly sacrifice the needs of endless other daughters; in feeding my cat, I irresponsibly abandon thousands of others. True, on Moriah, it is not knowledge of God or of the authenticity of his voice that is the issue, but difficult, *troubled* responsibility. But after that, Kierkegaard and Derrida part company.

First, for Kierkegaard not all responsibilities are universal, nor are they simultaneously binding. The Abraham-Isaac scenario raises the likely possibility precisely of a non-universal responsibility. If there is a "teleological suspension of the ethical" (where "the ethical" means "the universal"), then if Abraham is bound to sacrifice his son, that can only be because a unique, *non-universal* responsibility singles him out. To sacrifice Isaac is neither to assume nor to abandon a responsibility to sacrifice every son, anywhere. Abraham is not asked to bring every son to Moriah, nor does he model the universal principle that fathers should honor God's demand for sons whenever that demand is made. *Fear and Trembling* suggests, on the contrary, that a responsibility can be singular, targeting only *this* person, at *this* time and place. Or all we know, God may care equally for all, anywhere, at every moment. But finite creatures are not universally bound in that way. Without an obligation to generalize, they find the needs of this specific neighbor sufficient unto the day.

There is something metaphysically melodramatic and false about Derrida's understanding of responsibility – making each instance of responsibility also a principled demand requiring immediate *universal* fulfillment. But to attend in thought to absolutely *all* in need (present and future, here and everywhere) erases the full attention that neighbors and family and friends deserve. One swoons in illusion. It's *faux*-moral grandiosity to think that we owe

all to everyone every minute.[11] Is the mother weaning her child –
the motherly knight – to believe that in weaning her infant she is
– or ought to be – weaning, and abandoning, all others? If she is
anxious about the thousands of unseen infants she neglects as she
worries about her own, she is hardly a mother, and hardly of faith.

Second, Derrida has confused resignation and faith. Faith
requires trust that I *won't lose* those at risk as I act. A satisfied love
eludes the knight of infinite resignation; he must live in this pain.
Derrida laments he will never answer the needs of every claimant
on his heart. But faith is the trust that I will get Isaac back, that
in weaning the child, the child will not be lost, that in feeding my
cat, others will not starve. To lament inattention to endless others
is a counsel of despair, not the hope (*espoire*) that is faith. For de
silentio, faith is a double movement, a relinquishing and a receiving
back. It is the Gospel view that he who loses (gives up) his life shall
regain it. Giving up my Isaac is opening the portal to regaining
him. Giving up my selfish hold on him is releasing him for life and
conjointly releasing me for life. Giving up my selfish hold on the
whole world of cats, I get them back, undead, and am released to
feed mine, responding to a singular responsibility.

Kristeva: Silent approvals

In the 1930s in Paris, Kierkegaard, Hegel, Heidegger and Marx
were placed in many-sided contestations. At stake were a minimal
social order and stable institutions; the humanist imperative of
individual liberation from suffocating bourgeois conformity and
fascist regimentation; the libratory imperative of social change and
political revolution; the rational imperative of science and critique
in the formation of a viable society; and finally, the imperatives
of art and religion as these intersect social, political, and scientific
imperatives.

If Kierkegaard was center-stage in the 1930s, after 1950 his
presence began to decrease. Heidegger gave us anxiety, Sartre,
radical choice, Arendt, the critique of a stifling public "blob", while
Kierkegaard went into partial eclipse – no doubt a result of an
increased suspicion of religious thought, taken as inescapably over-
zealous and wild. Forms of phenomenology, post-structuralism,

and the increasing influence of Lacan and Foucault came to dominate the French milieu.

Kristeva entered the Parisian scene in the 1960s with a dissertation in hand on Bakhtin, who famously argues that the polyphony of voices in a novel like *The Brothers Karamazov* marks a polyphony of authorial standpoints. Accordingly, the assumption of a unitary authorial voice becomes problematic. "The" author disperses in a multiplex spread throughout the voices of characters.[12] The absence of a unified authorial identity has its parallel in the absence of a unified self, agent, or subjectivity.

Does a single authorial voice underlie Kierkegaard's pseud-onymous and veronymous works? Kristeva brings Bakhtin to her psychoanalytic writings, transporting a multiplicity of voices inward; Kierkegaard would approve. We are a fragile polyphony, reminiscent of the polyphony in the lyric sections of *Fear and Trembling*. Johannes is both garrulous and silent about many things, including his true center (if he has one). "The" self, for Kristeva, becomes a Kierkegaard-like ensemble of dialogical internal relations, reflecting an unfolding matrix of interpersonal child-parent and self-other relations.[13]

Kristeva's early work on Bakhtin also takes up his theme of the carnivalesque, a literary mixture of the grotesque, sensational, satir-ically comedic, and unblushing showmanship. These are striking features of the first third of *Fear and Trembling*. Copenhagen's new amusement park, Tivoli Gardens, was meant to outdo Paris, and opened in 1843, the year *Fear and Trembling*, was published. Johannes de silentio does not spare us the theatrical and macabre, the sensational, horrific, burlesque, and grotesque. Perhaps he is a carnival barker for a kind of freak show – as if Abraham were a three-headed monster, providing an occasion for gawkers to scream on the cheap, and crowds to line up for a view.[14] Here, we *see* faith!

It is not that Bahktin *found* the carnivalesque or a loss of a unified author in Kierkegaard. De silentio can be claimed as the ancestor who establishes the carnivalesque and disestablishes the unified substantial self as a matter of present identification – just as an adult might claim as a father someone other than his biological father. Kristeva claims Bahktin as her father, and we can claim Kierkegaard as *his* progenitor. In this vein, *Fear and Trembling* is dubbed the now-acknowledged mother of conti-nental philosophy of religion – quite apart from having to trace precise influences, a path of cultural DNA transmission, as it were.

This is not backward causality but renewing the present through new and creative adoptions of the past – what Robert Pogue Harrison (in *The Dominion of the Dead*) calls "Choosing your Ancestors."[15] Similarly, the actual knowledge Kristeva has of the four mothers weaning in *Fear and Trembling* is irrelevant to my interest. My claim is that Kristeva's thinking is so attuned to what we might call the deep meaning of religious separation, trauma, and the possibilities of rebirth, or birth itself, that we *cannot but* see her continuing Kierkegaard-silentio's depictions of the trauma and promise of weaning as homologous with faith.

Mine is not an invitation to speculate on a possible direct influence of Kierkegaard's portraits on Kristeva (perhaps such an influence will be established). Mine is an invitation to see Kristeva commenting on those portraits the way we might see my neighbor's struggles with affliction as commenting on the Book of Job. If Job can address my neighbor across centuries, Kristeva can address 1843 mothers weaning. I invite readers to an occasion of mutual address and acknowledgment.

Embodied significations

As she proceeds into a career in psychoanalysis, Kristeva elaborates what we could call the carnivalesque of inner life; carnivals are full of non-verbal pranks and tumbles. Her two faces of signification has a striking resemblance to Kierkegaard's two faces of communication. Her semiotic signification, the embodied speech and gesture that imparts a particular individual's feeling and passion, resembles Kierkegaard's indirect communication.

The contrast to semiotic signification would be abstract words reporting banal facts or objective directions, where an embodied speaker is inessential to the message. Kierkegaard would call this direct communication and Kristeva would call it symbolic signification. Both Kierkegaard and Kristeva affirm the centrality of embodied communication, the non-propositional imparting or transfer of affect, pathos and individualized perspective.

Neither Husserl nor Saussure has a place for embodied speech, for the voice of *this* person, speaking in *this* tone of voice – in *this* physical posture, with *this* gesture, among just *these* attentive, embodied, listeners. To give language a sort of theoretical and abstract sheen excises the dramatic, even theatrical context of living speech and expression. Speech has its genesis in a baby's coos, eyes fixed on its mom, who returns the look and the coo. It emerges later in an orator's sweating or calming exhortations. To insist on passion and embodiment does not denigrate the symbolic but resists the loss of particular speaking beings who avail themselves of the symbolic *and* semiotic, the abstract *and* the corporeally enacted.

Kierkegaard uses pseudonyms, dramatic narrative, and a variety of genres to set words in living motion in particular contexts, uttered by singular, passionate souls. He valorizes the singular individual, and it is a virtually embodied individual to whom he gives voice in the figures of Judge Wilhelm, Don Juan, the young man of *Repetition*, the seducer, and the professorial anti-professor, Johannes Climacus. Kierkegaard addresses the embodied individual as "My dear reader." Kristeva has no use for a theory of language that leaves language "removed from historical turmoil," floating "midair," words uttered, as she puts it, by "a sleeping body."

Tremors and traumas

We live episodically, our time punctuated by intrusions of the horrific. As a psychoanalyst, Kristeva is exquisitely attuned to the generative and dangerous drama of interlocking fathers, mothers, infants, and children. Thunder awakens us to mortality, finitude, and grandeur, and the chaos of cities awakens us to loss of place. Outbursts and communions can awaken us to the horrific and rejuvenating powers of family-ensembles. We can see Kristeva's schemas of familial tensions played out in *Fear and Trembling's* schema of trauma, near-death, and rebirth. The Abraham stories, as well as the quieter images of knights of faith, give us theatrical performance of our familial constraints and possibilities. They are dreams for our therapist that awaken us to nightmarish undercurrents in father-son, mother-infant, God-subject relations – and hold out an "absurd" hope for survival.

An old man remembers a childhood story. To whom does he tell it? Perhaps it's offered to the attentive ear of a confidant. Each of the early tableaux has a caption reflecting a weaning mother. The terror of the father in the act of severing is transposed to the anxiety of the mother severing. A nightmarish fright as Abraham raises his knife is transposed to an anxious nurturing calm. However difficult the severing of infant from mother, this scene of the mother will domesticate the horror of the near-sacrifice on Moriah. Yet even as the knife is partially blacked out, its afterlife transfers a minor horror to the act of weaning. Does the maternal severing now seem more like the paternal severing (and vice versa)? If Abraham becomes more like a mother, a mother becomes more like an Abraham. The trauma of severing, maternal or paternal, can live on.

A dreamy mother-infant scenario matches a dreamy father-son scenario – both dreamed under the demanding gaze of God. Isaac's trust that his father will protect him, Abraham's trust that God will protect him – a nursing infant's trust that its mother will protect her – are all placed at catastrophic risk. A person's moral sensibility – sense of up and down, good and bad, God and subjects, faith and reason – can be thrown into disarray. Do we awake from these nightmares to a world more or less restored?

Kristeva's writes on "the imaginary father" (colloquially, a "father figure") and the powerful yet expelled "mother figure." Both are larger-than-life impostors with counterparts in Father-God, weaning-Mother, and knife-wielding Abraham. Viewed from the positions of an infant or Isaac or Abraham as under duress, the near-destructions and wondrous escapes imply a divine Wholly Other. The nightmare of God's demand is the fright of mammoth waves, and the release from terror mimics awakening from a bad dream, awakening, in the best of times, to a rejuvenating wonder and delight – jouissance.

In *Fear and Trembling*, the tale is framed as a childhood memory of a beautiful fairy tale – by such modulation of register we handle our fears. But the possibility that God could make such a demand and that a father could heed it, remain disgusting, taboo, like mangled flesh. These are thoughts to vomit out, but they remain powerfully there, as what Kristeva will call *abjects*, marking a pollution of meaning, a fate to which any self is heir. Expelling the horrific is fantasized protection – casting it out.

Abraham's freedom might require casting off his internalized Isaac, setting Isaac free of him, and freeing him from Isaac. It might require that God cut off Abraham from God – temporarily suspending that relation. The survival of a son requires a father's and mother's ever-greater relinquishment of control and sovereignty – without relinquishing love. It is as if these difficult relinquishments were collapsed into three days approaching Moriah – and a moment of restoration, freedom, and independence. Just so, an infant's independence rests on a mother's casting off at weaning.

Johannes gives initiative to the mother who blackens her breast. Kristeva unabashedly defends the necessity of matricide – surely a hyperbole. Yet that is exactly the hyperbole at work in the Moriah tales of near-infanticide. Matricide is the necessity that the child separate from its mother in the name of independence: there is the necessary severing of the umbilical cord, and the later severing at weaning. However, each of these cuts are initiated by the mother, not by a matricidal child.

Abraham takes initiative at the behest of a Father who is in a position to order fathers. But we might wonder whether this Father is a model of constancy. It might seem that God capriciously flirts with the death of Abraham, at least with Abraham as father of faith. Isn't it plausible that Abraham will die of grief whether he obeys or disobeys, whether he loses Isaac (and retains God) or loses God (and retains Isaac)? Yet there is method in this madness. In *Postscript*, Kierkegaard says God's wants to give independence to persons over against Himself. God's apparent withdrawal of all succor might be a gift of independence.

The wide-screen drama of Isaac and Abraham haunts as a moment of *death*. But there are also moments of *birth*: the infant's cord is severed, and new life emerges in weaning – not to mention *rebirth* at Isaac's restoration.

Natality, mortality, and chora

We can figure separation not only as mortality but as natality, as coming to birth and independence. Then the infant's weaning, though awakening tremors, is also a foretaste of life. The weaning of Isaac from Abraham, and of both from God, is miraculous rebirth, as in the return of Isaac from the dead, and the return of Abraham to the ordinary of fatherhood.

Speaking of natality, it is striking that Kristeva ventures beneath language, signification, psychoanalysis, and politics, to hazard an image of primal womb. She ventures beneath discourses, disciplines, cultural practices, and institutions that crystallize, articulate, or edit a world. There in that under-world she imagines a place holding and giving birth to all levels and strands of the above-world. Lifting Plato's term, she calls this site of primal natality simply *Chora*. Not the stuff of the world – cultural, psychological, or otherwise – that becomes edited, organized, or constructed, *Chora* is whatever holds or contains that stuff, whatever "stuff" and its processes are "placed in." Of course, in the ordinary, above-world, a piece of "stuff" is born from its earlier, predecessor stuff. But infinite regresses are terrifying, and Plato and Kristeva venture that "stuff" and its processes are born from a womb that is held by nothing deeper, and so is absolute or primordial.

Socrates is midwife, male and female. He brings souls to birth, helps them emerge as individuals, emerge, that is, from wombs. Kristeva is enough a Bakhtinian and Socratic dialogical thinker to take psychoanalysis as a midwife's art. Insight comes as she helps readers or clients trace a genealogy of formative mothers, fathers, siblings, teachers, and neighbors – that is, trace generative ensembles working in embodied, speaking space. These deeply rooted familial and wider ensembles are all held in play in an unnamable place – of fright, but also of birth and nurture. Kierkegaard would call it the place of God, while Kristeva has it the place of natality or *Chora*, in its own way, divine. Therein the pain of dispersal and mortality's abyss are joyously, affirmatively, answered.

Notes

1 That John D. Caputo, who has worked to bringing continental philosophy of religion to birth in North America, is also indebted to *Fear and Trembling* is apparent from even a quick glance at his *Against Ethics* (Fordham, 1993).

2 For a discussion of choosing a progenitor, see Robert Pogue Harrison, *The Dominion of the Dead* (Chicago, 2003), Chapter 6, "Choosing your Ancestor."

3 For extended interpretation of *Fear and Trembling*, see my *On Søren Kierkegaard: Dialogue, Polemics, Lost Intimacy, and Time*

(Ashgate, 2007), Chapter 8; *Knights of Faith and Resignation: Reading Kierkegaard's Fear and Trembling* (SUNY, 1991); and *Selves in Discord and Resolve: Kierkegaard's Moral-Religious Psychology from "Either/Or to Sickness Unto Death"* (Routledge, 1996), Chapters 4 and 5.

4   For the best discussion of the tax man, and how his simple faith can sustain his joy and delight amidst a world of cruelty, boredom, and sin, see Sheridan Hough "What the Faithful Tax Collector Saw (Against the Understanding)," *International Kierkegaard Commentary*, Volume 18, Robert L. Perkins, Editor (October, 2006).

5   I discuss the Abraham scenarios as distractions from faith, in *On Søren Kierkegaard*, 140f.

6   Caputo is in love with *the impossible* – but not, as I see it, the impossibility of representing weaning mothers or dancing knights of faith. Plenty of impossibility remains: the impossibility that a weaning mother or a jaunty tax collector *is* a knight of faith, or that both are somehow *equivalent* to the father going up Moriah, or that Abraham can survive his trail, or that God could stage it.

7   I document these failings in *Knights of Faith*. In addition to the four "Attunement" versions, they occur in the Hannay translation at 21, 36, 52, 32, 119.

8   I show how Tivioli and Moriah are homologous in *On Søren Kierkegaard*, Chapter 8.

9   I discuss *de silentio's* allusion to giving birth to one's father, of being mother to one's father, and hence to oneself, in *Knights of Faith*, 40.

10 Jacques Derrida, *The Gift of Death*, trans. David Wills (Chicago, IL: University of Chicago Press, 1995), pp. 70–1. See John J. Davenport, "What Kierkegaard Adds to Alterity Ethics: How Levinas and Derrida Miss the Eschatological Dimension," in J. Aaron Simmons and David Wood, (eds), A *Conversation Between Neighbors: Emmanuel Levinas and Søren Kierkegaard in Dialogue* (Bloomington, IN: Indiana University Press, 2008).

11 Patrick Stokes has suggested that Derrida may be making a less extreme claim. "Derrida's point is perhaps more that in attending to the neighbor, we thereby fail to help others – we can't help everyone who we *could* help. Thus it's not necessarily that we have to attend to or focus on *everyone*, but that every moral act represents a failure to help someone else." My sense is that we can often distill a "reasonable" reading from points Derrida delivers with seductive hyperbole. But shouldn't we *challenge* hyperbole, if that's what we have?

12 See Chapter 3, above.

13 See Chapter 2, above.

14 I pursue the Tivoli-Fear and Trembling comparison at length in Chapter 8, *On Søren Kierkegaard* (first published as "Moriah in Tivoli: Introducing the Spectacular *Fear and Trembling*", *Kierkegaard Studies Yearbook, 2002*, de Gruyter, New York, 2002).

15 Harrison, 'Choosing Your Ancestor.'

7
Socratic Self-Sufficiency, Christian Dependency

Suspicion and need of metaphysics

Philosophical Crumbs – for years better known as *The Fragments* – is one of Johannes Climacus' excursions into philosophical theology, or abstract metaphysical thinking about Christianity. His other great quasi-philosophical excursion is the sequel to *Crumbs* (or *Trifles*), *Concluding Unscientific Postscript* – "unscientific," because Climacus is protesting the cultural-academic positivist shift toward venerating "science" as the sole vehicle of respectable discourse. We could say Climacus writes an "unscholarly postscript," but even scholarship was, as George Pattison puts it, "being colonized by positivist and instrumental thinking."[1] Before tracing the argument, let me say a bit about the philosophical background that Johannes, and Kierkegaard, inherit. Is Climacus a metaphysical thinker? Is he anti-metaphysical?

Ideas of form and matter, mind and body, substance, consciousness and freedom, passion and reason, and so on, are Greek concepts that have come to mark the field we now call "metaphysics." These concepts in various shapes and articulations have filtered down through the centuries. Periodically, in the interest of procuring a unified picture of reality, thinkers have tried to link these concepts systematically. But it's doubtful that they can be joined in a coherent system, or what comes to the same thing, that they can give us when so articulated any ultimate knowledge or practical insight.

Kierkegaard writes in the wake of Kant, who abandoned the search for knowledge of metaphysical structures. The world is properly studied by natural science, and metaphysics should step aside. Theology evokes virtues of the heart, but it will never prove the existence of God, or, for that matter, explain heaven or hell. Ethics may appeal to freedom but freedom, cannot be an item of certain knowledge.

Although the questions of metaphysics cannot be answered, nevertheless Kant makes a Quixotic, or tragic, concession. He concedes that it is hard to forget them or give them up. Metaphysics presented tasks he could neither "abandon nor carry to completion." These kinds of questions are hopeless, intractable, but we ask them anyway. Constantine Constantius, the writer from Kierkegaard's little book *Repetition*, echoes Kant when he announces a "new concept," repetition, which is both "the interest of all metaphysics and [also] the interest upon which metaphysics becomes stranded." (Kant would have spoken of the "foundering" of metaphysics – we have an inescapable interest in not abandoning a sinking ship, or, strange to say, forgetting that it's sinking.)

In *Fear and Trembling*, we are fascinated with the fact that, against all odds, Isaac is returned, or in the Book of Job, that against all odds, the world is returned to Job. Fascination grows toward a *metaphysical* interest. A metaphysical interest calls us to develop an abstract systematic, and rational account of how meaning and truth emerge, how worlds can be revealed, as if they were a divine gift – and delivered, in the case of Job or Abraham, as a voice from a storm, or a return of an son from the dead. Is the allure of a rational account – one that would make such strange things intelligible – inescapable? Is the allure like a love we can't give up, though we know it is (most likely) doomed to disappoint?

We can have a passion for metaphysics, for asking "why?", seeking a metaphysical answer, but that does not mean that there are answers to be found. Insofar as Job wonders why he has been deprived of a world, he has an interest in the quasi-metaphysical concept of repetition, which captures the idea of getting things back as a gift. But Job's faithful trust in restoration does not win him a metaphysical answer. He gets the wonder of a world returned, but he does not learn why he suffers.

Metaphysical *wonder* is uncoupled from metaphysical explanation. The wonderful reception of a life beyond dust and ashes throws the need for an answer aside. In nautical images, we would say that metaphysics (as knowledge, as answers, or explanations) will founder; its sailing will be suspended. Yet it sets out on its quest nevertheless. It assumes the risk (even the assurance) of failure. For Job, as for the poetic young man in *Repetition*, to seek repetition is to ache for a restorative intervention, a redemption.

The consolations of philosophical explanation or theory pale beside the shattering wonder of restoration. The impact of such experience overwhelms paltry attempts to theorize it. In a Kantian vein, Kierkegaard's (or Climacus') *Philosophical Crumbs* returns to the *impossibility* of metaphysical answers to our deepest questions. Metaphysics is stymied because the mind is not designed to answer questions that arise at the deepest level of metaphysical interest.

Socratic and biblical access to truth

A simplified Socratic position, as Climacus outlines it in *Philosophical Crumbs*, is the optimistic view that, under prompting, we can access truth stored in memory (though memory is not translucent); we are designed to have access to truth that's already indexed in the mind. The non-Socratic, biblical view is more pessimistic. We are flawed. Our design leaves us irremediably in error, insufficient to acquire on our own the truth we so desperately need. For Socrates, limits on knowledge reflect temporary ignorance that can be cured under proper tutelage. We are innately fitted out to make progress toward infinite knowledge. Inverting this position gives us the biblical position. We are not up to the task of acquiring infinite knowledge. Our basic design is flawed. We are in Error (or sin). Nevertheless, we yearn for the infinite.

Philosophy (or metaphysics) thus is a tragic passion. Metaphysics born as a youthful yearning for explanatory system comes to grief as an unrequited love, even as metaphysical interest, the passion for knowing why, continually, tragically, re-emerges as an aching desire. A biblical stance, installs a passion for God (rather than for systematic explanation). A passionate "Why?" is met (when all goes well) by a revelation that responds to the metaphysical "why" – even as it models a Truth that inexplicably "comes out of Nowhere" and fails the requirements of metaphysical expla-nation. For a yearning youth, the advent of love might relieve some metaphysical angst, but not in virtue of his gaining an explanation.

Love explains nothing. The event of repetition only qualifies an otherwise inexplicable pain, making it sufferable; the pain, lingering or not, remains inexplicable.

Socrates a biblical figure?

I mentioned that Johannes Climacus, in *Philosophical Crumbs* invokes a "simplified Socratic position." A fuller portrait of Socrates could accommodate elements of what I've called a biblical response to metaphysical yearnings. In *On Søren Kierkegaard* I argue that Socrates' trademark protest of ignorance signals his acknowledgment of wonders beyond our reach, and displays an implicit affirmation of finitude, of humility in matters of knowledge and comportment.[2] Furthermore, I argue that in his stance toward things he holds of utmost importance – that a good man cannot be harmed, that the oracle and Diotima speak truth – Socrates exemplifies something like a Kierkegaardian faith.[3] And there's another point to make here about the picture of Socrates Climacus sketches in *Crumbs*.

Let's concede that under the dominant model of modernity, selves are conceived as autonomous projects. This is a "self-sufficiency model" of selfhood. In *Crumbs,* Climacus calls this a "Socratic" position. It's helpful, however, to follow Rick Furtak, who suggests that it's better to call this "a Nietzschean" position.[4] The contrasting biblical position exemplifies the "insufficiency" model, where selves are bequeathed rather than autonomously sculpted. The rub is that in *Crumbs,* Climacus puts Socrates in the camp of self-sufficiency. But why call the self-sufficiency model "Socratic"? We know Socrates depended on his "god" or "voice" for guidance, and on his oracle. The image of Socrates in *Postscript* is closer to the truth than the "insufficiency model" of *Philosophical Crumbs* allows. If it is a stretch to call Socrates a biblical figure, we need a third model for Plato's Socrates, a hybrid of self-sufficiency and insufficiency.

Apart from his faith in Diotima and his oracle and divine voice, we find that in *Postscript*, Socrates dances solo before the divine. He dances for his audience, not just for himself, and is *dependent* on that audience. His actions do not have autonomous meaning, but find their completion as delivered to the divine. His life depends on relating to the oversight of the divine. Without having a personal audience before God or the divine, his life is insufficient, incomplete, His dancing is faithfully related to an establishing power. Contrary to the simplified Socrates of *Crumbs*, the *Postscript* has Socrates acknowledge insufficiency of self. His dancing recalls the biblical David dancing mightily before the Lord (while his wife laughed). Socrates did not find faith to be foolish, no matter how foolish he looks. He embodies a flowing, dancing, questioning, faith.

The little book *Repetition* continues the contrast between sufficiency and insufficiency of selves.[5] It holds out the promise of new and vivid registers of perception. A new world (or love) floats in for us experientially, awaiting poetic articulation. It appears as a site of marvel, praise, and astonishment, and flows healingly, working as a salve. Of course, we must be receptive to such an encounter. In letting go of the drive for explanation of hurt, we forgo a striving-to-achieve, forgo the impulse of an autonomous, executive self. This allows receptivity and willingness to supervene. A craving for self-sufficiency subsides. Such is the heart of *Repetition*. This is also the heart of the Christian option mapped out in *Philosophical Crumbs, or a Crumb of Philosophy*.

Philosophical crumbs

The book reads more like the philosophical first half of *Repetition* than the more poetic, literary and romantic second half. It might be philosophical-theology, although sometimes it sounds like a parody of it. Like *Repetition*, it unsettles our expectations, starting with the title. A serious heading would be "Philosophical Reflections" or "Philosophical Investigations." At its full length, however, we have the title *Philosophical Crumbs, or A Crumb of Philosophy*. We don't know whether to laugh at this poke at "serious" philosophy, or to weep at the thought that the only wisdom available is crumbs — or to scowl because the author is pulling our leg. Kierkegaard, or his present pseudonym, Johannes Climacus, is willing to provoke philosophers and theologians who are typically put off by wit and lightheartedness. The Danish word *"Smuler"* means "bits, scraps, crumbs, or trifles." For years it has been translated (in English) as "fragments." But "fragments" is not among a dictionary's favored options for "*Smuler*," and it guarantees that the nimble irony of that topsy-turvy title is lost.

Kierkegaard loved to satirize all-too-serious ponderous thinkers. Take his *Postscript*. The title signals an addendum to something considerably longer. But *Postscript* is a 500-page sequel to the 100-page *Crumbs*. At full length its title runs: *Concluding Unscholarly Postscript* to *Philosophical Crumbs*: *a Mimic-Pathetic-Dialectic Compilation: An Existential Intervention*. Seriously hilarious, he takes a poke at stiffness, keeps humour alive and minds alert, mocking the pretension to summon the whole universe or all history — and have it delivered in a three-course meal. He will toss you a crumb.

In the title *Philosophical Crumbs, or Crumbs of Philosophy*, the halves are divided by an "or" and they mirror each other in a whimsical repetition. Why should philosophy be somber? "*Smuler*" ("scraps," "bits," "crumbs") suggests the remains of a banquet. In the Gospel story, Lazarus was content to gather crumbs falling from the rich man's table (Luke 16: 21). Jesus broke bread into bits and scraps. *Philosophical Crumbs* is a parody of books that promise a banquet containing everything.

Reading Kierkegaard requires a rare combination of nimble wit, irreverence, and religious concern. He downplays his own part in the composition, putting forward Johannes Climacus as the author. But S. Kierkegaard' is "responsible for publication." We are set adrift, left to our own interpretative devices, sharing a raft with a speaker who has only scraps in his sack and who disguises his real name. The original St. John Climacus (*c.* 570–649) was a Christian monk whose name, meaning John of the Ladder, derives from the title of his treatise on monastic life, *The Ladder of Paradise*. Climacus might have been climbing to heaven. Yet he must know that God knocked down the Tower of Babel, also a ladder. A ladder might be no more than a logo to attract converts. Or it might offer a step up, not to storm heaven but to widen one's horizon, looking out over common ground. A better vantage on the vagaries of earthly life might improve one's sense of the contrast, which is religious virtue or Truth.

Beginning

The motto from Shakespeare at the start of the book, "Better well hanged than ill wed," can be read as "I'd rather be hung on the cross than bed down with fast talkers selling flashy 'truth' in a handful of propositions." A "Propositio" follows the preface, but it is not a "proposition to be defended." It reveals the writer's lack of self-certainty and direction: "The question [that motivates the book] is asked in ignorance by one who does not even know what can have led him to ask it." But this book is not a stumbling accident, so the author's pose as a bungler may be only a pose. Underselling himself shows up brash, self-important writers who know exactly what they're saying — who trumpet Truth and Themselves for all comers.

Climacus is not a learned hero or trumpeter or bungling understudy. He suggests in the Preface that he might be like Archimedes, the Greek mathematician, who finds a sword over his head after encircling armies break into the city. Archimedes does not beg for his life, but for his geometry. His circles, sketched in the sand, must not be disturbed. Climacus might bequeath gems hidden in scraps in the sand. He styles himself a bumpkin of little learning and no opinions, but this masks a clever urbanity. Climacus writes as a soul at risk. This precludes him from "having opinions," in this sense: if one is about to drown, one has not the luxury of opinions.

Diogenes appears, rolling his barrel as his city rushes this way and that preparing for siege. The citizens of Copenhagen are rushing about their business. Is Climacus another Diogenes, aimlessly tossing his crumbs? There follows a more remarkable image. Climacus is "a lively dancer in the service of thought," a dancer "to the honor of the god." (Compare the *Postscript* image of a Socrates dancing before the divine.) A few sentences later we learn that he dances with no human partner, for he is wed to another dancer, the nimble "thought of death." Here Socrates begins to undermine the standard opposition of Athens and Jerusalem. Perhaps he is a hybrid, half biblical Hebraic "foolishness," a multi-faced "typhon," and half Athenian "rationally interrogating wisdom."

In Chapter I the writer is an assistant professor, a talking head, pacing at the blackboard charting differences between Socratic and Christian sites of Truth. Earlier, he's a show-off tossing witty crumbs at those who couldn't care less. Later he is a poet in the service of imagination. And in the Preface, he's a dancer with death before the god. This is fluid, polyphonic identity. Each face carries its own mood. The face of philosophy counters the purveyor of crumbs, each laughing at or mocking the other. Disruptive wit is steadied by chapter-by-chapter argument on salvation and history, sin and error, change and necessity, the reliability of ancient testimony. These steady arguments respond to the questions on the title page. Can an eternal consciousness have a historical point of departure? Could such a thing be of more than historical interest? Can one build an eternal happiness on historical knowledge?

Historical Jesus, Christ of Faith

In the decades before and on through Kierkegaard's university and writing years, a controversy simmered in sophisticated circles about the relevance of historical scholarship to religious faith. "The search for the historical Jesus," championed first by German scholars, might be a great boon for Christians: faith might be confirmed through historical fact (with attendant reasoned argument) rather than through revelation or the authority of a priestly institution. On the other hand, the search might also be a fruitless diversion. Archeological digs and examination of texts might determine the historical truths round and about Christianity. One could compile a record of the life of a Jewish prophet, a political agitator, or the Son of God (as the case might be). Perhaps centuries of debate and bloody religious wars would cease, as truth replaced fiction, fact replaced myth. But Climacus never joins this parade. Faith or salvation can't be based on historical records. Just as there will always be gaps between the history of purported egalitarian societies and the egalitarian ideal, so there will always be gaps between the historical Jesus and the Christian ideal. Research won't detect a risen Christ.

Even if one tried, it is not easy to eke out credible narratives about Jesus. The record is scant, transmitted at third- and fourth-hand, and passed down through centuries with little check on accuracy of transmission. There are no "disinterested" spectators, disciples, reporters, editors, or curators. Even the best-case scenario yields only the most likely story. Second, faith seeks immediate assurance and conviction, while historical reports, even reports of revelation, speak from a cautious, narrative-building mind – not from the heart that testifies. Yet again, even if history gave some credence to the fact of a risen Christ, there would be no data confirming a Christ whose concern endures even to the present. In *Postscript*, Kierkegaard quotes Lessing's "leap over an enormous ditch." From this we get allusions to Kierkegaard's "leap of faith," pictured as a hero vaulting wildly over a pit of poisonous snakes. But Kierkegaard's "leap" is closer to the shifts from numbers to values, from the story of good Samaritans to answering a cry for help, or from evidence of atrocities to faith in (or despair of) humanity. To cross over to value or faith or faithful action of any sort, we must leap these sizeable gaps.

Impacts of truth

Sunsets touch us because we have receptors designed for us to be so touched. We learn simple mathematics so quickly because we are designed to handle arithmetic. We learn by "remembering how to do it," as it were. That is the Socratic model. Yet Truth can also strike us as utterly strange: it happened, but I'll never believe it! And in some cases, it strikes and we are changed in the knowing of it: I'll never be the same! Rather than our doing something to access truth, through its impact truth accesses us. Think of the horrors of battle exposing a soldier to a shattering revelation. It would be non-Socratic, because (a) he had not "always known" these truths (of brutality, or suffering, or the necessity of doing evil); (b) he is changed through and through by the encounter with them; (c) he can be broken under the impact, showing that he is not "designed" to handle them; (d) he can emerge a new man, as the misfit between who he was before and who he becomes, between his earlier self-sufficiency and his later humbling tremors, resolves itself.

In place of battle-trauma, imagine truth breaking through in soul-shattering conversion-trauma. Christ can make unbelievers Christians "in the twinkling of an eye." His Truth fits nothing we were or could know ("Love your enemies!"). Unlike Socrates, a savior provides a jolting awareness of the heterogeneous. In his technical jargon, Climacus says that Socrates gives us the occasion for the arrival of innate Truth, while a savior gives us the design feature and weakness required as a condition of receiving Truth. For a Christian, receiving Truth is receiving the savior who is Truth, whose intervention hollows out a space for his own reception. The Socratic models self-realization as becoming what we already "eternally" are. The Gospel models radical reconstruction, accepting new being with-and-for-others. But this offer will seem exorbitant and offensive in its demands. To accept appears to be participating in one's own extinction.

For a human to be Christian is as hard as for a fish to sing. A human's design must be totally altered; by nature, it is radically unsuited. "The god" has to "create a new being" that might not look that different after conversion. But while appearing only to swim, she would be newly fitted to sing, and perhaps do more singing than swimming. Refitting our condition happens in the "twinkling of an eye," in a poetic "flash of transforming vision." Yet the sense of that impact may remain strange. Wonder steps with humble ignorance and fearful unknowing.

Hebraic, Socratic, Christian

The idiom of "crumbs" mocks professorial chatter. If Climacus is to avoid the appearance of chatter, he must not appear to run on a radically Christian ticket against the Socratic-Hegelian alternative. At most he tenders a case for the possibility of a Christian position: if the Socratic stance is incomplete (as the plausibility of the alternative seems to show), then there is a chance that the alternative is correct – that insight arrives in the fullness of time wherein we are made new. Climacus doesn't worry about implications. He assumes the Truth exists; he doesn't consider nihilism, a dismal possibility. And if Truth comes through a revelation that I am powerless to summon, then I may be condemned to endless waiting. At least the Socratic option lets me hunt for a good teacher. Climacus assumes that Truth arrives either from outside or inside the human. But Truth might arise in a negotiation between the other and the familiar. A subject's initiative could be met halfway by an initiative from outside, and vice versa. Additionally, Truth might be non-Socratic and still not quite Christian. It might arrive through Job's Whirlwind – not Christ's incarnation. *Repetition*'s young man is not Christian, nor about to become one. If anything, he is Hebraic. The Socratic model of grasping an innate Truth does not fit the arrival of Job's "thunderclap" or the return of Isaac. But the advent of a God-man, a Christian revelation, is not quite what Job and Abraham undergo, either. Yet the young man of *Repetition* stands closer to Christianity than to Socratic recollection or Hegelian historicism. Neither his sweetheart nor his freedom can be regained through memory or time. An intervening "thunderclap" is somewhat akin to a savior's advent.

It is remarkable that what starts as a bare outline of a non-Socratic position stealthily acquires the ornaments of Christian theology. Climacus has the teacher become Teacher and Savior, ignorance become Error and Sin, the Savior become Atoning Redeemer and Judge, deciding our fate; the Moment becomes Fullness of Time, the beholder Repents, is Converted, becomes a New Creature. These adornments are acquired in only half-a-dozen sentences.

A king and a maiden

In Chapter II Kierkegaard introduces the fable of a king who finds himself in love with a poor maiden. Differences in class or wealth or power short-circuit understanding, and so short-circuit love. The king's robes and throne hide him, for she will see glory and power, not his love. He cannot be generous, showering her with wealth and privilege, for then she would see a bestower of bedazzling goods. To see him in his love, she can't see his largesse. Seeing his generosity will trigger gratitude, but love in repayment of debt is tainted. The king wants a love that would flow even if he offered nothing but crumbs. If he sheds his glory and power, appearing as only a poor servant, his love still might be hidden. She could pity him as just another beggar looking for leftovers she could spare. The analogy is with God's love. For it to show, God must shed his glory and power. Christian love is love not just of the mighty, but of the least. For the poor and homeless to see God as love rather than might, he must arrive poor and homeless, the equal of those he loves. Yet to appear as a humble servant makes it no easier to show love; the poor can assume he wants company in his affliction. If God is love, he can be neither visible nor invisible.

To break this double bind – love must be seen and not seen – we have to imagine a miracle. The maiden would have to be reborn and refitted in a way that ensured that her love would be blind, at least partially, to wealth, privilege, and power (or their absence) – free from inhibiting gratitude and bedazzlement, yet attuned to the other's love. If the maiden is remade by a transforming revelation (in a Christian reading of the fable), then she may express gratitude (how could she not!) and be innocently won over. Yet all the while she is made to see love as it is, apart from its worldly disguises: it might arrive as king or servant or both!

Paradox, passion, reason

Death as salvation, evil forgiven, power as powerlessness – each pair offends reason because each is recalcitrant to it. At a high pitch, this recalcitrance is the offense of Paradox, an incongruity that both stalls and arouses reason. Stalled and aroused, in Chapter III Climacus writes "a metaphysical caprice" or whimsy. He plays disarmingly with such oddities as a truth that seeks us; that unites temporal and eternal; a love needing miracles. Running up against such enigmas arouses the passion of reason, making it work that much harder. Then Climacus announces that passion seeks its own downfall. Why?

Perhaps love needs to subside in order to reflect back on itself, to measure its strengths. To test a beam's strength, we bring it to its breaking point. To know its strength, the passion of reason must seek its match and its downfall. What better adversary than paradox? We needn't fault reason for pushing to exhaustion and collapse; that is just the way of any passion. Short of a miracle, neither love nor reason can attain the peace and understanding that it seeks, for several reasons. Each harbors internal conflict: love of others needs self-love, but in ways they are opposites; effective practical reason and would-be imperial reason are mutually opposed. A strong self-love grounds the requirement that we love others as ourselves, yet being-for-others means keeping self-love in check.

The more expansive and detached imperial reason becomes, the less it is locally effective. And each faces external conflict: falling in love puts the passion of reason on hold, and the passion of reason can put opportunities for love on hold. But paradox can frustrate reason, with salutary effect. The ever-restless knower-reasoner can be transformed into someone else – someone humbled, and for a moment, full of wonder. This clears the decks for a "jolt" of transformation. From Climacus' perspective, the defeat of ever-expanding reason opens space for a God-man's arrival.

Offence

In an "Addendum" Climacus looks further into the offence to reason as it breaks against paradox. He alludes to an "acoustical illusion": the ear mishears. It is an illusion if reason hears a death-knell when it is frustrated, for reason can start again elsewhere. Paradox defeats reason, but not every defeat is a humiliation. There is nothing humiliating in reason's discovering its limits. Even the most powerful passions meet their match, if nowhere else, then in death, and there is no reason to take death as humiliation. Openness to otherness means suspending the passion of reason. We must be quieted, as Job was, to let the Other speak. Job "melts away" before the wonder of the whirlwind and all it delivers. He knows directly the futility of his former questions and stops asking.

The intrusion of paradox is coordinate with revelation that raises up life from the ashes of despair. If a person is a nest of self-expanding projects, rooted in desire or thought or imagination, each of these passions or projects can be self-valorizing. When out-reachings of the self are halted, time is ripe for refitting. Truth undoes and redoes the receptor to its own specifications. Job is reborn as an ear tuned to the poetry of the world. He is no longer a lawyer demanding his turn to speak, his turn to interrogate. Climacus takes a lead from the otherness of death; it suspends self-valorization. Death gives a sense to life's dance.

Interlude

Typically, an interlude is a moment of relaxation within a more taxing structure, as a musical interlude is. But Climacus makes the Interlude that follows Chapter IV the most condensed and difficult section in all of *Philosophical Crumbs*. It is worth wrestling with bits of it, though. For a start, he differentiates levels of faith. In ordinary knowing, say in simple historical knowing, faith operates at a familiar and uncontroversial level. We move from hints and possibilities to the assurance that we now know what happened, or are pretty sure about it. I may wonder if it is true that a well-known soldier was recently killed by "friendly fire." In fits and starts a record accumulates, full of gaps and contradictions. But as facts gather and cover-ups are exposed, a narrative emerges and my doubt subsides. I see that it is really true that, in a terrible mix-up, he was shot by his own troops. That occurs, if it does, on the basis of what we can call "first-level faith," faith as a confidence in some stock of empirical beliefs that grows in scope everyday.

A second-level faith is trust in a construal of first-level beliefs. I might construe history as an upward progress (or a slow decline), or construe persons as basically good (or bad, or neither). I might be assured that evil will be punished (or won't). These thoughts about "the way things are" can be idle musings, or relatively firm beliefs subject to discussion, or indeed, matters of deep and unshakable conviction. A first-level faith brings closure to my belief that there are untold instances of evil-doing. A second-level faith can focus those beliefs into the conviction that "men are inherently evil." The "existential grip" of unshakable conviction transcends what we would expect as a decision reached by discussion. Some might agree that Jesus comforted the poor (a first-level belief), and yet reach no agreement that his is the deepest compassion one could know (a second-level conviction). For Christians, second-level convictions are about the centrality of compassion, but also about rebirth and creation, history and change, the necessity of the past or the indeterminacy of the future. We can subject these convictions to a kind of metaphysical analysis.

Necessity, change, history

Whatever undergoes change, Climacus says, already exists. For any change, there is a "that" that changes. Now a change in being is marked by its invasion by something it is not. A possibility is "not-being." Coming into being, then, is the invasion of being by non-being, of a being by what it is not, of actuality by possibility. For someone who earlier was suspicious of metaphysical reason, Climacus seems all too adept at it. It is his chance to show off, but not only that, for he has a metaphysical interest in freedom. If the necessary is a precondition of something coming into existence, then the original necessity cannot itself have come into existence. It is the realm of the unchangeable, where nothing comes or goes. But freedom must enter any account of change, because persons bring things into existence. So Climacus posits a freely acting cause, a basis from which things come into existence. Causes reach bedrock in freedom.

This metaphysical picture is meant to allay two worries. We cannot stomach the anxiety raised by the thought of a universe of endlessly receding causal chains. We need to say, "In the beginning ..." Second, we cannot stomach the anxiety raised by the thought of a universe of nothing but lifeless causes; there must be room for freedom. To allay both anxieties, Climacus posits a first cause (no infinite regress) that is free (no exclusion of free agency). This sounds suspiciously like a positing God as first cause. Should we cheer Climacus for his brilliance or jeer him from the stage?

Climacus proceeds to differentiate two levels of history. Anything that comes into existence has a past and thus a history. Some things emerge as a matter of physics, chemistry, and physiology. Other things emerge through human choice and become embedded in culture. A natural history (without culture) has within itself the possibility of a "redoubled" coming into existence (history with culture and agency). The past isn't necessary, but nevertheless it can't be changed. Climacus concludes that to know history is to know a field of freedom. Thus it is not a matter of what had to be, or was fated from eternity.

Resolution and skepticism

What defeats skepticism, as Climacus sees it, is not so much cognition as will. The greater the contingency of something we would believe in, the greater the leaps required for conviction. We have three gaps to leap if we are to be convinced that a child born under a star is a savior. The first leap comes when we grant the near certainty that a particular mother gave birth to a child 2,000 years ago in a particular land. But another gap must be faced if we think it is important that this child, as an adult, is compassionate or healing. We need cultural, not merely biological, knowledge and resolution to believe that Jesus had compassion for others, or cried in anguish from the cross. And for some, there will be a third gap to leap. Perhaps this compassionate man is the Savior, the eternal in time. But a resolution at this third level will have a radically different structure from the first two resolutions.

I can bring myself into a cognitive position ready to embrace the fact that a child came into existence 2,000 years ago, or that Jesus was compassionate in life and in anguish at death. (I go over the texts and decide that the evidence tilts that way.) But in coming to believe that Jesus is the Eternal in Time (for instance), I do not bring myself into a cognitive position. Something displaces my cognitive position, obstructs and dismantles it. If I come to believe that the Eternal entered Time, it is not because I have assumed a position appropriate for making good cognitive judgments. My best cognitive positions are roundly dislodged. The eternal disables my expectations and shuts down reason. If I emerge with a positive Christian conviction, it is because my receptive equipment has been refitted. Closure at this third level comes primarily through an unseen initiative that undoes my preferred cognitive position and simultaneously provides new angles of orientation – at first unsettling and offensive, at last, satisfying and saving.

Can this third sort of resolution have any appeal to those who are not already Christians? Can it appeal – even to Christians! There are severe limits to reason's capacity to exhibit the allure of the biblical model to the unconvinced, or even to those who think to be a Christian is just to accept one's present social status, for instance. A reader might well stick with the Socratic model, might fail to see why one should acquiesce in having one's will shaped by another. Delineating, as Climacus does, the possibility of a non-Socratic position with regard to Truth may convey to skeptical others some small bit of the allure it holds – generally, and for a believer. But it also may utterly fail. Whether we are persuaded that a revelation of our insufficiency, if it happens, should stick as a plausible description of our condition, or whether we are actually given the sort of revelation he sketches, are matters out of his control, and ours. There is no forcing radical transformation.

Closing

The book comes to an end in Chapter V, and a final "moral of the story." Climacus discusses the question whether persons who were in close proximity to Jesus have an advantage over those from later generations and centuries, the "disciples at second hand," in grasping the Truth he embodies and speaks. He answers that those who were in close proximity have "gaps" to leap every bit as daunting as those faced by persons living centuries later. Being proximate requires faith at three levels, just as being distant would. Being near might even be thought harder, since the templates suitable to assimilate the stark events, refined over centuries of tempering interpretation, would be unavailable. On the other hand, 19th century would-be Christians have to unlearn those accumulated interpretations that make Christianity all-too familiar, a matter of simple socialization from the cradle to the grave. Christianity has to be made strange. But comparing difficulties in understanding across historical eras is a bit like comparing trauma or joy across centuries. For Climacus, the point is that a shattering jolt is inescapable – no one is raised a Christian. It becomes just as impertinent to ask "whose disruption is greater" as it is to ask "whose trauma is greater." A full human response to the witness and writing of Søren Kierkegaard in 1840s Copenhagen is not made less possible by the passage of 170 (or 300) years. Nor is a full human response to the witness and events witnessed now two millennia ago made less possible by the passage of time.

The final "moral of the story" is concise. We are invited to consider a non-Socratic alternative; and this is clearly the Christian alternative. Climacus avers that to go beyond Socrates requires assent to "a new organ: faith; a new presupposition: the consciousness of sin; a new decision: the moment; and a new teacher: the god in time." He does not conclude that the Socratic model is erroneous. The admonition is that Copenhagen's so-called Christians, if they are to surpass the Socratic presumption that truth lies within, cannot dodge the requirements: that there is a new organ, a new presupposition, a new decision, a new teacher. To be true to Socrates and to Christ, one's Christianity cannot be just another version of the Socratic. Yet as Climacus sees it, that is the radically un-Christian style of the philosophy and culture and religion around him.

Kierkegaard confessed late in life that his entire task as a writer had been Socratic. By that he meant, at the least, asking the deepest questions about how one should live, and pursuing them fearlessly. He also meant maintaining a certain irony about the limits of reason. Socrates professed ignorance, in part, to avoid the pretence that there were ready-made answers to deep questions, and to encourage those who listened to resolve these questions on their own, not on his authority. Kierkegaard was true to these features of the Socratic adventure and so characterized his career as Socratic, but he was also unmistakably Christian.[6]

Because *Crumbs* ends with accentuating the difference between the Socratic and the Christian, we should note that Kierkegaard finally brings them together. He exploited his Socratic inquisitive mind in sketching non-Socratic lives – some Christian, some nearly Christian, some anti-Christian – some anti-Socratic, some neither here nor there. He was Socratic in a venture to be Christian, and Christian in a venture to be Socratic. Climacus avers early in *Crumbs* that within the wonder of faith, "everything is structured Socratically." Later in his writings we hear Kierkegaard say, in his own voice, "*Socrates has become a Christian.*"[7] But to pursue further how one can be both Socratic and Christian brings one to new wilderness.

The great appeal of Kierkegaard's writing in the 21st century and beyond rests on two striking accomplishments. He had an alarmingly powerful capacity to challenge, perplex, and sustain Christian and Socratic intuitions and institutions (not to mention stand-apart aesthetic and ethical insights), that he then quilted into the shapes of a number of partially viable lives. And second, he conducted this venture passionately, poetically, and philosophically in a variety of wonderfully innovative genres, with a style and wit that the best of those who shape culture (poets and novelists, theologians and dramatists, philosophers and painters), have found strange and irresistible.

Notes

1 Personal correspondence.

2 (On Søren Kierkegaard: Dialogue, Polemics, Lost Intimacy, and Time (Aldershot, Ashgate, 2007, pp. 40–3, p. 46), I thank Rick Furtak for calling my attention to the contrast between a Socratic and non-Socratic (biblical-Christian) relation to truth is too simple, even in terms of the exposition Climacus offers here. Climacus is sympathetic to a Socrates imbued with a wonder bypassing a need for explanation. This makes him sound closer to what I call the "insufficiency" model of the human stance of metaphysical yearning or religious need.

3 *On SK*, p. 16.

4 See Furtak's unpublished remarks at the November 2011 AAR session, "Examples of Socratic (or, Kierkegaardian) Faith."

5 See my discussion, On Søren Kierkegaard, Chapter 9.

6 I explore Kierkegaard's collaborative Socratic-Christian identity in *On Søren Kierkegaard*, pp. 46–9.

7 "Socrates has become a Christian," *Point of View*, p. 41.

8

On Authenticity

Kierkegaard's account of authenticity seems uncannily prescient, a critique of our own age at least as much as of 19th century Copenhagen, that relatively small and provincial Danish market town. Especially prophetic is his scathing critique of a betrayed individuality, a lost authenticity, shunted aside by gossip and trendy opinions, by affectless politeness and decorum, where persons are degraded to interchangeable parts in a reigning public sphere. The shallow social directive of his native Copenhagen is apparently to see and be seen, and to "fit in" with a publicly sanctioned pattern of life that belongs to no one in particular, making individuals radically anonymous, non-existent, no matter how well-known their names might be. Perhaps *especially* those who are "names" in 1840s bourgeois Copenhagen mask with eloquence (and betray without shame) a banal emptiness within.

If these citizens of Copenhagen are precursors of T. S. Eliot's "hollow men," then authenticity could not even be an issue for them, for insofar as authenticity is bound up with being true to oneself, we suppose some sort of self to be true to. But if the prevalent condition of middle-class intelligentsia and striving capitalists is to be indifferent or blind to the possibility of a serious attention to whomever one is becoming – if the prevalent condition is mass complacency about inwardness or selfhood and a willingness to merge with mass opinion and mass comportment – without even a second's hesitation – then those suffering that forfeiture of self are lacking even the conception of a self they could honor or acknowledge as theirs to be true to.

Authenticity becomes a value, then, at least for Kierkegaard, precisely when its presence is an impressive and ominous *absence*. That absence might take one of at least three forms. There would be some for whom the idea of authenticity, being true to oneself, had some grip – yet in moments of clarity, they would see that they had failed themselves, had betrayed their deepest sense of what they were about. Then there would be others for whom the very idea of being true (or false) to oneself was absent, a ringing emptiness. Finally, for some, lip service would be paid to a venture in "finding oneself" – but only because "finding oneself," and associated patterns of narcissistic "seeking," were *de rigueur* in one's set. To be authentic then means to be inauthentic, to be *comme il faut*.[1]

Kierkegaard's account resonates with critiques of bourgeois life launched in his own century by Marx and Nietzsche, for example, and with the many critiques of consumer and suburban culture launched in the twentieth century and that continue in the twenty-first. His exposure of falsity will seem uncannily familiar to those acquainted with Heidegger's story of inauthentic "Das Man" in *Being and Time*.[2]

Fitting in

Heidegger's account is now widely recognized to be a modulation of Kierkegaard's *A Literary Review* (commonly referred to as *Two Ages*"), a slim book that carries out an attack on a city's faceless, affectless public.[3] The table of contents of this work from 1846 signals Kierkegaard's intention. He contrasts "The Age of Revolution" with "The Present Age."[4] He valorizes the passions and commitments of the generation of the French Revolution in counterpoint to his own generation, 60 years later, marked as it was by applause for citizens who merely "reflect" on states of affairs (forgoing individual action) and whose thought, comportment, and mood are no more than reflections of shifting opinion and fashion – everything from how to dress, what diva to praise, to when it was proper to stroll in the park, and at what speed.

Heidegger's definition of human being or *Dasein* can help focus Kierkegaard's story of fugitive authenticity. Heidegger starts with a rough formula that allows that humans, unlike pine trees or rocks, can lose themselves – can paradoxically, or ironically, *fail* to be human. They can fail by falling into indifferent oblivion regarding the options of being true or false to oneself, or fail by yielding to the relentless pressure to become one of a faceless public. On the other hand, they can dodge failure by opening themselves to a self-scrutiny and self-questioning that at last tilts toward the intimation that they are true to their singularity. Heidegger frames things pithily: "humans are those beings for whom their very being can be called into question."[5]

Kierkegaard's has many discussions of the seemingly inevitably failing of humans to become human, but he has no single formula that compares with Heidegger's. Two of Kierkegaard's best-known conceptual fixtures that bear on authenticity are the idea that the self is a relation that relates to itself, and the idea that truth is subjectivity. Failing to meet the normative demands these ideas impose is to fall into inauthenticity.

Relational ensemble

In the famous opening passages of *The Sickness Unto Death,* Kierkegaard's pseudonym "Anti-Climacus" proposes that "the self is a relation that relates to itself" [6] (p. 43) He goes on to add that the self, "in relating to itself relates to something else." What is this "something else"? Anti-Climacus holds that in relating to itself, and in wanting to be itself, the self is grounded transparently in the power that established it (p. 44)." [7] A self relating to itself is something like a musical ensemble or administrative committee relating to itself. And in each case the ensemble or committee finds its *raison d'être* or basis in something other than itself.[8] But why is a person or self defined as a "relation that relates to itself," and how does that formula epitomize the fact that a self can be perpetually and essentially a question or issue for itself – such that self-betrayal is an ever-present option?

The characterization of the self as an ensemble of relations relating to itself is a nineteenth century version of what Charles Taylor and Harry Frankfort propose in saying that persons are persons in virtue of their capacity to establish second-order relations to themselves.[9] A person's related parts, its "self-factors," might be interpreted as multiple and contrasting needs, projects, demands, desires, engagements or vulnerabilities. I might be vulnerable, for instance, to the contrasting needs or demands of being a father, a pilot, a friend.

These ways of being spun together in a web or ensemble are relations that I can step back from in determining how, or if, I will relate to them. Thus I am tiered. There is a) the self that has relations of engagement or disengagement b) to sub-selves or self-projects that maintain a kind of relative independence: my career, a love-life, a religious-life, a life of art, etc. I can avow or disavow, encourage or discourage, commit to or disengage from any or all or none of these identity strands. In this rough and ready picture, I am a relation to my relations. I can do better or worse in avowing the responsibilities of each "self-project," be better or worse in coordinating the opposed, often incommensurable demands in which the total self-ensemble consists, better or worse in avoiding self-betrayal, or in enacting the self I would and will be, thereby existing "in truth" (or not) as the singular individual I am.

In *The Sickness Unto Death*, Anti-Climacus does not produce the image of self-projects. He goes at the opposed elements of a self more abstractly, speaking of a relation to the pair "infinite-finite" for instance. I hear this as suggesting that I will be vulnerable to the call of "infinite things" and also to the call of "finite things." He mentions the pair "Freedom-Necessity," which I hear as being subject to aspirations that fly free of social constraints and being subject to social-life's necessities. The third pair of *relata* or self-factors in *Sickness* is named "Eternal-Temporal." These contrasting abstract pairs can point to concrete needs, desires, projects and so forth (as we saw earlier in Chapter 2). Rather than dwelling on this, however, let me turn to the wider issue.

An authentic self underway, in motion, as we saw, is evaluated and revised fairly constantly. The concrete realization or embodiment of this paired array of self-factors will be in question as the self-ensemble improvises its way ahead. This is a matter of weighing alternatives: one's family, it seems, needs more. One's career is bloated. One has relatives to contact or needs to nurture one's early love of music. Humans become an issue for themselves. Thus, authenticity comes into play. We can care for and take a stand on what we are about and what we will be. We will be true to (or betray) the identity roughly shaped by those stands and cares.

A person can evaluate whether she has been or will be true to herself. She will evaluate whether she has been in line with the self that over time she has articulated and become for herself (and others). She will ask whether she is in line with the self she most deeply, most truly, takes herself to be. Does she beam with satisfaction that, on reflection, she seems in tune with her deepest commitments? Does she blush with shame in the realization that she has betrayed the self she would be? Does she vacillate, especially in midnight hours, between negative and positive self-assessments?

Social and existential identity

In an important paper, "A Phenomenology of Inauthenticity," John Davenport provides a lucid summation of the approach to Kierkegaardian authenticity I've been taking.

> Personal authenticity [he writes] is often taken to signify simply being true to yourself in the sense of 'following your heart,' for example in not selling out your deepest interests for temporary advantages such as monetary gain. Here authenticity is primarily a mode of self-relation.

He continues:

> If the "self" to which one remains true involves commitment to moral principles or ideals of excellence, then authenticity can mean something very close to "integrity" in the sense of loyalty to one's principles and ideals.

Davenport then points out the difference between a publicly accessible social identity and a less publicly accessible *existential* identity. There is a difference between how a wider society might judge who we are, and in contrast, a more personal sense of who we are that emerges in self-reflective moments as we listen for intimations. We work for the feel of a different side of identity, for a felt-sense of what is urgent or central in our make-up, a sense that may or may not align with how others take us to be.

> Our social identity, including our interpersonally recognized roles, habits, and personality traits, has at its core an *existential identity* that can be – to a significant extent – a result of our effort to fashion a life worth living. [This] gives meaning *to the agent* living it.[10]

We mentioned in passing that Kierkegaard holds that self-relations are finally established in a power outside an ensemble of self-relations. To take that establishing power to be God would be an obvious possibility for would-be Christians. But even in the penultimate paragraph of *Sickness*, Anti-Climacus leaves God out of the formula, speaking, again, only of an "establishing power."[11] An alternative slant on that phrase is of considerable interest, whether or not it interests Anti-Climacus.

It might be a "wholly other" God to which the self relates in an establishing relation. On the other hand, we might consider the "establishing power" to be the ideals and commitments to which I am devoted – those bequeathed by a culture, offered as inheritance, say, of traditions of courage or compassion or worthy artistic living. To be myself is in an important way predicated on taking up with, making my own, meanings to which I can be devoted. Subjectively, I find myself established in a range of ideals, opportunities, demands, that community and time provide.[12]

Authenticity is a matter first and foremost of a subject's own evaluation of her alignments with her deepest self-establishing commitments to others and to the goods that function as struts and beams of her identity. Self-assessment is where the stress lies. Verdicts of one or another's authenticity or self-betrayal often circulate in a public sphere, coming to roost on this person or that. But these judgments generated from a more or less public space, when they are more than gossip, should function (as they single out their target) primarily as exhortations prodding the person addressed to consider, or reconsider, what she is about. The worth of these prods is measured by the speed with which that person's self-appraisal comes to the fore, *for her*.

Although verdicts of integrity or self-betrayal circulate loosely in registers of public praise or opprobrium, the focus of Kierkegaard's analysis is a specific measure of achievement or failure that is "inward" or "subjective" rather than powered by public appraisal. The relevant measure of self-betrayal or truth-to-self is one that in lucid moments the person in question will have adopted herself. A lip-synch of free-floating opinion is a symptom of self-loss and self-righteousness. Luxuriating in a smug moral superiority dodges our Socratic obligations. My self is at issue. Exposing untruthfulness in the anonymous public is a pedagogical gesture in Kierkegaard that teaches us what untruthfulness amounts to. After all, our concepts are learned among mentors in a context of application. But for Kierkegaard, such a grasp of social norms is not an end in itself. We are to consider the beam in our own eye, not the mote in another's.[13]

Truths and subjectivities

Kierkegaard's *Concluding Unscientific Postscript* (presented under the pseudonym Johannes Climacus) offers the signature slogan, "Truth is Subjectivity." The thought is developed over many pages, but here is a sampling from a section titled "The subjective truth, inwardness; truth is subjectivity." None of these citations mentions authenticity directly, but their gist evokes our theme. The existing individual has to be "making clear to himself ... what it *means to be there*" (p. 159, emphasis added); "If the truth is asked about subjectively, reflection is directed subjectively on the individual's relation [to itself, its tasks, its God]; if only the *how* of this relation is in truth, then the individual is in truth ..." (p. 168); "As Hamlet says, existence and non-existence [how one will determine oneself existentially] have only subjective significance" (p. 163).[14] Subjectivity concerns what a person "had in truth to do" (p. 192).[15]

To be in truth as a person, to aspire to *be* a person, has a practical dimension and delivers a normative status. We admire those who are truly persons, and aspire (on Kierkegaard's view) to achieve that status. Thus "truth is subjectivity" is not a subjectivist standard of true belief, announcing a measure that factual statements ought to meet. "*Existing* in truth" is "existing truly as a human being," which declares a *practical and vocational* aspiration. To want to be authentic is different from wanting to hold true beliefs. To be in subjective truth is to be truly human, a *mensch*. "To exist in truth is to make it clear what it means to be there" as an existing individual.[16] This is a moral truth concerning how I accomplish my own personhood. It applies to adults and future persons – adolescents who are on the threshold of responsible personhood, or children, some distance from it.

Subjectivity presents a practical goal that one fails if one becomes "objective." To live in objectivity (for Kierkegaard) is to refuse, or be oblivious to, the normative status of one's personhood. The crowds of *A Literary Review* are a "swarm," a citizenry without particular individuals moved by passions and commitments to constitutive values. The "public" relate to the media, to fashion, to recycles of stale social mores, or comic departures from them. To be immersed in "the objective" is to swim in Hegel's objective spirit. One replicates norms whether or not one is committed to them, or has taken them up in one's existential identity. Individuals relate one by one subjectively to their own subjectivity – even as it may turn out that one adopts the commonplace.[17]

"Authentic"

"Truth is Subjectivity" is not a remark about scientific knowledge or scholarly endeavor. It is a moral aspiration, not a value-neutral epistemological claim. To be morally true to myself, I must attend to myself, to my subjectivity, to who I am as a subjectivity underway. I am a human being whose being is an issue to myself.[18] Authenticity can't be the quest to line up true beliefs against the independent reality of a self that is mine. There is no way I can investigate whether the statement "this is *my* self" (when I utter it) is true or false. If I have a conviction or intimation or hazard of who I am, this is not to find it is true that something is a *self*, and that this something is *my* self.[19]

In ordinary parlance, to say that something is authentic is to say that something is a true (or fitting or exemplary) instance of its kind. An authentic 1857 silver dollar is a true 1857 silver dollar. If we have a true friend or a true Matisse, we presume that the friend or Matisse at hand is not false, traveling under false auspices as a fake or a phony. Each is a good, reliable, trustworthy instance of its kind. Truth here is meaning-laden, value-laden. True statements, from this angle, are good, reliable, trustworthy. But truth is a feature of more than statements. A true friend will not dupe me, will remain true to our friendship, and true to friendship itself. A true Matisse is what it is, and will not dupe me by turning out to be a forgery. If I am authentic, I must not be a fraud or a fake. Quite apart from consulting whether others take me to be good, reliable, trustworthy, in general, or in relation to *them,* some sense must be available to *me* of what it is to be a good or reliable or trustworthy *me*. My self-appraisal may be harsher, and appeal to different measures, than the appraisals of others. And if I have that sense of what is to be a non-phony me, I will also have a sense of what it is to *dupe* myself, be *false* to myself.

Am I a being that can find itself a question to itself? If so, then I am a being that evaluates itself. I engage in self-assessment, asking whether I am a good, reliable, trustworthy instance, not of a *general* kind of thing, but of the particular, singular being I would be. The evaluative standard against which I measure the particular being I am to myself will be a truth I can be true to or false to. It will be, as Kierkegaard puts it in his early *Gilleleje* testament, "a truth I can live and die for," a truth that is deeply *mine*. Once I have that sense of what I stand for, I will have a sense of what it would be to abandon or betray myself. I would then be able to judge whether I had in fact abandoned or betrayed myself.

Role diffusion

Each *true* subjectivity will evaluate herself responsibly, with care and attention, and will act to the furtherance of her projects responsibly, in light of that self-evaluation. Her truth, or her goal, her way or her light, will be the highest goods of her existence, as she sees it. She may find herself committed to a panoply of only loosely commensurable goods. But whatever the concrete speci-ficity of her commitment-array, there is a primal vow, as it were, to be self-aware and self-evaluating, to take seriously relations to others and to those goods that guide her ongoing self-evaluations. Her more concrete defining goods might include following a life of compassion, or a life devoted to family, a life of political action or a life devoted to poetry and the arts.

In an earlier age, one was likely to inherit a more or less fixed identity. One was, named John Farmer, or John Miller, or Peter Churchyard (Kierkegaard) because one's father, and most likely one's family line for generations back, tended farms or mills or graveyards (churchyards).[20] That was their trade, their identity, and the idea of forming a self around that trade just wouldn't arise – that identity had *already* arrived and settled in as a more or less inalienable possession.

One might be a failed farmer or miller, but one did not face forced options between being a miller or alienating that status to adopt the life and identity of a tinker. One couldn't occupy an extended adolescence agonizing over whether to become a farmer or fisher. An inherited compact identity descended on one, more or less unchosen, to live out or fail at. The increasing migrations in Western Europe from rural estates and feudal life into burgeoning cities together with Catholic hegemony being cracked by the Reformation collectively ushered in the possibility of more open, fluid, and complex identities.

A burgher could be "self-made," his identity somewhat self-shaped, rather than simply inherited as a fate. Fixed, compact identities, including religious ones, became less absolute as one encountered identity-options: one could decide on a trade, or modulate one's religious loyalties, or lead secret lives in the anonymous interstices of the city.[21] A Marrano in 16th century Spain could be Catholic in public and Jew in private.[22] There emerged in time the dream and reality of more mixed and hyphenated identities (a Catholic-feminist-banker, a New York-intellectual-jazz clarinetist, a gay-novelist-congressman). This trend culminates in the postmodern declaration of a polyphonic or baroque self. At a hyperbolic extreme, one might encounter proclamations of the very *death* of the self – so dispersed can its partial identities become.

The early Marx would have us be freed of a single-focus identity in order to fish in the morning, herd cattle in the afternoon, and write criticism or philosophy in the evening, as one wished.[23] In a different mood, a Marxist might hold that one could be a shopkeeper by day and a revolutionary by night. A man might be a nurse by night and by day, mother children. Kierkegaard manages a Socratic-Christian dual identity.[24] One might take his proliferation of pseudonyms and life-stages as indicative of the proliferation of identity-projects more or less available to the intelligentsia in a 19th century town like Copenhagen. That proliferation of identity-options is also a source of deep anxieties about whether one has stable or enduring roots. Anxiety or despair about one's existential identity, about what does, or should, matter most to oneself, becomes anxiety over whether one can confidently separate the true from the empty or phony.

The characteristic feature of the age of the "polyphonic" or "Baroque" self is the sense that to be human is to lack a compact center, and to find oneself relating to a relatively unfinished, shifting, reticulation of self-projects. We can hesitate before declaring this, or any time, as *the* age of modernism, the baroque, the post-secular, and so forth. Ages have precursors. They pile up and overlap, and seldom have absolute beginning and end points. We point to the sack of Rome, or the French Revolution, or the 9/11 World Trade Center Attack. We point to Kierkegaard for a sense of the disintegration or dispersal of self. Yet the sixteenth century Spanish Marranos also endured a disruption of single-consciousness. In any case, anxiety over the loss of a central magisterial and managerial self did not begin in post-structuralist Paris in the 1970s.

The multiplicity of self-strands tenuously negotiated by a contemporary "polyphonic" or "postmodern" self might seem to have an analogue in the concept of occupying multiple roles over time. A passage in the Talmud lets God study Torah in the morning, do works of justice and mercy in the afternoon, and sport with leviathan in the evening.[25] Perhaps God has three self-facets to cultivate and coordinate, but more likely, He is always one, in different roles. A feudal lord might have a compact, pre-modern identity, yet ride in the afternoon, survey his estates in the morning, and play music by evening. Surely both God and the feudal lord carry compact, pre-modern identities? Neither asks which of his projects most truly stands for his identity, and neither stays up nights agonizing over the answer.

Aspirations, irony

To be human is more than a *social* status (being a judge, pastor, or seducer) and more than a *biological* status (being female, male, mammalian). It is a *normative*, evaluative status. This normativity underwrites aspiration and hope, and exposes one to failure, self-betrayal, and corruption. We fall short of our self-constituting goods, endlessly. The gap between a norm to be attained and a present condition, between a need or lack and an aspiration underwrites the *irony* internal to the Kierkegaardian polyphonic or Baroque self.

We are good to our neighbors, but are we good enough? If we dare attest to our goodness it will only be under the sign of irony. I fail to attend to a distant cry. Is it a cry for help? I am culpable. But am I *that* bad? Whatever my judgment, it will be delivered under the sign of irony, for whatever my judgment, it tells only half the story, always. Irony lets us play one evaluation against another, and against itself, speaking of good and bad, for instance against an amorphous scale that keeps us constantly on edge about the true scale of our evaluations, of our accomplishments, of our failures.

You're bad! (Am I *Really*?) Well, then you're good! (*Really?*) Well, then you're ... what, mediocre? A moral bland between this and that. Where we *are* on a scale for moral evaluation becomes difficult to determine. The scale won't hold still in the run of routine things that fall short of less than gargantuan good or gargantuan evil. We can take time, if we will, to puzzle. To whom – or to what – shall we compare a difficult child, a difficult neighbor, a difficult spouse, a difficult teacher? The drop into irony or skepticism may seem inevitable.[26] Even the presumption of an *amorphous* scale may seem mistaken. But are we ready to dump the very idea of a *shining* goodness or a *good enough* goodness? Are we ready to dump the very idea of absolutely *repugnant* evil, or a banal, everyday corruption? Falsity to self presupposes a contrast between good and evil.

Taken up by another

We could gloss Kierkegaard's emphasis on subjectivity in a variety of ways, each having slightly different consequence for interpreting authenticity. Subjective Truth-as-authenticity is responsiveness to, and responsibility for, myself and those others integral to my self; is taking seriously one's relations to self, others, and those goods I take up as constitutive of myself; is not betraying oneself or what it is to be the human one is and will be; is acknowledging that to be human is to honor one's *self-relations* – to honor one's capacity as a subject to take oneself as a complex and ongoing issue for oneself.[27] The exhortation "Truth is Subjectivity" sounds an alarm, tries to shock us awake. These several enumerated truths are buried. They would not be news if persons were persons.[28]

In *The Sickness Unto Death*, as we've noted, the formula for self has a final component. The self *finds itself* or is *grounded* in something else, *a power that establishes it*.[29] Minimally, the point is that persons are relational not only inwardly to an array of tensed self-factors, but also outwardly to an array of goods and other persons (and for someone tracking a Christian existence, to God who emblemizes a convergence of ultimate good and particular personhood). The claim is that persons are tuned to and receptive to fields of indeterminate otherness, things initially other than themselves. Projects, persons, goods initially present themselves as outer possibilities can then (gradually or suddenly in a conversion-like event) become internalized. Often they appear first as outlying sources of enablement. They are then "taken up" – or better, they "*take us up*" – as demands, alluring prospects, or loci of admiration.

So persons are not just determinate objects like hammers or carriages or pine trees, stable objects in a determinate world. Despite a persistent tendency to deflect or deny this truth, we are beings for whom a resolution of their being will be partly their own doing.[30] We are best seen as indeterminate subjects in relation to an indeterminate world. We struggle with otherness, with exteriority, with a difficult reality. If we are to be selves, we will become committed to projects and values that first manifest as parts or sectors of this difficult reality. We find ourselves held by something that empowers us and simultaneously *calls us into question*.[31]

Things matter

The demand that one be true to oneself can't apply across the board to all creatures roughly human. Infants lack the capacity to bring their very being into question for themselves, and so cannot be in a position to judge whether they succeed or fail at resolving issues of self-identity. They can be neither true nor false to themselves, for in the relevant sense, they have not established a self to be true to. Adolescence might be taken as a threshold where, at least in modern European-traditions, matters of identity and self-constitution can enter the horizon of reflection. Of course the option of self-refusal remains. One can refuse to take the matter of self-choice or self-constitution to be a live issue in ones own case.[32]

Truth is related to values that *matter* to me, that I can *live by*, and that I can *betray*.[33] Authenticity, quite schematically, is first, relational and evaluative, not a static essence or set of fixed abstract properties: I ask whether I am (or my neighbor is) related properly to the values I (or my neighbor) overtly affirm or tacitly endorse.

Second, authenticity is a feature of becoming a self, and hence both a moral feature (linked to the *specific* values we affirm as ideals or aspirations) and a proto-moral feature (linked to our *capacity* to affirm or commit to any value whatsoever); it signals that we are the sort of creatures who can be self-evaluative, and also that we can succeed or fail both in the acuity of our self-evaluations and in the effort (or laxness) we devote to responding to those demands and commitments that our most lucid self-searching delivers.

And third, authenticity is something always at risk: self-betrayal haunts all projects I undertake to become who I am and want to be; thus my authenticity must be under question and reestablished (or allowed to degrade) endlessly unto death, placing me spiritually in a "sickness unto death."

Loss of self

There are numerous ways to undergo degradation or loss of oneself. The inauthentic being described in Kierkegaard's *Two Ages* features a would-be person who fails to undertake any self-modulating or self-shaping projects. Only a shallow anthropological or biological category of the "human" is in play. Biological humans can mimic the behavior and chatter of others, be crowd-beings in dress, action, thought and speech. But no normative status of what it is to achieve one's humanity is in play. With no ethical-moral status to achieve (or fail to achieve), there is no self (as yet) to be true to.

The beings described by Kierkegaard in the first volume of *Either/Or* are inhabitants of what he will call "the aesthetic" sphere or life-stage. These will include those who are bored and thus pursue nothing, and thus also fail to see action or thought as falling under the contrast between good and evil. Also included will be those who pursue pleasure without regard to its falling under the contrast between good and evil; they may be true to a diminished level of self-hood; they do not suffer the question of how pleasure as a good weighs in against other constitutive goods, so there is only a one-dimensional band of shallow evaluation possible: am I maximizing my pleasure (or not)? And finally, the rubric of the aesthetic will also include those who have an inkling of the contrast between good and evil but disregard it in manipulating others toward evil.[34]

In the second volume of *Either/Or*, we find a conventionally proper "Judge" who realizes that self-hood, humanity, requires seeing that the good-evil contrast matters. The Judge urges the "aesthete" of the first volume of *Either /Or*, and his young friend of the moment, to "choose yourself." That would be to choose to take *choice* seriously, to choose to evaluate one's projects and actions under the good/evil contrast. The Judge may be right about the aesthete not being committed to self-evaluation, but as we have mentioned, the question of authenticity ought first to be addressed to *oneself*. It seems likely that the Judge deceives himself about the extent of his vulnerabilities. Would a more conscientious assessor be wary of a whiff of self-righteousness, suspect one's own blindness to the trials of death and love that others live through? How wide does a range of goods need to be to fixed the array from which a less narrow judge would recruit? Can he be untrue to the pall the anxiety of death casts over every life?

The inauthentic beings described in *Concluding Unscholarly Postscript* value objective impersonal truth at the expense of the concrete array of truths of a properly full life. The inauthentic Johannes Climacus (in *Postscript*) only partially comes to recognize or acknowledge the pressing need of a vocation of some sort, a need that descends on him finally as he finds himself secret witness to a graveside scene. The *faux* speakers in *Repetition* either manipulate others in shallow disregard of the other's worth (can one be authentic in perversity or predation?), or like the young man in conversation with Constantine Constantius, have only an adolescent's view of the storms and trials of unrequited love (can a pre-teen or teenager be authentic?). The false creature of *Fear and Trembling* thinks that viewing the religious, watching the spectacle of Abraham climbing Moriah, cheering on Abraham's daring (as it were), has bearing on being a person of faith. The inauthentic beings of *Fear and Trembling* have no idea that in faith one gives birth to one's father, or that in faith one gets the finite world back and strides the world like a tax collector. They have no notion that a knight of faith might be one's grandmother knitting by the fireplace, or a mother nursing her child.

Except in passing, in considering the Judge, I have not mentioned a connection between authenticity and having a sharp sense of one's impending death. This is the connection Heidegger makes so paramount. Kierkegaard does make this connection, but focuses on other spurs to authenticity as well.[35] So this list is does not answer to all issues of authenticity, and is not exhaustive of Kierkegaard's many exposures of self-betrayal, or of those lacking enough of a self to betray it.

Dependence

Questions remain. What are we to make of the apparent presumption in Kierkegaard that authenticity-issues are *inescapable*? Making appeals to authenticity, and faulting its absence, is not a practice familiar to every human being who ever lived anywhere on earth but primarily familiar to those who inherit central features of the Greco-Roman-Biblical tradition that Charles Taylor traces in *Sources of the Self*, features especially prominent from Kierkegaard's time to the present.[36] Perhaps the authenticity-requirements falling on a "knight of faith" are of interest only to those who place value on becoming a Christian. Do the more specific and demanding rigors of a Christian existence have any bearing on those outside the fold of confessing Christians?

As we've seen, in *The Sickness Unto Death*, the relation that relates to itself is at last grounded in a power that constitutes it. Would it be false to the spirit of Kierkegaard to interpret this grounding power as partially lodged in the creative power of traditions and cultural kinetics? This lodgment need not exclude an appeal to divine power, and might compliment it, letting "grounding power" be less abrupt than a raw appeal to theological dogmatics. I elaborate this possibility in the final pages of Chapter 2. It must suffice here to quote George Pattison: "for those in the stream of Schleiermacherian thought (and I think Kierkegaard was), the choice is not: do I have to be a fundamentalist believer or a secularist, but: how can I best articulate this mysterious moment in which I realize my life is given to me, as if from another."[37] That moment would be a moment in which, even fleetingly, I sense my authenticity is secure.

The path I have taken here follows the urgent and bewildering elusiveness of the self. Whether focusing on others or focusing on our own benighted case, on what basis do we confidently (or tentatively) distinguish a phony from a *mensch*?[38] We want an answer that seems bent on eluding us. Perhaps at best we do not exile or defuse the quandary but learn to live with it, accepting the foreboding dissonance and disquiet without letting it derail our lives. Not having a surefire solution to the quandary of knowing if we are true to ourselves, we may nevertheless live forward in hope of at least partial success, and perhaps retrospectively have a better sense of the measure of our errancy.

Notes

1 See Jonathan Lear's discussion in *A Case for Irony* (Harvard 2011).

2 "The critique of *Das Man* is elaborated in *Being and Time* (trans. Macquarrie and Robinson, Harper, 1962), especially Chapter IV, pp. 149–68. The translators prefer "the they" to *Das Man*.

3 See, e.g. Theodore Shatzki, "Early Heidegger on Sociality", *A Companion to Heidegger*, Dreyfus and Wrathall (Blackwell, 2007), p. 241. For an argument that Heidegger's appropriation of Kierkegaard may be less egregious than it can sometimes appear, see George Pattison, in *The Future of Continental Philosophy of Religion*, ed. "Existence, Anxiety and the Moment of Vision: Fundamental Ontology and Existentiell Faith Revisited" After the Postsecular and the Postmodern, eds. Anthony Paul Smith and Daniel Whistler, Cambridge Scholars Press, 2010, Ch 6. 128–51.

4 See John Davenport's "Frankfurt and Kierkegaard on B. S., Wantonness, and Aestheticism: A Phenomenology of Inauthenticity," in Living Reasonably, Loving Well: Conversing with Frankfurt and Kierkegaard, Myron Penner and Søren Landkildehus, (eds) (forthcoming). There, Davenport writes of *A Literary Review*, "Nowhere in the existential tradition is this idea (of a loss of self) clearer than in Kierkegaard's riveting, direct, and devastating critique of "The Present Age" of his own culture. In this signed work, Kierkegaard portrays mid-nineteenth century Europe as a period of reflective detachment, indolence, shrewd egoism, and superficiality that has lost the passionate engagement and heroic will-power of the preceding revolutionary age (Two Ages, 1978, pp. 69, 77). The

revolutionary age had its demons, but it was not lukewarm. See
Harry Frankfurt, *On Bullshit*, (Princeton). His analysis of bullshit has
deep connections with existential "authenticity" and "inauthenticity"
in Kierkegaard. In the present age, a broad aestheticism is linked to
bullshit.

5 "The Being whose being is in 1n question", BN, 42/67 trans.
See Charles Taylor's use of this formulation in "Self-Interpreting
Animals."

6 p. 43.

7 p. 44, cf. "The self is grounded in the power that established it."
Later the formula becomes "Faith is: that the self in being itself and
wanting to be itself is grounded in God," *Sickness*, Hannay trans.
(p. 114). Yet on p. 165, the formula reverts to a being "grounding
transparently in the power that established it."

8 See my discussion of the self as an ensemble of relations, interpreted
as a musical sextet, as an ensemble relating to itself and to another, in
"Music of the Spheres: Kierkegaardian selves and transformations",
Chapter 8 in *Selves in Discord and Resolve* (London: Routledge,
1996).

9 See Charles Taylor, "Responsibility for Self," in *The Identities of
Persons*, (ed.) Amelie Oksenberg Rorty (Berkeley): University of
California Press, 1976), reprinted as "Self-Interpreting Animals" in
Taylor, *Philosophy and the Human Sciences, Philosophical Papers*, II
(Cambridge, 1985); Harry Frankfurt, "Freedom of the Will and the
Concept of a Person", *Journal of Philosophy*, 68.I, January 1971,
reprinted in Frankfurt, *The Importance of What We Care About*
(Cambridge, 1988); and John Davenport, *Will as Commitment and
Resolve: An Existential Account of Creativity, Love, Virtue, and
Happiness* (Fordham, 2007).

10 Davenport's essay will have a longer title, "Kierkegaard and Frankfurt
on BS, Wantonness, and Aestheticism," and is forthcoming in *Living
Reasonably, Loving Well: Conversing with Frankfurt and Kierkegaard*,
Myron Penner and Søren Landkildehus, (eds) (forthcoming). He
interweaves Frankfurt's analysis of bullshit with Kierkegaard's analysis
of self-loss in *A Literary Review*. I have benefited immeasurably from
this essay. See Frankfurt, *On Bullshit* (Princeton, 2005); also found in
The Importance of What We Care About.

11 Interestingly, Lowrie does not like the indeterminancy of ending
Sickness with the thought that the self rests transparently in "the power
that established it." He translates the end of the next to last paragraph,
"rests transparently in God." Hannay resists this distortion.

12 For some thinkers, rooting our understanding of God in our
    inheritance of certain traditions is either self-evidently the way we
    connect to God as establishing power, or is at least compatible with
    a proper connection. In *Postscript*, Climacus intimates that cultural
    traditions cannot "mediate" our understanding in this way, that to
    confront God as establishing power is to confront "the paradox,"
    nothing as amenable to understanding as the rich traditions one
    inherits. Whether this is in fact Kierkegaard's position is a matter
    of debate. See George Pattison's discussion in *Kierkegaard and 19th
    Century Philosophy* (Cambridge,forthcoming).

13 Matthew 7:1–5.

14 *Sickness,* p. 163.

15 Page numbers refer to *Concluding Unscientific Postscript*, trans.
    Alastair Hannay (Cambridge: Cambridge University Press), 2009.

16 See my discussion in "*Postscript* Ethics: Putting Personality on
    Stage", *Ethics, Love, and Faith in Kierkegaard: Philosophical
    Engagements*, Edward F. Mooney, (ed.) (Indiana, 2008).

17 A social science can be committed to methodological individualism,
    so that explaining group behavior at some point leaves the level of
    an aggregate to locate the role of individual desire and choice that
    "feeds into" any description of aggregate or institutional behavior.
    Social malaise, then, in Kierkegaard's view, would be fed by
    individual malaise. Focusing on the latter is focusing on subjectivity.

18 We could look at culture spheres, and identify various truth
    commitments implicit in the search for political or aesthetic or moral
    or pedagogical value, making explicit various truth commitments
    internal to the practices that each sphere enshrines. Taking this
    approach, the search for scientific truth is just one of a culture's
    truth-tracking activities. The search for "political rightness" would
    be a search for political truth; and so forth. A crucial truth more or
    less underlying all others is that one must take seriously whatever it
    is that a self adheres to and articulates as his or her identity (partial
    and unfolding and retreating as that identity might be); one must
    take seriously who she or he is *as a subjectivity underway*, as a
    human being whose being is an issue to herself.

19 Here we don't seek propositional truth or truth attached to
    statements. (There's no good label for the truth at issue here. Would
    "truth of being" suffice?) Kierkegaard pursues truths of supreme
    significance, yet have little if anything to do with true belief or
    doctrine or statement. If epistemology concerns grounding something
    in evidence or argument, this is not seeking epistemological truth.

20 Hannay adds that Søren's grandfather was "Kierkegaard" in light of his job of "looking after the church property (usually a farm as well as a cemetery or graveyard). He might have been called 'Churchfarmer'" (personal correspondence).

21 In *Postscript*, Climacus devotes several pages to satirical comment on the Priest's Sunday declaration that we can do nothing, are nothing, and the converse, that we are capable in every respect: the rich are rich, the poor are poor, the priest preaches powerlessness from the pulpit of power: we precisely *don't* know what to think or to do, what we can and can't do. Presumably this loss of an identity center is distinctive of post-medieval persons. Hannay, p. 391f.

22 In a fascinating study of the Marranos (and Conversos) of 16th century Spain and later, Yirmiyahu Yovel argues persuasively that these Jew-Christians and Christian-Jews are the first to establish (and suffer) the common contemporary phenomenon of hyphenated identities. See *The Other Within: The Marranos: Split Identity and Emerging Modernity* (Princeton, 2009).

23 See Marx, *German Ideology*, second paragraph in "Private Property and Communism": "For as soon as the distribution of labour comes into being, each man has a particular, exclusive sphere of activity, which is forced upon him and from which he cannot escape. He is a hunter, a fisherman, a herdsman, or a critical critic, and must remain so if he does not want to lose his means of livelihood; while in communist society, where nobody has one exclusive sphere of activity but each can become accomplished in any branch he wishes, society regulates the general production and thus makes it possible for me to do one thing today and another tomorrow, to hunt in the morning, fish in the afternoon, rear cattle in the evening, criticise after dinner, just as I have a mind [to], without ever becoming hunter, fisherman, herdsman or critic."

24 See my discussion in Chapter 3, "Kierkegaard's Double Vocation: Socrates Becomes Christian", *On Søren Kierkegaard: Dialogue, Polemics, Lost Intimacy, and Time* (Ashgate, 2007), especially 46–54.

25 See Hilary Putnam, 'Jewish Ethics,' in *The Blackwell Companion to Religious Ethics,* William Schweiker, (ed.), p. 159 (The account of God's day is given at TB Avodah Zarah 3b).

26 See Jonathan Lear's fine discussion of "living an ironic existence" in *A Case for Irony* (Harvard, 2011). He interprets Kierkegaardian, Socratic irony as something we can endorse as a worthy way of life.

27 The possibility that truth is not "value neutral" but belongs to the good is jarring. But Habermas (for example) holds that truth and morality are analogous, both requiring rational debate and the aspiration and

effort toward warranting claims entered in debate. Despite the loss
of religiously or metaphysical guarantees, morality can be "right"
or "wrong" as the outcome of inclusive, dialogical inquiry into the
worthiness of attributions of "right and wrong" and recognition of
these outcomes as normative. See Habermas, "Rightness versus Truth:
On the Sense of Normative Validity in Moral Judgments and Norms,"
Truth and Justification, trans. Barbara Fultner (Cambridge: MIT Press,
2005), pp. 237–75, 246. Habermas claims that "truth" asserts what
is the case, empirically, while "morality" asserts what *ought* to be the
case, in the shared symbolically structured social world. Yet it might
be that asserting what *is* the case presupposes standards of "what
ought to be the case, in the shared symbolically structured social
world" – i.e. it presupposes what (valued) standards empirical truth
claims ought to meet. If so, "ought" precedes what we discover "is" or
fact presupposes value. Value always already infiltrates fact. "Thick"
moral phenomena like rudeness or courage are fact-values or value-
facts – the contrast has no grip. Hilary Putnam challenges the fact-value
dichotomy in *The Collapse of the Fact/Value Dichotomy and Other
Essays* (Harvard University Press, 2002).

28 See Jonathan Lear, *A Case for Irony* (Harvard, 2011), on whether
among all Christians, there is a Christian, or among all professors,
there is a professor – or among all persons, there is a person.

29 See Hubert Dreyfus, "Kierkegaard on the self," in *Ethics, Love, and
Faith in Kierkegaard: Philosophical Engagements*.

30 Sartre makes self-deception a reigning motif of his *Being and
Nothingness*.

31 Kierkegaardian selves are not acosmic or worldless. Rick Furtak
points out that commitments to self-projects typically involve
commitments to others. If I tilt toward more time with my family, the
constitutive good is a social relation. I look inward in self-assessment
and outward to consider the relations I value. For there to be an "I"
of motivational and passionate substance there will be moments both
of self-assessment and "other-assessment." As Furtak puts it, "we
need to sort out who it is that 'I' cares about, to whom I'm devoted
– as well as who it is that is the 'I' is who cares. Thus authenticity
is not an exclusively a private ideal." Additionally, in favor of
authenticity, "it's not good for society if everyone is unreflectively
conforming" (Furtak, personal correspondence).

32 What are we to make of the apparent presumption in Kierkegaard
of the *inescapability* of authenticity-issues? Making appeals to
authenticity, and faulting its absence, is not a practice familiar to
every human being who ever lived anywhere but primarily familiar

to those who inherit central features of the Greco-Roman-biblical tradition that Charles Taylor traces in *Sources of the Self*, or to most of those reading these sentences here and now.

33   Authenticity is perhaps best figured as an ongoing process or activity rather than as an enduring mental or moral state. See Chapter 2, above. Charles Taylor calls self-interrogation or confession "deep evaluation" in his classic essay "Responsibility for self" (also, in "Interpretation and the Sciences of Man"). My life undergoes evaluation and interpretation under the gaze of deep-seated goods, ideals, or "absolutes" – fundamental values in terms of which my life is at issue, and found wanting (or not).

34   There is a good deal of scholarly debate over whether one can be true to oneself if one is shallowly aesthetic – committed, and so in a self relation, but committed only to pleasure. By the time we reach *E/O II*, the idea is that one must put a good-evil standard into self-evaluation if one is to be a self. But should we go along with Judge William in this? Can't there be a committed profligate or rake who is a self (capable of being inauthentic or authentic) in virtue of making a commitment to a project (distasteful and narrow as it may be) and then capable evaluating himself in terms of achieving or failing the demands of that project? Can there be an authentic mobster? The answer will depend on how we interpret what Taylor calls constitutive goods. This brings us to the account of authenticity, or being true to oneself, in *E/O II*.

35   See "From the Garden of the Dead: Climacus on interpersonal inwardness", Chapter 9 of this book.

36   Taylor.

37   Pattison, personal correspondence. See his important discussions in *Kierkegaard and 19th Century Theology* (Kierkegaard and the Theology of the Nineteenth Century: The Paradox and the 'Point of Contact' Cambridge, 2012).

38   Wittgenstein would say that we ineluctable live lives where a central range of conflicting judgments and perspectives just exists – so our lives proceed (despite the conceptual mess) roughly on trust (rather than on some reason-certified epistemology that provides philosophical security in the judgment, for example, that our uncle is *for certain* a *mensch* and a local politician is certainly a phony). We can tell stories to elaborate, but these do not provide rock-solid foundations for our judgments. For a very accessible account of this avoidance of skepticism and dogmatism in evaluative judgment, see Hillary Putnam, *Renewing Philosophy*, or Stanley Cavell's classic essay "Knowing as Acknowledgment" in *Must we mean what we say*.

9

The Garden of Death: Faith as Interpersonal

Here in the span of a hand we have the worlds of the "Postscript" engraved. Or, as in Hamlet's "Mousetrap," have a play within a play to catch our conscience by surprise, and return us to the sufferings and smiles that are the wonder of life.

Setting to steal his heart

Climacus reports a scene overheard, seen in a fugitive glance through leaves as he sat on a bench at twilight in "the garden of the dead," a cemetery, most likely Copenhagen's *Assistens Kirkegård*. The scene is the grief of a grandfather mourning at the grave of his son, and speaking tearfully of the meaning of that death to a ten-year-old boy, his grandson, now fatherless. The "garden of the dead," as it is called, is not at the city's center, but at some remove, not out in the wooded parklands, but nevertheless sufficiently alive with nature's leafy shadows and open skies that Climacus can exalt in a kind of minor ecstasy over the coming of night – as if night were an invitation for a "nocturnal tryst," a beautiful prelude to the more tearful tableau ahead, where a grandfather's grief will spill over as an anguished admonition to his barely understanding grandson. But what can the night tell us of mood, yearning, and heartache? Night beckons with promise of a

> tryst … with the infinite, persuaded by the night's breeze as
> in a monotone it repeats itself, breathing through forest and
> meadow, and sighing as though in search of something, urged
> by the distant echo in oneself of the stillness as if intimating
> something, urged by the sublime calm of the heavens, as if this
> something had been found, persuaded by the palpable silence
> of the dew as if this were the explanation and infinitude's
> refreshment, like the fecundity of a quiet night, only half under-
> stood like the night's semi-diaphanous mist.[1]

The coming of night is only half-understood, like an uncanny mist, hard to frame, and so like a Kantian sublime. Yet the preferred example of the sublime for Kant would be a towering, awesome occasion: the violence of ocean storms, the wonder of starry heavens. In our *Postscript* passage, the sublime is a downscaled scene of allure and fear. Death haunts, but the surround is the half-understood gentle breathing, sighing, of a breeze, the "semi-diaphanous mist" of the night, the "palpable silence of the dew."

This gentle sublime leaves us in a tremulous, restless repose. An invitation to a nocturnal tryst foretells both refreshment and anxiety, like Kant's mix of pleasure and fear. We yearn for the infinite repose of a beckoning night, as a Christian might yearn for the infinite repose of a savior, seen through a glass darkly. But Climacus is a romantic, not a Christian. He yearns for the comfort not of a savior but sensed in the "silence of the dew," in a "semi-diaphanous mist." His evocations of night breeze and dew bear comparison with the elegies to the lilies of the fields and the birds of the air (in Kierkegaard's discourses of 1849). As George Pattison notes, here nature "signals a kind of transcendence" that evokes "the anxiety of self-relation."[2] The repose of a lily or bird signals the contentment humans yearn for but lack. The anxious dark of the night and dark of the soul implicate each other in mutual resonance.

Grave critiques

Our *mise en scène* is a condensed and powerful meditation on death and grief, held by sky above and fresh grave below. Stepping beyond this garden of death, we might consider what's meant by "truth is subjectivity," or "true inwardness" but such disquisitions would remove us from the settings from which things and persons speak, from a man broken in grief, a frightened grandson, a fresh grave, an anxious night, a screen of leafy boughs behind which Climacus hides and listens. This tryst with the infinite realizes an "objective uncertainty" held in "the most passionate inwardness," a restless inwardness:

> the night's breeze … repeats itself, breathing through forest and meadow, and sighing as though in search of something, urged by the distant echo in oneself of the stillness as if intimating something.[3]

The sighing of night reflects a sighing soul, and a sighing soul reflects the night breeze, both yearning for a rest signaled by silent dew. It's not as though the physiology of anxiety *caused* the skies to spin, or the spin of the sky *caused* the brain to spin. It's a matter of poetic fit, as lightening portends shock to the heart, and shock to the heart portends lightening.

Death disrupts the living, puts the dead under judgment, and warns the living to take heed. Death speaks indirectly through a night breeze and also through words overheard. The grief-wrought old man does not intend his words for the eavesdropping Climacus. As they float by more or less anonymously, Climacus is *taken* by them, and takes them up as his *own*. Climacus is a sometime mimic of the subjective thinker, so perhaps he *appropriates* the grief that floats his way. In its primary sense, however, to appropriate is to illicitly seize – as in an illicit appropriation, theft, of land or funds, and Climacus is no thief. What is stolen away is his composure, in the way a love or beauty or truth might steal up and overcome him. Grief and its lessons of death and life, *steal into* his heart. He makes his *own* what has in the first instance captured *him*. The subjective thinker *appropriates* what first *appropriates him*.

What are the lessons of life and death revealed in this setting? The old man fears for the soul of the departed, for his son was caught up in the cultural illusion that philosophical or historical speculation or debate *about* faith could be a substitute for *being* of faith. Now, through tears, he pleads with his grandson. Beware! Erudite scholarly engagement with a religion is not a work of faith but of an alienating and distracting objectivity. A perfect analysis of faith does not give me faith: I might be no more than an atheist, humorist, or scholar.

Romance, comedy, revelation

Grief wafts contagiously through the night. Climacus grieves not for the corpse in the grave but for the old man who is denied a restful old age, trembling that his son faces perdition, having taken up with abstract philosophy as a substitute for faith. If the old man correctly identifies the cause of his son's downfall, and furthermore, if Climacus is at a loss, utterly *bored* with his life, then this setting suggests a resolve. Climacus can launch a crusade against abstract philosophy. But does Climacus realize that a crusade against objective philosophy, however worthy, will not move him an inch toward Christian faith? He will annoy cognoscenti trumpeting philosophy as a high form of Christianity, or replacement of it. But to crusade against the arrogance of theory is not to *become* a Christian. As a self-described humorist, Climacus perhaps knows no that a demolition of theory will not fill the void hollowed out by his own absence of faith. A humorist will understand what's wrong with theory and what's right with the available Christian cure. But Climacus won't take the cure. He is fundamentally uninterested in becoming Christian himself.

This scene of inadvertent spying opens disarmingly: "What happened is quite simple. It was four years ago ... " [4] we're told. The writer simply sat on a bench, becoming inadvertently privy to a conversation. Yet that moment triggers vocation. Climacus hears a "decisive summons [for him] to come on a definite track" (p. 202). And why should *this* be the moment of revelation or conversion? He works through the moment out loud. "You are after all, tired of life's diversions, you are tired of girls that you love only in passing, you must have something that fully occupies your time. Here it is" (ibid.). But this is comedy central! He mocks the gravity of losing one's soul (hence needing a summons) by pairing it with ridiculousness of loosing interest in pretty girls. This puts the need for religious or moral salvation on a par with the need to be tickled by girls.

Graveside weeping awakens Climacus to a need for direction, but his understanding is comically inept. He needs a replacement for chasing pretty girls, but wonders exactly *what* this replacement looks like. He is at the threshold of a new life, but how will he find out what his vocation will be? His suggestion of a method of discovery once more is utter comedy. He must face "something like an intricate criminal case in which the very complex circumstances [make] pursuit of the truth difficult" (p. 202). He says he faces a *detective's* puzzle, as if he faced a "Who done it?" of a crime mystery. But "How should I live?" is an *existential* question. *Who did it* is not *what do I do*. One answer is massively *inessential* to my life; the other is massively essential. Amidst the flailings of comedy, however, we find traces of truth.

Death does alert one to the need for "a definite track" even though Climacus stumbles absurdly in trying to absorb what that need amounts to. The anxious "whence-and-whither" of his life is not just a police matter, a challenge for gumshoes with flashlights. In a moment of lucidity, he bravely reflects, you are tired of girls that you love only in passing. He grabs his detective's flashlight to spot what comes next in his life. He has managed to shift from idle flirtation to sense the need for a serious vocation, the other side of his hearing a summons to do *something*. And he musters a *resolve* to take up "a definite track": he'll become a critic of abstract philosophizing, of misplaced objectivity. *Postscript*, in fact, becomes the fulfillment of his graveside summons. Before we move on to his critique of theory, as an aside we should remember that a defense of existential subjectivity does not make one a subjective thinker any more than knowing, as the humorist does, what is essential to becoming a Christian makes one closer to actually *becoming* a Christian. Now what *is* the subjectivity that Climacus defends?

Interpersonal subjectivity, nature-immersed

Climacus' graveside testimony leaves a rich sketch of existential subjectivity – *not* just a pinpoint of agency or choice, or a moment of appropriation or responsibility, or a locus of "hidden inwardness." Subjectivity is a boundless sphere in which nature, death, and other persons interweave in mutual resonance. This resonance awakens Climacus to his own subjectivity – his relations, for instance, to nature, death, and other persons. Far from an isolated impenetrable inner space, subjectivity is *a* natural, embodied, interpersonal space.

The author of this 600 page "postscript" seems to be mainly an objective thinker, defending the truth that truth is subjectivity. Does this make sense? In the early 1960s Stanley Cavell noted that there was something quixotic in this venture – the attempt (if that's what it is) to *defend* subjectivity. Philosophical defense by definition is an objective project, isn't it? Yet on second thought, that sort of quixotic project is not very foreign to philosophy. Kant, after all, uses reason to limit reason. In any case, Climacus is not really *interested* in offering a philosophical defense. He's conducting a kind of thought-experiment, trying out sketches that exemplify features of what, if it is to have weight, must be wrapped up in a way of life, or in a way of living into a life – he is not trying to *justify* that life. Nevertheless, it can surely *seem* at times that Climacus is doing something academic and philosophical – objective.

Later in the 1960s Henry Allison argued that the arguments Climacus delivers are so *patently* flawed that Climacus must be talking tongue-in-cheek. If he *knows* it's bad philosophy, perhaps it's a good mimic or parody. The point might be to parody his rival, Hegel – a kind of hoax at the expense of Hegelians or academics generally. The *Postscript*, like the "Hegelian System" that it mocks, collapses on itself like a house of cards – to our great amusement. But we shouldn't laugh too hard at Climacus for the foolishness of the *Postscript*. He knows what he's doing, and does it very well. So well, in fact, that ever-so-many professors think he's producing *bona fide* philosophy! The joke's on Hegel and anyone else who thinks he's serious about his "mimic-pathetic-dialectic," that most *unscholarly* anti-systematic postscript to some unassuming philo-sophical crumbs.

Have we digressed? The cemetery scene is hardly a straight-forward defense of subjectivity. It is rather an evocation. Here, Climacus slips into a confessional mood that places him well within *subjective* space, describing it from within, enacting its moves. He's subject to intimations of night mist, to sudden earnestness about his life's orientation, to being taken by effusions from a gravesite that *address* him. Subjectivity includes capacity to assume the space of other subjectivities. Climacus is the old man who sees the ruse of philosophy – is the child subjected to an insistence that he disavow his father's life – is the fearsome corpse, reminder of a life squandered.[5]

Chalked with age, the old man anchors a social and subjective space that links three generations and an invisible listener, a space activated by a corpse who prompts inwardness – all this embraced by a surrounding night. This listening and speaking, this passive and active ensemble, is not just a lonely and solitary affair, but ultimately social. Climacus calls it a "natural form of interpersonal association,"[6] thus a *social* space, free from the seductions of an indifferent, third-personal objectivity. Climacus waits "womanlike" for the infinite to half-appear, in "the night's semi-diaphanous mist."

Farewells to the dead

Climacus is welcomed to a nocturnal tryst, yet no such tryst is offered the old man. He lives under an anxious sky, knowing he must die, that his son has just died, that his grandson must live under clouds of his father's death and then under his grandfather's impending demise. Soon enough he must live alone, only a child. The old man abides the enigmas of farewell.

> Evening's leave-taking of the day, and of the one who has lived that day, is a speech in a riddle. Its reminder [of danger] is like the solicitous mother's admonition to the child to be home in good time.[7]

Farewells, leave-takings, are exchanged in the confidence that the sun will rise, that the world will return, that our friends will *not* enter the grave in the night – even as we know darkly that a *final* farewell awaits. Then there will be *no* tomorrow, we *won't* awake, the beloved will *not* return. A therapist must have a lively sense of death.[8] Termination, and respect for it, hangs over all developing therapeutic attachments. Climacus offers the disquieting riddle of a mother fearfully holding her child yet bravely letting go in bidding farewell. To "hold" the anxieties of a child (or an analysand) is always also to anticipate the day when the child (or analysand) will depart to live in freedom (or depart in death, abandoned all around). Good mothering, good mentoring, good therapy embodies and emboldens a "being toward death," an eye on termination that colors all action and thought even as hope is also conveyed. Here is a primal riddle of foreboding farewells and irrepressible hopes, of being toward death and toward birth. A "tryst with the infinite" brings love and death in tow amidst abiding uncertainties.

Climacus has no particular grave to visit. Yet perhaps he is already somewhat dead, and so *does* have a grave close by. Can he commune with himself as one communes with the dead?

> There is always in this garden, among the visitors, a beautiful understanding that one does not come out here to see and to be seen, ... Nor does one need company, here where all is eloquence, where the dead greet one with the brief word placed on his grave, not like a clergyman who gives sermons on that word far and wide, but as a silent man does who says no more than this yet says it with a passion as though the dead would burst open the tomb – or is it not strange to have on his grave "we shall meet again" and to remain down there?[9]

The night speaks without words. Now the dead speak, ready to burst eloquently from the grave, yet "remain down there." The dead declare, "We shall meet again!" and the living agree. Visitors speak with their *risen* dead. The dead speak with those on the edge or halfway down.

Inward and outward heartfeltness

Inwardness permeates our subjectivity and our communion with the dead. But we should substitute "heartfeltness" for "inwardness" for we are concerned with how we abide with another or others in modes of interpersonal address. Here is Alastair Hannay:

"Inwardness" is by no means a perfect translation of *"Inderlighed."* As with Hegel's *Innerlichkeit*, the sense is not that of inward-directedness [but of] an inner warmth, sincerity, seriousness and wholeheartedness in one's concern for what matters, a "heartfeltness" not applied to something but which comes *from* within.[10]

"Inwardness" brings psychologists to picture introspection or inner-direction, and philosophers to picture Cartesian divides between private consciousness and public world. Yet in his graveyard meditations, Climacus sidesteps all this as he relays how we do and don't convey who we are to each other, expressing ourselves from the heart (or not), under the burden of death. And Cartesian splits disappear in whispers of night or serenities of dew.

Subjectivity is of the world and others, not a pervasive breach with the world. What might seem like a steel wall is instead porous: it engages the whisper of night and the tears of a neighbor. It flows into the soul of a grandfather, of a dead son, of an abandoned child. Climacus rides the flow of grief to enter them, as they enter him. Climacus advocates *"hidden* inwardness" as a counterweight to "outward bawling" (as he puts it). Hysterical grief or outrage can mask an *absence* of heartfeltness, both outward and inward bound.[11] Courage or truthfulness reach out toward others and things. We are earnest *about* something, heartfelt *with regard to* something. Heartfeltness is a *reciprocal*, interpersonal relation: the heavens offer heartfelt invitation, accepted or refused, passionately or indifferently; a grandfather's grief is for another, who can return a concern. Heavens invite, an old man pleads. Climacus has ears open, the world pores in; he pores out in response to the world. Such give and take presupposes "interpersonal association."

Why advocate hidden inwardness?

There are false passions and true. "Inwardness [will be] untrue to the same degree as the outward expression ... in words and assurance, is *there, ready to hand* for instant use." [12] Whatever is there "ready to hand" gives the mimic ample material. True grief will be true to something beyond merely conventional "outward expression." "Ready to hand" expressions give only "everyday understanding of inwardness." [13] Mimics only *mimic* subjectivity.

Commonplace weeping and gesticulations can be true. Recoil in disgust can be perfectly true to one's affect and circumstance. Yet deep grief will be more than momentary bursts of emotion. Climacus observes that true grief is preserved "not as an instant's excitement, but as the eternal which has been won through death." [14] Deep grief will veer from momentary excitement toward the lastingly eternal, eternity gained insofar as one dies to a passion's outward ephemerality and preserves something deeper. Changeable love or grief is "less true" than its eternal counterpart. We grieve a dead child beyond immediate outbursts. Momentary passion is forgetful; deep inwardness has long memory. "[I]t is not unlovely that a woman gushes over in momentary inwardness nor is it unlovely for her soon to forget it again." [15] Sexism aside, it is lovely to weep at the moment but lasting grief, eternal grief, is not an outburst from which we move on. Climacus: "Praise be to the one living who relates as a dead man to his inwardness." The dead do not burst with public gesticulation. *To all the world* it may seem as if I am dead to my grief – it does not pester me to be taken out into the world.

Climacus would endorse the Stoic aim to eradicate false emotion. He differs in thinking that love or grief can be true, and so, worth *preserving*. It's the false media and marketplace fuss and bother, and shallow attempts to sell one's emotions, seeking publicity's profits, that deserve scorn. We might display grief among friends for a month, or on the anniversary of a death, but the time for public displays will soon pass. Then we enter twilight. Weeping may end, but grief over the loss of a child survives the cessation of weeping. Deep love will sustain grief for one departed. A grief extending timelessly after the death of a child might be so entrenched as to have become a very mark of a mother's identity, neither to be scorned or eradicated, nor to be put on public display. Climacus:

It has always stung my shame to witness another person's expression of feeling when he abandons himself to it as one does only in the belief that one is unobserved; for there is an inwardness of emotion which is befittingly hidden and only revealed to God. [16]

If emotion can be "befittingly hidden and only revealed to God," then we can expect great reserve in the expression of lasting love or grief. Heartfeltness may be hidden to the wider world yet expressed elsewhere nonetheless. The old man weeps as he speaks alone to his grandson in a nearly deserted cemetery. He is not mute. Otherwise hidden grief can become unhidden in revelation to God. The limiting case of the truth that inwardness is interpersonal is the occasion when affect arises for God only – bypassing one's neighbor, priest, spouse, or friend.

Preserving the living and the dead

What is living in Kierkegaard? A dialectical lens gives us an interweave of nature, subjectivity, and sociality as these mix with vocation, anxiety, and death. Working through these matters will not end tomorrow. A lyrical Kierkegaard sings through image, setting, and passion, providing poetic entry to a luminous dark. Such allures and satisfactions will not end tomorrow.

Midway in his monstrous book of satire and dialectical battle, Climacus sketches a garden of the dead as a lyrical-dialectical miniature of the larger effort. Enter the strolling critic of Copenhagen, the false-heaven of intellectualistic disputation, the true hells and redemptions of stricken fathers, and the worlds of only briefly innocent sons – the worlds of diaphanous mists and nocturnal trysts, and of the many tensed layers of the heart. In the span of barely half-a-dozen pages, this miniature provides a proof text for all that Climacus tells us elsewhere of truth and subjectivity, double reflection and indirect communication, confession of faith and its revocation, the inward recesses of the heart and their expression, the easy chatter of the classroom and the mystery of inheritance from star-crossed fathers, of farewells from anxious mothers, of receiving word from the risen dead and knowing the costs of a soul's self-betrayal.

Notes

1 *Concluding Unscientific Postscript*, trans Alastair Hannay, 2009, p. 197.

2 See *"Poor Paris!" Kierkegaard's Critique of the Spectacular City* (Berlin: de Gruyter, 1999), pp. 128f.

3 *CUP*, p. 197.

4 Ibid.

5 *CUP*, p. 200.

6 *CUP*, p. 203. More accurately, proper inwardness corrects an "unnatural form of interpersonal association."

7 *CUP*, p. 197.

8 Jonathan Lear, *Therapeutic Action: An Earnest Plea for Irony* (New York: Other Press, 2003), pp. 54–7.

9 *CUP*, p. 197.

10 Hannay, Concluding Unscientific Postscript, trans. ed. Alastair Hannay, Cambridge, 2009, xxxviii–xxxix.

11 *CUP*, p. 220.

12 *CUP*, p. 198.

13 Ibid.

14 Ibid.

15 Ibid.

16 Ibid.

10

When is Death?

Mid-way through his fluid meditations in *Moby Dick*, Melville presents us with a particularly hair-raising incident. A 14th century English commander has conquered the French town of Calais and demands his fair tribute in victory. He asks for six citizens to step forward to be hanged. The mayor and five others advance with halters around their necks.[1] This fright snaps us alert – not just to cruelty, but to our mortality. And within a page, Melville assures us that a philosopher, sitting by the fire contemplating death, can be as aware, afraid, and deeply cognizant of death as anyone mounting the gallows. We all live, as he puts it, with halters around our necks.[2] He has us aware of our own halters by delivering us to the terror of others – not unlike Kierkegaard's giving us the terror of Abraham, knife drawn, to incite our own worries about faith and the terrible divine.

These intrusions of death can snap us awake the way imminent danger can, but we would hope to learn more than naked fear. Such fear can be overcome, and with courage, it should be, but an awareness of death is *more* than fear, and it should *not* be overcome. For Kierkegaard, it can be a sustaining and continuously transforming spring of life. For Melville, it can impress us with the melancholy tragedy of life, even amidst life's joys and celebrations. Perhaps, it can also figure as a lifting inspiration, infusing us with breath and life.

Dancing

If we credit the testimony of his last days, for Socrates death is nothing to fear. It brings out moral majesty, and need not obtrude, as with Melville, as a terrifying nightmare one must master. In *Phaedo* we are taught that the philosopher "practices" death, or takes up with it philosophically; living-toward-death is of a piece with good thinking. One does not *battle* death so much as *move fluidly* with it in dialogue. Kierkegaard may seem close to Socrates here. For him, awareness of death can be a well-spring of good life; it can, as he says, "accelerate life."[3] But if Socratic meditation on death seems like *a preparation for death*, Kierkegaard's meditations seem like an *intensification* of life. And far from a nightmare or terror, Kierkegaard and Climacus figure death as an amorous partner.

Kierkegaard rejects the possibility that death teaches only fear and trembling, or teaches only *through* fear and trembling. It does not paralyze, or serve as a counterweight to vivid life. The fluid light steps of life are a *dance* with death. In the passages that have us linger, death is not a traumatic event so much as a transfiguring, intimate, mobile partner.

Note as well that neither for a tragic Melville, depicting death in its gritty terror, nor for a pagan Socrates, depicting it with serenity, is death a portal to afterlife. Nor is it a portal for the would-be Christian Kierkegaard.[4] Death adds luster to *this* life. In his discourse "At a Graveside," Kierkegaard is unambiguously emphatic: "Then [at death] all is over!."[5] Death is a teacher and mentor, a disturber of selves and minister to souls, in *this* life. Death obtrudes in a revelatory restructuring of the attentive soul.[6]

Transformation is often figured as a flash of light, or as the transforming jolt of thunder. True, the thunderclap of death may instill fear and startle one into awareness of one's finitude. It may firm one's resolution to take up the serious, and lose not an instant! Its visceral intrusion can clear out the trivial. "[T]he thought of death ... *accelerate(s) the living*," as Kierkegaard puts it.[7] "Earnestness (or seriousness) grasps the present *this very day*."[8] But however instructive the thunderclap may be as a figure, in his dialectical works, and even in his discourses, Kierkegaard favors another, surprisingly gentle, image.[9] Climacus takes his writing in *Philosophical Crumbs* as "*a dance with the thought of death*."[10] In a mid-period discourse, Kierkegaard evokes a man's graveside grieving, and remarks, "death invites him *also to the dance*".[11] In *Concluding Unscientific Postscript*, Climacus figures Socrates as performing a "solo dance" before the divine.[12] If we credit *Phaedo*, Socrates in his thinking should be accompanied by and rehearsing the thought of death, for as Plato has it in that dialogue, philosophy is a preparation or rehearsal for death.[13] Perhaps the moral earnestness death brings in her train is a matter of lightness and grace, not puritanical fear, hard labor and struggle.

Although it's seldom the focus of dialectical exchange, Plato must think that wrestling with death is a kind of ground project for the philosopher. If not directly, nevertheless through one's reflective practice, a person on the path to wisdom is never far from coming to terms with its idea and reality. Joining images from *Postscript* and *Philosophical Crumbs*, we get a dialectical Socrates thinking in a rehearsal for death that, as Climacus says, is a *dance* with the thought of death. This secures the intuition that Socrates is more than a thinking-talking head. He will enact a flowing, embodied artistry that somehow is the expressive equivalent of dialectic, and an expressive outpouring of a life-in-the-presence-of-death.

In *Phaedo,* Socrates confides that he has often been visited by a dream that urges him to "make music and compose." This unassuming unkempt conversationalist known for nagging interrogation reveals only hours before death that he has been haunted by a recurrent dream. We perk up, for this may be his parting revelation. It is passed on to us with artless simplicity.

These "last words" are easily forgotten or overlooked, buried in the wash of powerful and labored proofs for the immortality of the soul that follows. If he is immortal, and can prove it, he has nothing to fear, and neither do his companions. Yet what if a careful listener lets Socrates' opening dream whispering "make music and compose" hover over these dialectical exercises, as if to qualify or contain their reach? At the least, Socrates has us wonder whether this is the right time for a show of dialectical prowess. After all, death will overtake him the moment he's ready. Are these admittedly inconclusive logical structures a diversion, keeping his audience from tears? Perhaps the philosopher's last hours are better spent dwelling on his opening revelation, setting aside logical power for vulnerable exposure to the ministrations of a dream? Does this dream reveal a wistful regret?

It's possible to imagine this dream as calling his life in question, as framing a regret rather than pride in a life well spent, as naming a path not taken. Does the voice advising him to make music betray his wish to have lived his life *otherwise* – being *lyrical* rather than dialectical? There is an alternative. I like to hear this voice not as regret, but as reminding him of what he has been doing all along – the deep meaning of his doing, his life's apt epitaph. He has spent a life self-composing, in concert and contest with others, in response to a muse who prompts in night dreams. He makes music through conversation, and we are to remember him for that.

In *Postscript* Climacus gives us Socrates without speech or inter-rogation and if not making music, then composing himself with bodily lyricism in solitude. His dance, as Climacus has it, is "solo," not a dialogue in the public square. It does not involve public speech partly because it is silent reflection still seeking words, and also because identity is established, it seems, not only in speech but non-conversationally in comportment. This brings Socrates and Climacus close to Nietzsche, who wishes for a "music playing Socrates" and a "God who would dance."[14]

In *Phaedo, Crito,* and *Apology* it is Socrates' calm composure and steady posture (as much as any words he utters) that convince us – or many of us – of the wisdom of both his convictions and his way of life. If philosophy is a way of life expressed not only in words but also in comportment and posture, it can be dance. There one's thinking is unspoken in the double sense of being no part of a conversation (with others or with oneself) and of being expressed in comportment, in the way one moves. One thinks here of the artistry of Thoreau's thinking-in-walking.[15] Dance is music made flesh. Here we have Socratic artistry rendered as a solo dance before a watchful, appreciative eye.

Always attentive

Because this thought of death is danced "solo" before the divine, the dance and thought will not be apparent to others, and not expressed in dialogue (though perhaps it will be evident as a serene comportment to a sharp observer). How much in focus is this thought? At one point Climacus says that the subjective thinker must think of death "every moment." "To think this uncertainty [of death] once and for all, or once a year at matins on New Year's morning, is not to think it at all... . Therefore it becomes more and more important to me to think it into every moment of my life."[16]

Does the ever-presentness of the thought of death mean that death is an obsessive and explicit focus that always floods one's awareness? That would ruin life, and rule out the obvious, that Socrates is aware of so much that is *not* explicitly death: his interlocutors, his path toward a dinner party, his enjoyment of good wine. He might have any number of thoughts (including the thought of death) that *stand at the ready* every moment – without any of these being the constant focus of my *explicit* attention or action.

That I love my child, or will be loyal to my friend might be thoughts "at the ready" every moment – even as I stay fully focused on avoiding a traffic jam or remedying a bump in line of poetry. I close my letter to a distant friend, "You will always be close to my heart!" *Always*! This must mean "always at the ready." Climacus speaks of the necessary presentness of such essential thoughts in order to rule out a kind of spiritual cheating.

Having the passing thought only once a year that I will die, or only once a year that I love my child, does not count as truly taking up with my death, or my love. If the thought of death arrives only for a moment on the anniversary of my father's death, or if the thought of love for my child arrives only as a calendar reminds me of her birthday, then neither death nor love will be a compelling, subjective center of my existence. Having the thought of death at the ready *every moment*, is not *dwelling morbidly* on death. Thinking death is an "acceleration of life," Kierkegaard says. "Death in earnest gives life force as nothing else does."[17]

Intimations of birth and death

In *"Poor Paris!": Kierkegaard's Critique of the Spectacular City,* George Pattison reflects on the unfolding of life from an enigmatic beginning to an enigmatic finale.[18] What links my sense of death and birth is loss and bereavement. I mourn and yearn for continuities lost at the limits of life itself. In birth, I lose continuity "with the life that bore my life," as if birth were the breaking of a primal bond and in death, I lose continuity with the self that is mine, as if death were the breaking of a primal bond.[19] We are, as Melville avers, born haltered. Here is Pattison:

> The primal loss of continuity with the life that bore my life and the final loss of self in death mark out boundaries that are reinforced by the repeated experience of the births and deaths of others. Both this retrospective primal loss and prospective final loss are implicated in every important life-decision that I make, because they fundamentally condition my sense of life and my sense of myself as belonging or not belonging to it.[20]

What is the basis in my experience for this sense of bereavement and loss? The actual events of my birth and death can't be the source, because the event of my birth begins *before* I have the capacity for experience, and the event of my death ends *after* I have the capacity for experience.[21] Retrospectively I *imagine* a moment before birth or prospectively, a moment after death, and thus delineate, in imagination, a start to the event of birth and an end to the event of death. And I no doubt extrapolate from experience of births and deaths of others, encountered directly or through literature or conversation or the media. Thus experiencing the event of another's birth ort death gives me a model for imagining my own. Imagination may give experience of what I cannot have experienced directly, but is it the whole story?[22]

My sense of my having entered life before memory and of having to leave it without memory of that event, reminds me that access to events experienced or remembered is not the only way I get a sense of my life. It's not only *events* that affect me deeply. A sense of promise or failure, of impending doom or celebration, can suffuse my life, and these moods are neither events nor sets of events. The blow of life's loss can be experienced as the *looming* or *screaming* or *whispering* of something yet to come. A dark *aura* can jolt me awake, or invite me to dance. A melancholy aura drifting in as a distant wind can intimate a time before I was born, a virgin time, as it were, to cherish as loss. Such looming, ahead or behind, is palpable to the senses. Overarching moods afford access to deep futures and deep pasts, beyond the experience of events. I express them, and find them expressed, in posture, in tone of voice, in quickness or languor of stride, in specifics of diction or countenance, in the look of a face. Moods afford entry to the tonality of deep temporality, a tonality conveyed in poetry and art and liturgy. Such posthumous and prenatal spans have an enigmatic, intimate agency in my life.

To consider my own past and future as carrying earnest, transformative import requires that they are compelling, through mood or imagination, *to me*.[23] A detached, patrician overview of a field that contains me will yield nothing of subjective, existential import. Perhaps not everyone can say to herself, "my *own* death or birth is inflected by loss, and I'm gripped by it." My death and birth might not matter to *me*.[24] If this indifference were not feigned, Kierkegaard would not argue abstractly about meaning but rather intervene with words that might *shake* such a person *out* of indifference. Indifference can be selective: she might not care for her own life but care intensely about her children, say. Conversely, she might be indifferent to the births and deaths of others, but intensely responsive to her own traumas before and ahead. Pervasive indifference to others would subtract from the *moral* gravity she accords her life. The earnestness Kierkegaard sees death bring into view is not just a self-centered will to survive. Awareness of my own mortality (or natality) may be only loosely connected with moral care for others, and moral care for others, be only loosely connected with care for my own mortality (or natality).

Transgressing boundaries

If my sense of my *own* death can shadow all my actions and inactions, as Pattison and Kierkegaard declare, infusing them with moral seriousness, this reveals something profound yet commonplace, about human subjectivity. This capacity to have something *outside* the limit of my life have transformative agency on what lies *within* those limits brings to the fore our capacity to occupy two temporal and spatial standpoints simultaneously. I need to think of myself as separate from myself – for instance, as separate from the life that bore me and *was* once mine, and separate from the night that will claim me and *will* be mine. And this means I apparently transgress my temporal limits. Of course we can *wish* or *long* to live in another century, in the wholeness of an Eden behind. But in thinking the agency of death I speak from a position that *enacts a transgression* of temporal limits. Let me give two examples.

A condition of Job's being able to curse the day he was born is his capacity to imaginatively project himself to a time before he was born, and (quite enigmatically) speak and think and imagine from that emptiness. From that pre-natal position he resolves that he doesn't want to pass through birth and over into life. Likewise, if *silenus* or Ecclesiastes suggests it might be better never to have been born, we're asked to consider from the *midst* of life what it would be like to consider from a time before birth whether being born is worth the effort. So now as we deliberate are we standing in the midst of life – or before our birth, wondering whether to *enter*? Clearly, we are in both times, both places, at once.

Similarly, a condition of Achilles' being able to rue the day he will die is his capacity to imaginatively project himself to a time *after* death. He can attain a posthumous position from which, enigmatically, he can speak, think, and imagine ruefully, lamenting what he has lost. From that position, he resolves fiercely that he does not want *ever* to pass through the portal of death, to pass out of life. He knows from the other side, as it were, that the other side is ruefully deficient without him.

A double standpoint is not so obviously at work in assessing the immediate grittiness of death, as with Melville.[25] Kierkegaard highlights death as bringing an awareness of temporality that can instill moral urgency. But as we've seen, that means we occupy a double standpoint. I am here amidst fellows and calendar time, and yet also, in thought, out of calendar time. I dance elsewhere with the otherness that is death. This sounds obscure. But consider more familiar occasions of our being *temporally and spatially* both here and elsewhere. Take our capacity to "step into another's shoes."

Times of death

It's a platitude that moral attentiveness means seeing and feeling things the way another person sees or feels them, to "step into their shoes," as we say. Now perhaps that's just a metaphor, but I don't think so. I may not slip into your house and slip into your shoes, picking the loafers that fit. Nevertheless, there's nothing *"merely* metaphorical" in my saying that I step into your shoes when I try to adopt your perspective, to empathize with it, to see things from your standpoint.[26]

Let's say that moral maturity requires being able to step into another's shoes. How is this relevant to understanding death? Well, if I try to see my life backward from the shadow that is death, it's like stepping into the shoes of death and looking back toward the world – my world – from that shadowed position. I am taking in a span of life from outside that span of life, yet I am, as viewer and viewed, both inside and outside my life. This parallels being in my shoes as I transport myself spatially to slip into your shoes, while still being back in my own. From the position of death, I dance with my life, and from the position of my life I dance with my death, and either way, my dance transgresses temporal and spatial limits, as if I slip into the shoes of death even as I stay in my own.

Most of Pattison's *Poor Paris!* deals with Kierkegaard's spatial locations, in and around Copenhagen. The city is place of spectacle, the place to see and be seen. Even the large family home on Nytorv was there to be seen and admired, looking down on the market square it ruled. And perhaps its interior had spaces for minor spectacles – a drawing room in which to be seen and to see, strict protocol governing who was to be seen and heard by whom and when and about what.

The more obvious sites of spectacles, however, were the bustling streets, the woods and parks newly designed for carriage rides and for viewing the king on his daily row on the lake – visible to all and sundry. There were the churches Kierkegaard entered for worship, or the university with the buzz or drone of lectures. Although these spaces were separate, they also were conjoined and layered. Amidst the drone of university lectures, Kierkegaard, like any student, might be more or less asleep to that space – yet quite alive in that moment to the space of carriage rides in verdant parkland, vivid in his mind's eye. Or amidst the sobriety of worshipers in Vor Frue Kirke, he might be swept into a lively room some blocks away filled with conversation, and with the presence of a pert and pretty girl he fancied.

Considering the way spaces can be conjoined or layered in a "multiple exposure" helps us grasp the strange business of seeing our life from beyond the grave, from the standpoint of death, even dancing with death. When spaces are layered, rather than merely laid side by side, an ambiguity of spatial location can sink in. If Kierkegaard dreams of a carriage ride in the midst of a lecture, *where*, exactly, is he? His classroom professor might speak either way: "You're *here* (in class), Søren – don't be *there*!" Or equally, "you're *there* (in the carriage), Søren – come back *here*!" This testifies to our spatially and temporally anomalous existence. Søren is on a carriage ride and equally in class, flirting in living rooms and equally in church.

Layered space, anomalous time

Anomalous results in science beg to be explained, and explained away, by new paradigms or laws. Life and death are not anomalous in *that* way. Life and death do not fall under any uncontested "normative" or "law-like" background against which their shifting shapes can be charted. [27] It's as hard to locate Søren (in church – or not; in class – or not) as it is hard to find a "nomos" or overarching pattern to locate life or death.

If the background for fixing "death" is the field of coroners or county clerks, death will be located more or less definitively in clock or calendar time. "Life ceased at 12:01 am!" But if the background in play is the work of cultural critics, then another meaning of "time of death" will become pertinent. Kierkegaard may be dead for the coroner yet for the critic be alive in *my* generation, well past the coroner's declaration. Then the coroner's announcement of death lies strangely idle. One's estimate of Kierkegaard's cultural life may be also unfixed: will he be alive 50 years from now? *How* alive or moribund? Kierkegaard may be still in his youth. The grid operative for cultural critics can undermine the grid operative for county clerks, and vice versa. The meaning of "*the* time of Kierkegaard's death" radically shifts; that's what makes death anomalous.

We can superimpose a third temporal grid for locating "time of death," increasing the play of anomaly. Beyond the backdrop of cultural history and the practices of county clerks is the arena of family dynamics. Kierkegaard's death then seems to leap over his burial to invade the life of his elder brother, becoming a toxin that brought on *Peter's* death. Peter seems to have died years before his clerk-registered burial.[28] Peter Kierkegaard, the august and powerful church dignitary, died biologically decades after Søren's biological death. Yet Peter became ever more convinced that he had failed his younger brother, and he declined under a burden of guilt, finally resigning his claim to legal competency and delivering himself to the state as its ward. Søren's biological death was the start of his impressive post-burial cultural life. The younger brother's biological death was the onset of Peter's spiritual death, which was complete long before biological heart stopped.

To call death anomalous is to register an ever-expanding set of possible meanings to "death," each presupposing a background making its occurrence dateable, but none particularly congruent with others. To fix a time of death we might check a coroner's report, a critics' evocation, a family drama.[29]

Asking when death arrives (or is left behind) is a little like asking when love arrives or is left behind, or when birth arrives or is left behind. Birth might begin with the exchange of a glance between lovers, with a midwife's cry of delight, with the utterance of a first word, or with setting out from home. Death might begin with birth, or with the first failed love, or with a final gasp of the lungs, or with the departure from memory of all those who might have remembered one – as one was when alive.

There is no "mother of all contexts," no "map of all maps." We are, in some mysterious sense, flying without maps when we ask – as if there were a general, all-purpose answer – *when did death occur, what is death*? From that elevated, irreal but irresistible vantage, death becomes amorphous, anomalous. Luckily we soon enough descend to schooled second nature and inherited intuition to get around without collisions, without exhaustively pinning down by regressive demonstration the full grounds of intelligibility – a ridiculous aspiration and impossible task.

When death shows up will depend on who, locally, is keeping time, and on the time-zone we are presumed to inhabit. A family watching their child succumb to a prolonged illness may well sense an elongated time in which death hovers – or not – while the coroner takes quick note of its arrival and departs. Kierkegaard has death an extended dialectical dance, and Socrates has death co-extensive with philosophy. For many of us, death may show up momentarily in "gritty" accounts of war and murder, in reading a novel, in a medical lab report, or less momentarily in the death of a relative. And then there is the strange presence of death paradoxically in the smile of a child.

Leakage of time

Kierkegaard lived a number of generative life-segments (or phases) during his 40 odd Copenhagen years, phases that were layered and endlessly extending. Figuring out a narrative of what holds them together brings out, from a different angle, the complexity of pinning down how that narrative unfolds. The point is not to determine how his life "really" unfolded biographically, but to see how aspects of a life are focused by agencies from a difference phase than the aspect in question. Looking back at a phase of his life from the region of death can, as we've seen, *accelerate* life. That's one way to find his life focused by agency outside it that nevertheless invades it. Kierkegaard is not alone in finding himself writing from "outside of life," as it were, from a posthumous position. Stanley Cavell, living relatively hale and hearty these days, speaks of his autobiography as a piece of *posthumous* writing.[30] Kierkegaard suggests a subtitle, "A *Posthumous* Work of a Solitary Human Being."[31] His writing rooted him beyond the time of his living, as he saw it, and a century and a half later, we too find him alive, rooting him in a posthumous life. His presence hovers over numerous conversations and library carrels day in, day out, any recent decade. Clerks and tombstones tell only a bit of the story.

The time of Kierkegaard's childhood (an early phase of life) has a "post-childhood" resonance. Just so, the evening of his life has a post-burial, posthumous resonance. His childhood is marked by his exposure to other children, to those who laughed, for instance, at the uneven length of his trousers – an exposure that caused interior hurt. That early hurt might resonate in "post-childhood," translated into a new register, as Kierkegaard turned the tables through the verve and bite of his writing: he would expose the uneven spiritual trousers of others. His early hurt was thus transfigured. It leaked forward into mid-life and then was transfigured through the agency of seeing it retrospectively.

Does maturity lie in being able to leave childhood hurt and uneven trousers behind, not letting their toxin leak into mid-life?

Does maturity lies in leaving death to the dead, not giving its toxin leak into the bloom of life? We *want* childhood hurts not to leak forward – however much the child and its wounds ride on past childhood. Similarly, we *want* to stop thoughts of post-burial time leaking backward. Excessive concern with childhood hurt or future annihilation can lead to morbid self-preoccupation, self-pity, or a sense of victimization. But deficient attention to early afflictions or inescapable mortality can lead to recklessness, self-aggrandizement, or overweening pride.

Thinking of the overlap and leakage permeating successive phases of life – childhood hurt reaching forward, then being transfigured mid-life, for instance – we might ponder a second incident where turmoil from early adulthood works forward, somewhat underground, to provide the impetus for transfiguration later in life. Breaking his engagement exposed Kierkegaard to ridicule and opprobrium. [32] It began as a more or less dateable occurrence and continued through a powerful afterlife. It's not implausible to find it translated into new keys and transformed through his writing. The backward facing agency of his writing takes up the toxic forward flowing waves of opprobrium in ways not unlike the agency of his writing taking up the demands and decisions flowing backward from impending death. His writing transfigures the breakup, making it sufferable, perhaps turning the tables. He exposes *others* to the sort of ridicule he had suffered by exposing the shabby unevenness of bourgeois Copenhagen life.

Dancing in amorphous time

It may become blurred whether Kierkegaard is in church or elsewhere while in church; and it may become blurred whether as he writes he occupies the time of his earlier hurt, or has left that time behind. He can be alive in two *spaces* at once, and be alive in two *times* at once. If human time is amorphous, there is no ready answer to how the agency of hurt begins or ends, or how far it invades the future. There is no ready answer to how the agency of future emptiness invades the present or induces seriousness or earnestness that "accelerates life."[33] Kierkegaard says that a passion is like a river whose source and endpoint we will never know.[34] Now if we are cartographers in a blimp, we can probably chart the source of a river and its final merging with the sea. But if we are swimming in its midst and middle, both source and endpoint will be hidden, however much both have agency over our present.

Does the imprint of uneven commitments to Regine wash away once Kierkegaard decides to shatter the engagement and get on with his life? If we were in a blimp, perhaps we could pinpoint the source of a hurt and its final merging with wider currents down the river of time. But hurt in his soul no doubt lies out of a cartographer's view, its tendrils receding backward and reaching forward indefinitely, despite the fact that some vivid moments of hurt may erupt in a tick of time. Death, too, might leave an imprint of indeterminate duration erupting from a place that is only strangely apprehensible. The death of Kierkegaard's best friend, or of his father or his mother, enters the city clerk's records as a well-defined occurrence. But the meaning of those deaths ripples forward, back, and sideways in his life, as aftershocks that defy precise dating and tracking. This agency of death, rebounding from the deaths of others, is other than the effect of anticipating my own death, looking at my own life from beyond the grave, earnestly. In mid-life, I can occupy the position of an earlier phase of life, putting myself, say, in the shoes of a child humiliated by the length of his pants, or in the shoes of an early adult scorned for his vacillation or for his refusal of love and marriage. And in mid-life I can occupy the position of a later phase, or end-time, of life, putting myself, in the shoes of one dead looking back on life, assessing its vitality or debility. In fact, if death has agency that "gives force [to living] like nothing else does," that occurs only insofar as temporality, like spatiality, is amorphous.

I can project myself into shoes that give a prospect on my life from beyond, so that I see I-am-alive-and-will-die. From that spot, I participate in death's retrospective transfigurations of earlier life, as a dancer embraces and moves with her partner. My dance with the thought of death is my dance in the present and with a time not of this present, as I partake of an amorphous existence. That other in whose shoes I step is myself looking back as from beyond the grave, and that self-from-beyond-the-grave is every bit as much me as the self-this-side-of–the-grave, caught up in eating, drinking, paying taxes, being with family, a solitary walker as companionable with death as with life.

Glimmers of light

If not a river whose source and terminus is unknown, life might be a moment of daylight before the darkness of night sets in, or the moment a sparrow spends in the vaults of a great hall. As the Venerable Bede will tell us,

> Your Majesty, when we compare the present life of man on earth with that time of which we have no knowledge, it seems to me like the swift flight of a single sparrow through the banqueting hall where you are sitting at dinner on a winter's day with your commanders and counselors. In the midst there is a comforting fire to warm the hall; outside the storms of winter rain or snow are raging. The sparrow flies swiftly in through one door of the hall, and out through another. While he is inside, he is safe from the winter storms; but after a few moments of comfort, he vanishes from sight into the wintery world from which he came. Even so, man appears on earth for a little while; but of what went before this life or of what follows, we know nothing.[35]

In his discourse "At a Graveside," Kierkegaard suggests the image of life not as a moment of light within a great hall that we are granted as we dart through the rafters, but as a moment of light before darkness sets in.

We can picture Kierkegaard's life as a luminous daytime during which he dons his trousers and wrestles his uneven commitments, and dons a way of being in Copenhagen, a person with these opportunities, these talents, these anxieties, these parents, this insufferable older brother – or perhaps it's more having a role or talent thrust upon him – throughout, dancing with the shadow of death. Here he refutes the Epicurean claim that my death and I cannot co-exist.[36] For others, Kierkegaard's death is his public burial, a time his body was again exposed to praise and opprobrium.

Even for outsiders, watching in a way Kierkegaard couldn't, it's natural to see the funeral as continuous with his writing, his last days in hospital, and his earlier attacks on the church. The scandal of his life lived through and after his burial. There is the posthumous vantage he assumes pre-burial in surveying his writing and life, and the posthumous vantage we assume from after his burial. His life vaults over the time of his interment, just as earlier death vaults back into the flow of his scandalous and writerly life. All this wreaks havoc with a simple image of life as a glimmer of light, with darkness before and after.

Posthumous authorship

In Christian theology God initiates transfiguration: we don't change ourselves solo. At best we perform and interpret transfiguring poetized roles that descend, as it were, from above. We cannot know but have faith alone that the taxpaying Kierkegaard is transfigured as the author of authors who speak from the pages of multiple texts. He cannot know but have faith that as author of lives he will pass transfigured into unperishing poetry. Joseph Westphall reminds us in *The Kierkegaardian Author*, that "The author comes to be understood by his or her readers as both author and work, *simultaneously* but *separately* the creator of the work and a created element within it." Here, God is not the sole initiator. The to-be-transfigured author "gives birth to him- or herself by writing the work in which he or she is written."[37] This gives the text an existence beyond death, with the consequence, among other things, that the author can't fix the meaning of a part or the whole of the authorship with any authority exceeding that of any other reader. He can't provide an "incontrovertible last word on Kierkegaardian authorship."[38]

Westfall develops Kierkegaard's view that writers give their work a kind of imperishable existence, a kind of immortality.[39] Death and resurrection are in play as tax-liable Kierkegaard dies, and implied-author of authors Kierkegaard rises up from the grave. Accordingly, the true poet is engaged in "posthumous production," as one of Kierkegaard's subtitles implies: "A Posthumous Work of a Solitary Human Being."[40] The posthumous work transfigures the life it looks back on, manifesting the agency of death to take up a life and cull out the flesh-and-blood tax-paying author, and resurrect a writer known as his papers that reveal a post-burial immortal author of authors. This view raises havoc for deflationary biography that foregrounds the mortal taxpayer and flawed suitor.

"The freedom of literature – its true immortality – is its absolute distance from the factual."[41]

Kierkegaard was polemical and cagey enough to revel in the changing shadows of a self and in the difficulties others would have in finding him. And he was moral and religious enough to exploit another possibility: only where radical openness to change is present – that is, only where a solid self *can't* be pinned down – can there be hope of transfiguration.

Is this the thought that death and life, love and hurt, are amorphous, anomalous? That they can appear from one angle sharply etched in space and time – and from another, diaphanous, elusive, indefinite, and infinite?

Mystery

The earnestness that retrospectively befalls me as I dance with the thought of death is like the earnestness that befalls me when I suddenly see things from the shoes of another and realize that I must change my ways. My friend is in pain and I just hadn't been taking its impact and importance seriously, earnestly enough (but how much is enough?). I reconfigure my sense of how it is with her. I haven't changed any fact about her life and what I learn is elusive – I grasp, or am grasped by, the extent and intensity of things for her – which is to say that I find myself compelled where I wasn't before. Things that matter for *her* now drive *me* into recognition. The insight can be frightening and in any case will transform my comportment toward her – will become my dance with her pain, one could say.

Death is enigmatic, Kierkegaard tells us, and an enigma isn't something utterly opaque, but appears under varied aspects: something I see this moment and don't see the next, or see first as profound and then as superficial, or see first as liberating and then as constraining, first as fearful then as wonderful. Like time and love and hurt, death is enigmatic because it is *now* – but tomorrow; it is *here* – but elsewhere. All who read these words, or read Kierkegaard's words, cannot have failed to think them partially – now *more* fully, now less so; and cannot have failed to think something like Tolstoy's syllogism: All persons die; I am a person; I will die.[42] And let the conclusion fall shallow and limp.

We cannot have failed to think: Now he is dead nothing matters to him; what mattered was his life as he lived it; when I am dead nothing will matter to me; what matters is my life, this very day, as I live it. Part of the enigma of death is that I can find this flow of thought inevitable and transparent and compelling to *me*; and that I can, as if under a spell of indifference, follow this thought utterly lacking conviction – hearing words yet not hearing them, hearing-and-not-hearing, you will die, act now: Let the thought of death deliver earnestness that your life may be changed!

I say to myself, "Those emaciated children in a Sudanese camp ... put yourself in *their* shoes, or in the shoes of their *parents!* Doesn't their death matter?" Or I ask myself (but don't really ask), "Was I too brusque? – Can't I do better?" I dance and don't dance with the thought of death. Of course I may sadly not hear because I find my life not to matter. Then I am other to myself: That person (who is none other than me) is afflicted by indifference, her morale and soul are emaciated – put yourself in her shoes! Can't you see that she matters, that her death matters to me – *is* me?

I can look at myself, and so can separate myself from myself, occupying two postures at once toward a soul that slips in and out of view yet is one – and doubled – and my own. Things can matter or not, and I can know and not know that my life matters or that your life matters or that the fall of a sparrow matters. My doubleness is requisite both to finding that my life matters and to finding that your life matters. Taking my life with earnestness (or not) is inextricably, mysteriously, tied to taking your life with earnestness (or not). The brute or subtle presence of mattering descends in resonance for and with one and all. From a discrete moment it seems to radiate in all directions, infinitely, as part of a fluid and sustained dance with death.

The strangeness of dancing with the thought of death is like the moral mystery, the human mystery, that seeing that my life matters, I see that yours does; seeing that your life matters, I see that mine does. Death brings us there (and love might, as well).

A dance with these thoughts is neither abrasive debate nor competitive exchange – nor even entirely vocal. But it nonetheless can be finally inviting and mutually satisfying. It is, perhaps that moment when we can affirm that we belong to each other and to the world.

A dance with death is not a death-struggle. It can be the consummate embrace of the other, part of a life with the other, with the other who is stranger, friend, neighbor, or lover – and the other even to myself that I am.

** **

Death is, in a way, a last word. But it is also a first. It can usher in a reception or rebirth of life with others in the world. This is a moment of vision or revelation that Kierkegaard knows as repetition. In that event we do not repossess but happily undergo – once more – life's suffering and smiles, madness and marvels.

Notes

1 George Pattison writes that a sculpture of the event by Rodin is found in the gardens adjacent to the UK Houses of Parliament.

2 Herman Melville, *Moby Dick, or The Whale* with commentary by Tom Quirk (London: Penguin, 2001), Chapter 60, "The Line" p. 305f.

3 *Three Discourses on Imagined Occasions*, trans. Howard V Hong and Edna H. Hong, Princeton, 1993, p. 83.

4 Kierkegaard is a "would-be Christian" in the sense all inhabitants of Christendom are: it's as if to be a Christian is to *not yet* be a Christian, and so, be a *would-be* Christian. See Jonathan Lear's marvelous account in *A Case for Irony* (Harvard University Press, 2011).

5 *Three Discourses*, p. 71

6 *Philosophical Crumbs* gives an extended treatment of the way non-Socratic learning occurs through the invasive, restructuring of revelation. See *Kierkegaard's Repetition and Philosophical Crumbs*, ed. with introduction, Edward F. Mooney, trans. M. L. Piety (Oxford World Classics, 2009), discussed above, Chapter 7.

7 *Three Discourses*, p. 83.

8 Ibid.

9 In *Repetition*, the young man awaits transformation arriving as a thunderbolt, or as Job's whirlwind.

10 *Fragments*, p. x, emphasis mine. I follow the Oxford World Classics title, *Philosophical Crumbs*.

11 *Three Discourses*, p. 87.

12 *Postscript*, p. 89 "Socrates is a solo dancer before the divine (or 'the god')." A proposed author for *Fear and Trembling* was "Simon Stylites, Solo Dancer and Private Individual."

13 *Phaedo*, 64-a

14 For "a music playing Socrates," see *Birth of Tragedy*: trans. and intro. Douglas Smith (Oxford: Oxford University Press 2000), sections 15 and 17, pp. 85, 93; for "a God who would dance," see *Thus Spoke Zarathustra*, trans. and intro. Graham Parkes, (Oxford: Oxford University Press 2005), First Part, section 7, "on reading and writing" p. 36.

15 In his essay "Walking," Thoreau claims that only one or two persons of his acquaintance have learned "the art of walking" – not exactly dancing but nevertheless a corporeally lyrical, kind of meditative pilgrimage among the things of creation. See "Walking," *The Essays of Henry D. Thoreau*, selected and ed. Lewis Hyde (North Point Press, 2002), p. 149.

16 *Postscript*, p. 1: 166–7 Patrick Stokes pointed out this passage. See his discussion in *Kierkegaard's Mirrors, Interest, Self, and Moral Vision*, (Palgrave-Macmillan, 2010), p. 126.

17 *Three Discourses*, p. 83. My emphasis.

18 Pattison, George *Poor Paris! Kierkegaard's Critique of the Spectacular City* (Berlin: de Gruyter, 1999), p. 140.

19 Patrick Stokes points out (in correspondence) that unlike birth, where continuity with the mother is clearly broken as a newborn emerges into the world, it's not so clear that at death the newly dead have emerged into a new world. Thus "broken continuity" can't be the same in the two cases. In the first case (birth), a prior state of being is severed *as that being enters a subsequent state* (say, a being moves free of the womb). In the second case (death), a previously intact person is severed from its status of "person" *without* entering a subsequent state (existence comes to a complete halt). In the latter case, the continuity that is broken is the continuity manifested in of those *past* moments that constituted a life now extinct. In the former case, the continuity is found in the steady progress of fetal development and is broken as fetal development henceforth is infant development. At death we do not have a bridge to new phases of development, but the end of any development at all.

20 Pattison *Poor Paris!* p. 140.

21 See Wittgenstein, Ludwig *Tractatus Logico-Philosophicus* trans. C.K. Ogden (Routledge: London, 1996), p. 185, on death as not an event I live through.

22 See the excellent discussions in Stokes, *Kierkegaard's Mirrors*.

23 See Stokes, *Kierkegaard's Mirrors*, p. 5 and elsewhere.

24 Compare Heidegger's picture in *Being and Time* of human life being a structure of care tilting toward death, and death tilting back.

25 Thoreau finds the death of John Brown sublime and transformative; both Kant and Burke see the presence of *my* death to be an ingredient in any experience of the sublime. See my "Wonder and Affliction: Thoreau's Dionysian World," forthcoming in *Thoreau as Philosopher*, Rick Furtak, (ed.), and *Lost Intimacy in American Thought: Recovering Personal Philosophy from Thoreau to Cavell* (Continuum, 2009), Chapters 4 and 12.

26 It's merely churlish to insist that the proper statement is "*It's as if I 'stepped in your shoes'*." There's nothing second best in saying "I step into your shoes" any more than saying "I see what you mean" (rather than "*It's as if I see what you mean.*"

27 See J. David Velleman's "So it Goes," *The Amherst Lecture in Philosophy* 1 (2006): 1–23 http://www.amherstlecture.org/velleman2006/. What I call "anomalous" about locating self and death and hurt, he calls "incoherent." Is his designation less forgiving? I attribute a difficulty to our sense of reality whereas his designation, to my ear, calls on us more directly to clean up our act. I feel ashamed if I'm called incoherent, but only baffled if my experience is anomalous.

28 See the accounts of Peter's late life in the biographies of Kierkegaard by Alastair Hannay, *Kierkegaard: A Biography* (Cambridge: Cambridge University Press, 2001) p. 423 and Joakim Garff, *Søren Kierkegaard: A Biography* trans. Bruce H. Kirmmse (Princeton, NJ and Oxford: Princeton University Press, 2005) pp. 807–10. John Thoreau dies of lockjaw in his brother Henry's arms; a few days later, Henry takes on all the death agony and symptoms of John; later still Henry writes a memorial to John, *A Week on The Concord and Merrimack*. See *Henry Thoreau, A Life of the Mind*, Robert D. Richardson Jr. (Berkeley: University of California Press, 1986) pp. 113–16.

29 We might ask, in this age of heart transplants, whether the dead live on in the living – since a heart of the dead may live on.

30 Stanley Cavell, *Little Did I Know: Excerpts from Memory*, (Stanford, 2010), p. 5.

31 Without Authority, 51, my emphasis.

32 Against the background of his writerly vocation and talent, his failing to achieve marriage might not be the lamentable fiasco some

take it to be. In *Fear and Trembling*, those who fail as knights of faith (or resignation) are consigned to the ridiculous status of "frogs in life's swamp" – complainers croaking in life's swamp. Could our retrospective assessment of his life (an overview unavailable to him as he faced breaking his engagement) find the suffering he caused her vindicated by the flowering of his marvelous art?

33   *Three Discourses*, p. 83

34   *Postscript*, 1: 237, trans. altered. The passage is discussed in Pattison, *Poor Paris!* p. 97. The importance of a specific *calendar* date for the writing of a note that shattered an engagement diminishes as we track its *meaning*.

35   Patrick Stokes provides this marvelous passage from Bede's *Ecclesiastical History of England*: Bede, *Ecclesiastical History of the English People: With Bede's Letter to Egbert and Cuthbert's Letter on the Death of Bede* trans. David Hugh Farmer and Leo Sherley-Price (London: Penguin, 1990) pp. 129–30.

36   See Patrick Stokes, "The Power of Death: Retroactivity, Narrative, and Interest" in Robert L. Perkins, (ed.) *International Kierkegaard Commentary: Prefaces/Writing Sampler and Three Discourses on Imagined Occasions* (Macon, GA: Mercer University Press, 2006) pp. 387–417.

37   Joseph Westfall,*The Kierkegaardian Author: Authorship and Performance in Kierkegaard's Literary and Dramatic Criticism* (Berlin: de Gruyter, 2007), p. 143.

38   Ibid.

39   Westfall *The Kierkegaardian Author*, p. 51.

40   As noted earlier, Cavell calls his "Excerpts from Memory" his *posthumous* writing. *Little Did I Know*, p. 5.

41   Westfall *The Kierkegaardian Author* p. 135, and p. 77.

42   Tolstoy isn't endorsing such a syllogism himself; he has Ivan Ilyich quote it at second hand: "The example of a syllogism which he had learned in Kiezewetter's *Logic*: 'Caius is a man, men are mortal, therefore Caius is mortal,' had seemed to him all his life to be true as applied to Caius but certainly not as regards himself." Leo Tolstoy, *The Death of Ivan Ilyich and Other Stories* trans. Rosemary Edmondson (London: Penguin, 1960), p. 137.

INDEX